A Note to *Instructors* about the Pre-Release Edition

As we refine *The Entpreneurial Journey* for eventual publication in the spring of 2003, we are hopeful that you will contribute your thoughts for improving function, performance, and look and feel by returning this comment card. Comments are also being solicited at htttp://omalia.swcollege.com, if you prefer to provide your feedback to us online. **So, tell us, what are you thinking? We look forward to hearing from you.**

Molly Flynn
South-Western/Thomson Learning
molly.flynn@swcollege.com

Dear Molly:
Here is something I would like you to know. The two or three things that you must absolutely do to retain my adoption are:

Overall, how well did *The Entrepreneurial Journey* work in your course?

- ❐ Excellent! I was very well satisfied.
- ❐ Good. I was pretty well satisfied.
- ❐ Above average. I was moderately well satisfied.
- ❐ Only so-so. I was less satisfied than I had hoped.
- ❐ Not well. I will be looking for another text.

Sincerely yours

Name: _____

Please provide contact information.

School: _____

Email: _____

I teach:
- ❐ freshman / sophomores
- ❐ juniors / seniors
- ❐ graduates
- ❐ executives

My students are:
- ❐ business majors
- ❐ nonbusiness majors
- ❐ both

A Note to *Students* about the Pre-Release Edition

The inaugural edition of *The Entrepreneurial Journey* will be officially released in the spring of 2003. This Pre-Release has been made available to you now to ensure that student voices are heard as *The Entrepreneurial Journey* is being refined for publication. If you would like to convey your suggestions for improvements via this comment card, we would welcome the feedback. Comments are also being solicited at htttp://omalia.swcollege.com, if you prefer to provide your feedback to us online. **So, tell us, what are you thinking? We look forward to hearing from you.**

Molly Flynn, South-Western/Thomson Learning
molly.flynn@swcollege.com

Dear Molly:
Here is something I would like you to know. What I found MOST helpful was:

Overall, my experience of *The Entrepreneurial Journey*, in terms of my readiness to pursue an entrepreneurial career, made me feel:

confused	somewhat shaky	so-so	prepared	very well prepared
❐	❐	❐	❐	❐

Sincerely yours

Name: _____

Please provide contact information.

School: _____

Email: _____

I am enrolled as a/an (check all that apply

undergraduate	graduate	executive	bu...ess
❐	❐	❐	

NO POSTAGE
NECESSARY
IF MAILED
IN THE
UNITED STATES

BUSINESS REPLY MAIL
FIRST CLASS MAIL   PERMIT NO. 5191   MASON, OH

POSTAGE WILL BE PAID BY ADDRESSEE

MOLLY FLYNN
SOUTH-WESTERN/THOMSON LEARNING
5191 NATORP BOULEVARD
MASON, OH 45040-7135

Pre-Release

The Entrepreneurial Journey

Thomas J. O'Malia

Kinko's Endowed Chair and Director
Lloyd Greif Center for Entrepreneurial Studies
Marshall School of Business
University of Southern California

Margaret H. Whistler

Director of Operations
MedReviews, LLC

THOMSON

SOUTH-WESTERN

Australia · Canada · Mexico · Singapore · Spain · United Kingdom · United States

THOMSON

SOUTH-WESTERN

Pre-Release for The Entrepreneurial Journey
Thomas J. O'Malia and Margaret H. Whistler

Editor-in-Chief:
Jack W. Calhoun

Vice President, Team Director:
Michael P. Roche

Acquisitions Editor:
John Szilagyi

Developmental Editor:
Judith O'Neill

Marketing Manager:
Rob Bloom

Production Editor:
Emily S. Gross

Manufacturing Coordinator:
Rhonda Utley

Compositor:
A.W. Kingston Publishing Services

Printer:
Edwards Brothers
Ann Arbor, Michigan

Design Project Manager:
Tippy McIntosh

Cover Designer:
Tippy McIntosh

Cover Illustrator:
Artville® by Getty Images™

Library of Congress
Cataloging-in-Publication Data

O'Malia, Thomas J.
   Pre-release for the entrepreneurial
journey / Thomas J. O'Malia, Margaret
H. Whistler
      p.   cm.
   ISBN: 0-324-17688-0 (alk. paper)
   1. Entrepreneurship. I. Whistler,
Margaret H., II. Title.

   HB615 .045 2002
   658.4'21–dc21

                        20022066891

Table of Contents

Chapter Five: Getting Past the Idea

Chapter Six: Feasibility

Chapter Seven: Entrepreneurial Marketing

Chapter Eight: How Do I Sell?

Chapter Nine: Developing Your Benefit

Chapter Ten: Money Tool Kit

Chapter Eleven: How And Where Do I Find The Money?

Chapter Twelve: Feasibility Part Two

Chapter Thirteen: The Business Plan

Preface

The entrepreneurial revolution is upon us! Never before in the history of commerce have so many sought to start a business, be their own boss, and control their own destiny. It truly is the era having the greatest impact on the vast majority of the population.

Nowhere is this as evident as it is in the colleges and universities of America. Almost every business school in the country offers some type of course in entrepreneurship; many offer multiple courses, and others have full programs with a major or emphasis in entrepreneurship. This phenomenon is not limited to one class of schools; it spans the Harvards and Stanfords through to the smallest of junior colleges and trade schools. It is offered in executive MBA courses and in distance learning programs. Further, it is touted in the popular press and in dedicated entrepreneur magazines. It is everywhere.

It is even more extraordinary to think that the word *entrepreneur* was not even part of the common vocabulary just two decades ago. Its rise to prominence in both the business world and secular world give testament to its importance. And well it should.

Over this same period of time, close to 35 million new jobs were created while the Fortune 500 companies lost upward of 5 million. The end of the cold war and the related emphasis on defense spending could have begun an era of great recession or even a depression. To some extent they have, and throughout many economies.

The United States, however, has experienced the greatest growth in its history. More jobs have been created than there are workers available to fill them. More companies have been started than ever before in history. More money has been raised to start and grow firms than ever imagined. The magic of the entrepreneur has fostered all of this.

There was a time when a limited few, if any, dared start their own firms. Today, almost everyone is in the hunt to do just that—whether it be a new technology or service firm employing hundreds or a lifestyle business employing one—entrepreneurship has moved from a dream to reality.

It is the explicit goal of this text to answer three big questions:

1. **Who are these entrepreneurs?** Are they super humans capable of abnormal feats of commerce? Do they have a gift not shared by the masses? Are their skills sets so advanced that they cannot be emulated?

The answer to all of the above is no, and you will learn why. We will explore the vast range of entrepreneurs and review their characteristics, mind-sets, and motivations. We will look at and dispel the most common myths associated with entrepreneurs and explore their common attributes and why those qualities enhance success. We will learn that there are no rules in entrepreneurship and that every entrepreneurial journey is unique.

2. **How do entrepreneurs start companies?** Is it the same way that large companies expand their offerings? Are the start technologies today the same as a generation ago? Is money the big factor in success?

Just as no two entrepreneurs fit the same mold, no two entrepreneurs started their firms in exactly the same manner. Each is unique to the time and opportunity of the moment, as well as to the talents and motivation of the individual. Many new ventures, however, seem to follow a common structure, a common thought process. Examining how entrepreneurs think is a crucial part of this text. Seeing what they see and testing as they test is part of the learning process. It will help you achieve your goal while also enabling you to avoid the land mines stepped on by many.

3. **Why do entrepreneurs start new companies?** Are they motivated by greed, the ultimate dream of getting rich quickly and retiring to a life of leisure? Are they seeking to be king or queen of the mountain because they can't get along in an existing company or job?

Again, each journey is unique and every entrepreneur starts and is motivated to continue by desires, goals, and needs unique to him or her. Everybody reacts differently to his or her surrounding world, and each journey is independent of age, race, creed, and education level. There are also hundreds of wonderful journeys of entrepreneurs who started nonprofit companies to do community service and to help others. Beginning with an acquisition or inheritance is another starting point for a journey. The whys are as plentiful as those who journey.

It is our hope and desire that once you know
 who is an entrepreneur
 how do they start companies
 why do they start companies

you can answer
 are *you* an entrepreneur?
 given *your* skills and mind-set, do *you* wish to start *your* entrepreneurial journey?
 what is the motivation that will carry *you* forward to *your* goal?

This is not a text about entrepreneurs, but we will meet many on our travels.

This is not a text about how others did it. It is about how *you* will do it—your way with their tools.

This is not a text that purports a formula or a process. This is a text written and executed with the singular purpose of paving the way for your entrepreneurial journey. It is about you following in the footsteps of all who have traveled this exciting road before you.

Are you ready to begin your entrepreneurial journey?

"You get ideas everywhere. I mean, the most unexpected
places you can get an idea to help you start your business.
You just have to keep your eyes open."
-Paul Orfalea, Founder, Kinko's Inc.

Organization

The Entrepreneurial Journey is more than a simple textbook. The information herein provides the framework for the phenomenon of entrepreneurship. It guides you through the many steps that are necessary in deciding how, when, and why to start your own venture. The text is based on the application of the entrepreneurial process and does not place heavy emphasis on theory.

The chapters are organized around fundamental concepts of entrepreneurship. At the beginning of each chapter is a list of the major concepts covered in that chapter. At the end of each chapter is a featured entrepreneurial journey that provides a real-life example of an entrepreneur in action. These journeys highlight what the entrepreneurs have accomplished and the trials and tribulations they have endured in so doing. Learning from those who have experienced or are experiencing the journey gives meaning and insight to the text, enabling you to simulate the challenges, exercise the skills sets, learn from the experiences, and embrace the accomplishments, as opposed to memorizing theories. "Up Front and Personal" stories are also strewn throughout each chapter for the same reason.

Additionally, each chapter includes "entrepreneurial exercises" designed to enhance your learning experience. It is our hope that you will perform each of these exercises to the best of your ability and, where appropriate, apply the concepts to your own journey. A notation at the bottom of each exercise instructs you to tear them out and move them to your "entrepreneurial road map binder." We encourage you to create your own binder while reading this text. Pull out all sections you think are particularly relevant to your potential business and organize them in this binder.

The text was designed to cover all the bases of the entrepreneurial journey. It begins with an assessment of entrepreneurs themselves, with in-depth coverage of their characteristics and passion for the journeys. Also discussed are the many myths commonly associated with entrepreneurs and the reality behind them. A tool for determining the best entrepreneurial journey for each individual, the model business, is also introduced.

The essence of entrepreneurship is covered with a detailed analysis of opportunity recognition and the importance of creativity and innovation. Finding a structure and framework within which to proceed is an important aspect of the journey.

"The Customer Is King" is a mantra that all entrepreneurs must live by to succeed. This text highlights the importance of the customer and emphasizes clearly defining the customer and the need. The customer is also explored in relation to selling. How do you reach the customer you seek?

Feasibility—the study of testing the business concept—is also examined. If the answer is yes, what is the question? The notion of a feasibility funnel and a structure by which to test the feasibility of business concepts are explored.

Several chapters are devoted to the benefit of the product or service being offered in terms of the patterns of change, creativity, and product development. How this benefit is transferred to the customer—that is, the method of distribution—is highlighted as a crucial area of opportunity.

Chapters on money needs and sources are included to give you the knowledge you'll need to assess and meet your financial requirements.

A discussion of business plans, what they should and should not contain, and their direct purpose is the primary topic in a later chapter. The notion of bringing everything together and of creating an execution strategy is emphasized here.

Essence of This Book

Who You Are

The Entrepreneurial Journey is about who you are, what you do, and why you do it. The *who you are* looks at the persona of many successful entrepreneurs. What do they possess? How did they get it? It assesses the myths surrounding the stereotypical entrepreneur and uncovers the passion that drives all entrepreneurs. You will be forced to assess whether your own attitudes and mind-set match any that are presented in the text.

What You Do

The *what you do* is about learning to think like an entrepreneur and acquiring the necessary tool sets to become successful. Entrepreneurs face the challenge of starting, acquiring, or expanding a firm through a process known as *feasibility*. Feasibility seeks to answer the question, Under what conditions are you willing to proceed? The *what you do* incorporates (a) learning about the entrepreneurial business concept and how to test that concept, (b) defining your customer as well as your sales and distribution channels, (c) dealing with patterns of change in your industry of choice, (d) translating the features of your product or service into benefits, and (e) defining how much and what type of money you will need to start your business.

Why You Do It

The *why you do it* centers around the goal of harvesting the business. You will create something of value and then decide whether it will remain a lifestyle business supporting your chosen level of living or whether it has a value that should be harvested. What is your strategy: lifestyle or exit?

All of these topics and many more are explored as our journey proceeds.

Chapter One
Do You Have What It Takes?

Chapter One Major Concepts

- Thinking outside the box
- What does it take to be an entrepreneur?
- What is entrepreneurship?
- Entrepreneurial mindset
- The model business

Journey One: Border Grill

Up Front & Personal: Todd Q. Smart

Up Front & Personal: Avanteer

The Beginning of the Journey

Greatest love affair in the world.

Congratulations! You are about to embark on the greatest journey of your life. The Entrepreneurial Journey is one that is based on passion, perseverance, and hard work. It is about desire, learning new skill sets, and recognizing that **you are responsible** for you. The journey is the greatest love affair in the world—the marriage of an idea, a product, a customer, and an entrepreneur. You begin with a clean slate and your success is not dependent on any one thing that you have learned, but rather, is dependent on everything that you will learn as you study entrepreneurship. To learn these skills, you will have to force yourself to do things that you may not like to do, such as contacting people, selling, dealing with the unknown, or working with others. It is a journey of hard, but rewarding work.

Journey of hard work.

It is time to realize that you will get out of this journey what you are willing to put into it. In other words, you will get what you give. The journey can be compared to a marathon in that you must train and prepare yourself for the event. You cannot expect to be able to run a marathon without having prepared yourself, both physically and mentally. Likewise, you cannot expect to begin a successful entrepreneurial journey without proper training. But, you must be willing to do the training. Are you willing? Are you prepared to pay the price?

Journey of reality.

You have to make the decision to be a part of this journey. By choosing to partake, you are going to control your destiny. You will change the way you look at things and find out if you are an entrepreneur. The 11th commandment will be your guiding force: "Thou Shalt Not BS Thyself" because this is a journey based in reality. This is not the first day of the rest of your life; it is the **first day of your real life**.

Journey of passion.

This is a journey of passion. It is doing what you want to do, when you want to do it. Ask yourself what you would do if you could work for free for the rest of your life. The answer to that question will help you begin to determine the area in which you should focus your studies. If you could work for free, what would you be doing? It may not be the easiest question to answer, but you need an initial direction.

Journey is unique to you.

The journey is unique to each and every individual. There is no formula, are no guarantees and is no right or wrong answer. There are only opportunities and you will learn to recognize these opportunities and become sensitive to when and how they arise. You will need to be receptive to new ideas, to new creativity, and to new ways of thinking. Are you ready to begin the journey?

Practical knowledge.

The focus of this text is to learn from those who have "been there and done that." It is not a class <u>about</u> entrepreneurship, it is a class <u>of</u> entrepreneurship in which you will meet and learn from many successful entrepreneurs. You will learn who these entrepreneurs are and what kind of person wants to and is able to take this journey. You will also be given a set of tools that you can add to your "toolbox" of entrepreneurial skill sets. Can you be the person? Can you acquire the skills? The effort must come from you and not from your professor.

What Does It Take To Be An Entrepreneur?

Issues you must face.

In learning to think like an entrepreneur, there are many issues that you will face that are unlike other issues you may have dealt with in your life thus far. Entrepreneurship is about a mindset and about a set of tools and skills that will help you to realize your entrepreneurial dream. On the journey, however, you will have to understand and embrace new ways of thinking and be open to different ideas and paradigms.

Is money needed?

For example, is money needed to start a business? Most people would say yes, that it is definitely a needed ingredient. However, many successful entrepreneurs have started without a lot of money. When two 19 year olds sold a van and a calculator for $1,600, Apple Computer was started and five years later reached $500,000,000 in sales. Another company, Absolute Towing and Transport, began when the founder, Todd Smart, sold his used car for a used tow truck. The company grew to 53 trucks and was sold for $8 million after 8 years in business. Money is the great big excuse that many people use for not starting a business. It does not take a lot of money to become an entrepreneur.

Is a great idea needed?

Do you need a great idea to start a business? Again, most people would say yes, but think outside the box and perhaps a new idea is not necessary. For example, Michael Dell did not invent the personal computer. As a college senior, he simply found a new way to sell the computer—directly to consumers. Today, Dell is the third largest United States computer company.

Can you think outside the box?

Entrepreneurs are individuals who think outside the box. They step outside of the normal realms of thinking in order to discover solutions to problems defined by others as unsolvable. There are no hard-fast rules in the entrepreneurial world because the rules are constantly changing and innovative ways of accomplishing tasks are being discovered. Entrepreneurship is about reversing a lifelong set of personal myths. You must be able to understand and adopt this new way of thinking. Can you change? Can you face the world with an open mind? Can you free your mindset to see alternatives?

Income tax: good or bad?

What is your first reaction when you think about income tax? Is it good or bad? Most people would respond that it is bad, that they do not like writing checks to the government for income tax. However, if you think outside the box about income tax, you may be able to see it in a different way. The founder of Absolute Towing did when he had to write a check for $500,000 to the IRS because it meant that he had incoming revenue from selling his business of $8 million. So, why are taxes good?

Can Americans save?

We live in the midst of one of the greatest economies of all times. Why are we so fortunate? The general consensus has been that historically Americans were unable to save money; however, currently $25 billion a month is put into IRAs, 401(k)s and such, which is often reinvested in the stock market. Many believe this is a primary driver of our growth. But why do people invest in Keoughs, IRAs, and 401(k)s? People do this so that they can receive a tax deduction and thus are postponing the taxes on gains from their investment to some point in the future when they will not have to pay as much in taxes on their withdrawal.

Postponing taxes.

Why taxes are good?

So, where would the economy be without taxes? Where would entrepreneurs find the funds to start businesses without tax advantages? Without capital gains?

The point is simple. Can you be open to change, to new ways of looking at the world around you? Can you see the opportunity and not the problem?

> *"They're all kinds of entrepreneurs. There's no one class. 'Lot of 'em are scumbags."*
> -Joe Coulombe, Founder, Trader Joe's Inc.

Rule for Conduct of Entrepreneurs

A tenet that entrepreneurs must live by is that the most important word in business is customer. Without a customer you cannot start or maintain your company. Therefore, how you treat your customer is your most important responsibility. The customer is king.

Always treat your associates, your faculty, your network, your friends, and everyone as you would a customer and remember that the customer is king. That is, always be on time, always be prepared, always excuse yourself properly if you cannot make a meeting, and always present any written materials in a professional manner. Treating everyone as you would a customer builds an environment for success.

What We Know About Entrepreneurs

Entrepreneurs are open to exploring and willing to form their own opinions. They will see the opportunity and challenge in a situation, never the problem. By examining the entrepreneur's world and focusing on how entrepreneurs think outside the box, we can begin to get an understanding for the entrepreneurial mindset.

Child's most creative years from age zero to five.

Psychologists have told us that a child's most creative years are from birth to the age of five. During these years, children are extremely creative because everything is new; there are no preconceived notions, no paradigms to live by, and everything that children do during these years is rewarded, encouraged, and applauded. After turning five, kids are sent to the first grade and the paradigms of society begin to emerge. "Raise your hand if you have to go to the bathroom." "Don't talk during nap time." Permission is needed for everything thereby forcing individuality and creativity inward.

For example, when a child is learning to walk, he/she is encouraged when failure occurs. The effort and progress made is congratulated, supported, and the child is helped back onto his/her feet. If employees try something and fail, they are seen as failures and fall from the limelight. As we get more involved in the world, we are told not just what to think but how to think as well.

New ideas, new possibilities.

If you want to succeed as an entrepreneur, though, if you want to do something that others have not been able to do, then you will have to stop thinking like other people. You will have to open yourself up to new ideas and new possibilities. For example, when creating their service departments, personal-computer companies traditionally focused on establishing an easy way for consumers to bring the product back for repairs, a hassle at best. Dell Computer Corporation, however, provided on-site service instead, thereby implementing a new concept in the industry and setting itself apart from its competitors.

Think outside the box.

The message is very simple: all of your life you have been trained to think one way; today, you are going to throw away all of those paradigms and start to think outside of the box. Begin to look at the total picture, explore everything that is of interest to you and find the positive, the opportunity in everything. Do not be constrained by the forced paradigms of society.

Entrepreneurial Exercise

Before moving onto the next section, reflect for a moment on your definition of an entrepreneur. What are the characteristics and traits of an entrepreneur? Write down some notes on your thoughts and feelings about an entrepreneur and be prepared to share them in class. After reading the following section, return to these notes and write down any new thoughts that have come to mind.

What is an Entrepreneur?

_____

_____

_____

_____

_____

New thoughts:

_____

_____

_____

_____

_____

⇒   **Tear out and move to your entrepreneurial road map binder.**

Definition and Evolution of Entrepreneurship

Classic approach.

There are many definitions of an entrepreneur and much controversy over what actually constitutes an entrepreneur. The definition has also evolved a great deal throughout this century and the nature of entrepreneurship has changed dramatically. Refer to the table on the next page, which highlights this evolution and identifies various scholars' different definitions of entrepreneurship. We have moved from the super hero person who was product driven to the entrepreneurial team with a customer focus that exists today. The changes in definition are the result of a changing set of rules and standards in the economy, the availability and rate of technology, and finally the education level of the masses. These changes, coupled with the vast funds available to start new firms, are continuing to alter the entrepreneurial landscape. Most scholars today would describe this as the third wave in a series of economic cycles that began with early man.

First wave - land is king.

From the beginning of time up to the early 1800s, the main source of power (and the cause of most wars) was land. He that had the land was king. All else were the fiefs who toiled on behalf of their lord. Ninety-seven percent of all people worked on and received their livelihood from the lord.

Second wave - capital is king.

With the beginning of the Industrial Revolution, society started to move to the cities. As agriculture became automated, individuals moved to the factory. The factory was the domain of a new king—a king based on capital. He that had capital, had the gold, or ruled because capital was held by the elite few. The options available to those not born into resources were limited.

Third wave - brain matter is king.

Today, we are in the third wave. We are in the era of intellectual property. Resources are not a constrain—resources abound. The deciding factors today are the things that lie between your ears. It is the gray matter that creates new benefits, new concepts, and new ideas. It is the brain matter that recognizes and exploits opportunity. It is truly the age of enterprise.

Entrepreneurship is a phenomenon.

Many scholars prefer to think of entrepreneurship as a phenomenon. It is not totally explainable. It is a phenomenon driven by one's attitudes, skill sets, and personal characteristics and traits. Combining these elements of one's being leads to the creation of new ventures and enables an individual to begin his or her own entrepreneurial journey. Again, it is important to remember that each journey is different and that there is no right or wrong way of doing things, only the way that is most appropriate for the individual entrepreneur.

Analogous to baseball.

This entrepreneurial phenomenon that is driven by attitudes, skill sets, and personal characteristics and traits is analogous to baseball. If you ask the question what is a baseball player, you will typically elicit the response that it is a person who runs, hits, and throws a baseball.

A good baseball player is good because of his attitude and skill sets. He is good because he is driven, passionate, and devoted. He is not passive.

In order to become a good baseball player, one must learn the skill sets, understand his individual definition of success and develop a positive attitude. This mindset can be applied to many different talents: another example would be a violinist.

Analogous to a violinist.

A violinist is one who pulls and pushes a bow across a string. It requires an attitude that this is something that he/she wants to do and is committed to doing well. It also requires skill sets that must be developed and improved. And finally, the violinist must have a goal or aspiration for which to aspire.

The skills are learnable.

Just as no one can guarantee that you will be the worlds greatest baseball player or violinist, no one can guarantee that anyone will be a successful entrepreneur. But, almost anyone can play baseball or learn the violin at some level of expertise for which they receive great satisfaction and reward. The same applies to entrepreneurship. Your ability and desire to combine the right attitudes, skill sets, personal characteristics and traits will make for a rewarding entrepreneurial journey.

The Changing Definition of Entrepreneurship

Author	Date	Definition
Say	1816	The agent who unites all means of production and who finds in the value of the products...the reestablishment of the entire capital he employs, and the value of the wages, the interest and the rent which he pays, as well as the profits belonging to himself.
Schumpeter	1934	... entrepreneurship, as defined, essentially, consists in doing things that are not generally done in the ordinary course of business routine, it is essentially a phenomenon that comes under the wider aspect of leadership.
Stauss	1944	This paper is an argument to advance the proposition that the firm is the entrepreneur.
Cole	1959	... the purposeful activity (including an integrated sequence of decision) of an individual or group of individuals, undertaken to initiate, maintain or aggrandize a profit-oriented business unit for the production or distribution of economic goods and services.
Liles	1974	We have examined the entrepreneur who is involved in substantial ventures and have considered what we found in light of traditional thinking that he is a special type of individual—somehow an unusual and uncommon man—a man apart. It probably is true that very successful entrepreneurs beome men apart. But, at the beginning, when they make the decision to start an entrepreneurial career, they are in most respects very much like many other ambitious, striving individuals.
Mescon et al	1981	Entrepreneurs are, by definition, founders of new businesses.
Stevenson et al	1985	The pursuit of opportunity without regard to resources currently controlled.
Gartner	1988	The entrepreneur is not a fixed state of existence, rather, entrepreneurship is a role that individuals undertake to create organizations.
Shane	1999	One who recognizes and exploits opportunities.

Sources: Cole, A.H. (1959) *Business Enterprise in its social setting.* Cambridge: Harvard University Press, p. 7; Gartner, W. (1989) "Who is an Entrepreneur?" Is the Wrong Question. *Entrepreneurship Theory and Practice.* University of Baltimore Education Foundation, p. 64; Liles, P. (1974) Who are the entrepreneurs? *MSU Business Topics,* 22, p. 14; Mescon T., & Montanari, J. (1981) The personalities of independent and franchise entrepreneurs: An empirical analysis of concepts. *Journal of Enterprise Management,* 3(2), 149-159; Say, J.A., (1816) *A Treatise on Political Economy.* London: Sherwood, Neeley and Jones, p. 28-29; Schumpeter, J.A. (1934) *The theory of economic development.* Translated by R. Opie. Cambridge: Harvard University Press, p. 254; Shane, S. & Venkataraman, S. (1999) The Promise of Entrepreneurship as a Field of Research. *Revised for Academy of Management Review;* Stauss, J.H. (1944) The entrepreneur: The firm. *Journal of Political Economy,* 52(2), 112-127; Stevenson, H., Roberts, M., & Grousbeck, H. (1999) *New Business Ventures and the Entrepreneur,* The McGraw-Hill Companies, Inc. p. 5.

Entrepreneurial Mindset

In addition to opening your mind to new ways of thinking and attempting to break the paradigms that have been placed on you since childhood, there are several other notions that you must embrace if you are to become a successful entrepreneur. The entrepreneurial mindset is comprised of accepting ambiguity, letting the market be your judge, experiencing many rounds of trial and error, learning to network and seek mentors, and making no excuses.

Ambiguity

Chaos, confusion, and change equal opportunity.

The world is not definite and obvious and clear-cut. Ambiguity and uncertainty have a major impact on our lives. In the entrepreneurial world, ambiguity reigns supreme. It is not looked upon as a negative, it is a positive. Without chaos, confusion, change and ambiguity, there would be no opportunity for entrepreneurs.

During periods of change, entrepreneurs can use their special advantage of speed and nimbleness to reach customers and try new ideas faster than their larger competitors.

There are no rules in entrepreneurship.

Think in terms of yourself, as a student, for example. You are very bright, have gotten through school to this point, and have had the opportunity to grow in life. You have done that primarily by learning to understand and then to maximize the rules. In high school, it took you only a short while to figure out what your teacher wanted and what it would take to get an A or to get a C in the class. You knew the rules and then made a decision and you were able to control the outcome. You understood the paradigms and then you applied them. One of the biggest challenges facing you today is that there are no rules in entrepreneurship. It is completely ambiguous. You must accept that and know that you will never start a business if your goal is to know every single fact. It just does not happen.

Market is your only judge

Don't look to friends and family for acceptance—look to the market for approval.

It does not matter how many people love your idea and how many people hate your idea. What matters is the market and what the market says about your idea. We have become dependent on being accepted by other people and being encouraged by other people. However, their beliefs, their encouragement, and their compliments do not count. In the entrepreneurial world, there is only one voice that does count and that is the voice of the market. If the market says "I agree," then the idea has potential.

In the real world, it often happens that long shots pay off and sure winners come up short. In the 1950s, Ford Motors thought the Edsel would be a huge hit—Henry Ford even named it after his son. But, despite all expectations, the Edsel flopped. On the other hand, Decca Recording rejected the Beatles in 1962, saying, "we don't like their sound, and guitar music is on the way out."

Experts are not always right.

A student at Yale University in New Haven, Connecticut was pleased when a care package arrived from his mom who lived in San Francisco. He raced to his room in anticipation of the homemade cookies, fruits, and snacks he knew awaited him.

Only crumbs.

But, much to his disappointment, he found a mass of crumbs, a broken container of stale jelly beans, and over ripened fruit. As he closed the box, he noticed that his mom had sent the parcel three weeks earlier.

If we can put a man on the moon, he reasoned, why can we not get a package across the country in under three weeks? He sought to answer the question and after calls to the post office and small parcel freight companies, he was convinced that their excuses of time to sort packages and time in warehouses were wrong. So, he set out to create an alternative and adopted it as his senior thesis.

What he envisioned was an airplane with a custom interior filled with bins and a central conveyor belt. His logic was that if sorting could be done while the plane was en route across the country, then the parcels could be dispersed by region and delivered that morning.

He got a C!

He proudly presented his findings to his Professor who saw the idea as impractical and overly expensive. The Professors comment on the cover page of his thesis was that it was the stupidest idea he had ever heard and gave it a C grade.

Despite the setback, young Fred Smith went forward and the story of Federal Express is now an entrepreneurial legend.

In the long run there is only one judge—your customer.

Trial and error

Entrepreneurs live under an umbrella of experimentation without the fear of failure.

With no definite rules and no automatic formulas, the only way to learn and succeed is through trial and error. In the entrepreneurial world, you will live by trial and error. Experimentation is the key to success; you are going to have to look at 100 ideas, 100 business opportunities and explore every one of them and you still might not find the right business for you. However, every project that does not pan out is a learning lesson that brings you closer to your eventual success. Entrepreneurs live under an umbrella of experimentation without a fear of failure. Part of their persona is an acceptance that they will consider every new opportunity and they will learn from their failures.

A successful salesman was asked by a new salesperson what was his key to success. The veteran explained that it was his experience, that every sale was different, and that he would have to call ten prospects to get one meeting. Just then the phone rang and the salesman answered it as the junior observed. Despite a perfect positioning, the sale did not come on this call. The young salesman asked if he was disappointed. The elder salesman answered that he learned something in the call and only needed to make nine more to get his next sale.

Networking and mentors

Networking opens doors, provides feedback and offers guidance.

A very critical part of the entrepreneur's world is networking and mentors. One way to make the trial-and-error process more meaningful is to find someone who is already an experienced entrepreneur and turn that person into a mentor who can guide you past the most dangerous points and the least obvious mistakes.

Join associations, attend trade shows, exchange ideas.

Because entrepreneurs are without organizations within which to share ideas, they find other ways to do that, primarily through networking. They find people in similar situations, join associations, attend trade shows, and essentially do anything possible to encourage and partake in the exchange of ideas. Furthermore, networking allows you to surround yourself with people who can give you honest feedback, open doors, and offer guidance. They can spot the land mines and guide you through without injury.

Meet 250 new people.

According to William Gartner of the University of Southern California, a leading researcher in entrepreneurial start ups, to get into business you need to know at least 250 people that you did not know before beginning the journey. In order to expand your network, begin by asking your family and friends to introduce you to people they know in your industry. Who do they know that might be helpful to you in starting your business? Help yourself by learning of and attending industry functions. Learn from the players.

Find a mentor.

In the process of networking, entrepreneurs seek to find mentors. Mentors are individual entrepreneurs who have already experienced the journey. You might ask why someone would want to be a mentor. Consider that often times a mentor is a successful, recovering entrepreneur who has already ended his or her journey, but the passion is still there. By looking at and being a part of the aspiring entrepreneur's world, the mentor is able to relive their passionate journey while giving you a great deal of guidance. As such, mentoring is a critical part of the entrepreneurial mindset.

No excuses

What is the great big excuse?

Entrepreneurship is based in reality. You are your business and your business is you. That is the entrepreneur's motto, and it means that your success is up to you. Mistakes? They are your mistakes. Victories? They are your victories. Either way, it comes down to you. Entrepreneurs live by the 11th commandment: thou shalt not lie to (BS) thyself. There are no excuses, there is no one to blame. You cannot say that the sun got in your eyes, that someone failed to do something, or that you looked the wrong way. You can not say someone else did not deliver your supplies or the sales rep did not close the deal. These are only players—you are the driving force. It is all about you and you are the only one that counts.

Entrepreneurship is not dependent on intelligence, it does not matter what your race, your color, or your creed, it does not matter if you are tall or short, fat or thin. There are no excuses. Entrepreneurship is your journey. Embrace the entrepreneurial mindset and you will be on the road to success, on the pathway to your dream, on your entrepreneurial journey.

> *"I tell the kids who live in poor neighborhoods like I did. They always have excuses why they cannot get ahead, why they haven't done something, why they're not doing it now or why they won't do it in the future. I ask them how many of you were born in a single family household? How many of you grew up in a foster home? How many of you grew up on welfare, how mnay of you dropped out of school? I did and I'm here to tell you that you can still go forward, that has happened to me."*
> -Vidal Herrerra, Founder, Autopsy/Post Services

Up Front & Personal: Todd Q. Smart

Todd Q. Smart is an outgoing adventurer who thrives on adrenaline pumping activities such as motorcycle racing, helicopter skiing, snowboarding, skydiving, bungee jumping, and hang gliding. Although comfortable with risk, Smart always looks to manage the dangers of his favorite activities, including his business ventures. To minimize the risk of a start up business, he believes in obtaining a "customer in hand," before ever opening the door to any enterprise.

Smart began his first entrepreneurial venture at the ripe old age of 10 while living in Salt Lake City, Utah. After a considerable amount of begging and pleading, Todd's parents bought him a riding lawn mower for Christmas and off he went to mow the lawn of every neighbor on the block. At age 12, Smart did become employed putting bicycles together. However, in so doing, he was merely getting paid for what he loved to do: fix bikes.

Smart's entrepreneurial tendencies were inspired by his father, who never seemed to succeed in his own business ventures. As a child, Smart recalls each time one of his father's businesses failed, primarily because it meant being uprooted, which happened four times during his youth. Smart attributes his father's failures to an unwillingness to both face the full risk of business ownership and invest the level of resources, whether they be human or monetary, necessary for success. Recognizing this helped to motivate Smart to persevere when faced with challenges.

Among his fathers ventures were an attempt at selling used industrial equipment, becoming involved with a lube refiner distributor, and working on a business in the tire industry. As is evident, the nature of these businesses was "non-glamorous," which also influenced Smart and kept his mind open. He recognized that successful entrepreneurs and high levels of profit were not only found in Silicon Valley, but also in Grease Alley.

In 1985, after two years at the University of Boulder at Colorado, Smart was on a quest for a more dynamic academic curriculum than he was experiencing. He embarked on a motorcycle tour the summer following his sophomore year at Boulder, ending in Southern California. Having heard of the USC Entrepreneur Program and knowing that his ultimate goal upon graduation was a start up business, he felt that the Entrepreneur Program with its exposure to the USC Network was the perfect location at which to finish his undergraduate education. Without knowing a single person in Los Angeles, he uprooted himself to pursue his dreams.

While in school, the concept of a "customer in hand" was first introduced. Smart had a strong belief in his competence to build a successful organization with an infrastructure to support virtually any business concept, but he realized that without customers the business entity could never succeed. So, he began his search for a customer to provide the foundation of a profitable entity.

Todd had always considered himself "opportunity sensitive" and this characteristic, along with his open-mind (cultivated by his father's ventures), led him to believe that when a *needy customer* came along, he would recognize it.

He recognized that customer when the founder of Insurance Auto Auctions (IAA), spoke as a guest in one of classes. At that time, IAA was a young company but was growing. Smart listened as the founder identified his biggest problem as being the $600,000 per year IAA spent on towing costs because he had to contract with seven separate towing companies to handle his towing needs. With such a fragmented market, the founder was certain that these companies were not servicing his needs as efficiently as was possible. After hearing this speaker, Smart's *opportunity sensors* were immediately buzzing. He recognized that IAA was a customer in need who had over a half-million-dollars, thus, Smart's business concept was born.

Smart traded his car and paid a bit of cash for a single two-car carrier. The beginning years consisted of hustling business, driving his tow truck, personally repairing and servicing trucks, and building "sweat equity" to acquire additional used tow trucks.

Absolute Towing was built around the notion of being a customer service oriented company in a service industry that typically neglects this critical area. Absolute Towing distinguishes itself with such value added benefits as state of the art equipment, on-line vehicle assignment and invoicing with all insurance customers, "Teletrac" Fleet Management computerized tracking of all tow vehicles, professional and clean uniformed drivers, and the ability to accomplish out of the ordinary requests.

The operational side of Absolute Towing is also unique to the industry; a majority of the trucks used to tow customers are owned by full time sub-contractors who pay all associated expenses for their operation. By establishing a network of dependable sub-contractors and loyal employees, the company has been able to provide superior customer service, limit the downside financial and liability exposure, and handle extreme spikes in volume unlike other competitors (i.e., the flood of Jan. 95 provided an additional 2500 cars for that month).

Annual sales for 1997 reached $5 million dollars for approximately 90,000 vehicles. Since inception in June 1987 (one month after Smart graduated from the Entrepreneur Program), the company has experienced an increase in gross sales of 15 – 200% annually.

Recently, Todd successfully harvested his business and at the age of 28, sold Absolute Towing and Transporting, Inc. for approximately $8 million.

The greatest lesson Smart learned is that a combination of perseverance and integrity are the primary factors in the success of a business. This combination must be present in all members of the organization. Absolute Towing developed a reputation for meeting any challenges its customers presented and if a promise was made, they delivered. Smart says, "this may sound naive, but in today's world, the firms that can deliver what they promise and avoid short cuts for quick gains are the ones that will be present 10 years from today."

The Model Business

What business is right for you?

Within the entrepreneurial mindset, there remain a wide variety of styles, projects, and types of businesses. When choosing the right business for you, you have to be sure to take into account your own personality, your own preferences, and your own skill sets. Every business is different with vastly different external components. Which kind of business will meet your needs, will allow you to be successful? The model business is a tool that will help you decide which business is the "ideal" business for you.

Do what you enjoy and you can persevere.

Successful entrepreneurs do things they love and for which they have a great passion. Have you ever heard of anyone who has been extremely successful doing something they hate? To begin, you should ask yourself what you would do if you could work for free for the rest of your life. The answer to that question reveals your passion, which is what you should pursue.

The model business examines several differentiating factors and you must determine how you personally feel about each criteria. There are no right or wrong answers, just different styles of accomplishing tasks and different business environments. The way you think about each factor will help you to determine your own model business.

Hunting or fishing

Bait your hook and wait or stalk your prey?

A silly metaphor is helpful in understanding the first aspect of the model business. Are you a hunter or are you a fisher? If you like businesses where you can go after and stalk customers, then you are more of a hunter. You can make a list of potential customers and strategize the best means of attracting those customers.

However, if you prefer to bait your hook and wait for your customers to come to you, then you are a fisherman. Fishing is dependent upon action by the customer. It does not matter how well you build your pizza shop or your flower shop, you can only put it there and it then depends on the customer to enter the store before your business is truly started.

It is a matter of being proactive or being dependent. Neither approach is intrinsically better; both are different. The purpose of the model business is for you to decide with which one you are more comfortable and which one matches your personality.

Labor

Enjoy managing people?

You must ask yourself how you feel about labor. Are you the type of person that enjoys managing people regardless of the type of business or, are you embarking on an entrepreneurial journey in order to escape from having to manage people? The nature of the labor also plays an important role. If you are starting a computer software company, you will have to recognize that some of your best employees will begin at ten o'clock at night and work until six o'clock in the morning. They are free spirits and will probably not be available for a Friday afternoon staff meeting.

They do not meet the normal daytime schedule. Is this something that will bother you or something with which you are comfortable? Will you be able to allow your employees some flexibility or do you need to run a tight ship on your time line?

Is labor an issue?

Similarly, you may be passionate about cooking and want to start a restaurant. In your third month of success, you may get a call telling you that three of your waiters will not be coming in today. Your business has changed and you are no longer in the food business about which you are passionate, you are in the business of managing minimum wage people. You must decide how you feel about these challenges and what type of business makes more sense for you.

Paul Orfalea, founder of Kinko's, wanted to start a business that made money while he slept. He knew he would have to be dependent on his employees and build Kinko's on a culture where everyone was an associate or co-worker, not an employee. This attitude toward labor has been a key part of Kinko's success.

Investment

What are the investment options you are comfortable with?

The amount of investment needed, your ability to raise capital, and ownership issues are all considerations in deciding your model business. Do you want to start a business that needs a lot of start-up capital? Are you capable of raising a lot of money? Are you comfortable with giving up ownership, if necessary? Revisiting the restaurant example and assuming that you wanted the perfect restaurant in the perfect location with the perfect ambiance, then it may cost several million dollars. Are you capable of raising that much money and what percent of ownership do you end up with when it is all done?

There may be alternative routes if you do not want to give up ownership or cannot raise several million dollars. Entrepreneurship is about alternatives and finding different solutions. Perhaps you should start a catering business that would not require such a large investment. You could eventually move into the restaurant once your catering business is successful. How dependent do you want to be on outside money and how much control you want to maintain are critical questions that you must answer in choosing your model business.

Risk

Risk taker or risk manager?

Learning to manage risk is another important aspect of the model business. How do you feel about risk? Are you the type of person who can't sleep at night if you owe someone money? How do you feel about putting a second mortgage on your house to raise the start-up money? Will that keep you up for a week? You must deal with risk. If you are risk-averse, you might want to seek businesses that allow you to find your first customer before making a heavy investment.

Entrepreneurs perceive themselves as risk managers. You can manage your risk by choosing a business that you can start with a customer in hand, and then the only risk is your ability to fulfill the customer's order.

Up Front & Personal: Avanteer

Stefan Bean's journey began with much turmoil. As an orphaned child in Vietnam, he was in the wrong place in line when the polio vaccination was being administered. The country was too poor to vaccinate each child, thus, every other one was chosen. As a result, Bean contracted polio and now relies on a wheelchair and/or crutches to get around.

Luck took a turn for the better during a government-sponsored program, Operation Baby Lift, which brought orphaned children out of Vietnam. With 400 orphans, two planes were necessary to deport all of the children. Given that his last name is in the beginning of the alphabet, he should have been on the first plane; however, his files were out of order. The North Vietnamese shot down the first plane and nearly all of the 200 orphans perished in the crash. Bean, who was on the second plane, made it through to the United States, where he was adopted by American parents. This is where Stefan's true journey in life began.

Bean credits his mother with teaching him compassion; a trait he feels an entrepreneur must possess because "you need compassion for what you do, must have compassion for people because you are dealing with people all the time." His parents also instilled a sense of independence in Bean and did not "baby" him because he was in a wheelchair or used crutches. He had to walk to school and do his chores, just like every other child. Bean feels that these things built him both physically and mentally and gave him a "toughness." He attributes everything he is today to his parents and to God.

In High School, Bean was a natural fund-raiser and realized he had a talent for making money in creative ways. His class raised the most money in the history of the high school and Bean acknowledges that he truly enjoyed generating money by being creative.

Bean learned at an early age that he has a purpose in life and refers to a special poem as a guiding force: "Within me lives a purpose, A reason I am here, And one day soon, it will say to me Hi there, the world needs you, Are you ready?" Part of his purpose was to survive the plane crash and the obstacles he faced as a little child thereby enabling him to make a difference in people's lives. Also, because he has had to live with a disability, he has learned how to adapt to any kind of situation. As an entrepreneur, he feels those two traits are essential. "If you are going to start a company, there has to be a purpose behind that company, and then you need to be able to adapt to any type of situation."

Tony Rochon had a different path in life before meeting Bean and came into entrepreneurship by way of the music industry. He had been involved in concert promotions, and on the management team of a successful band, Striper. Tony describes himself as always being very independent and a sort of "maverick." "I think entrepreneurs are mavericks by nature. Always wanting to do things different." Rochon's reasons for getting into entrepreneurship include his desire for independence, to be in control of his own time, to not be limited by how much money he can make, and to avoid the confines of a corporate structure.

When discussing success and failure, Rochon feels that his "so-called" failures are really successes. Every venture that he has attempted has contributed to what he is today and has allowed him to learn and grow. As a result, he does not view anything he has done as a failure, but rather a successful learning opportunity.

The two met at the University of Southern California in the entrepreneur program. They each liked what the other had accomplished to date and expressed an interest in doing business together post-college. They both had energy and enthusiasm to build a business with unlimited potential, which led them to the Internet. They saw it as "the new frontier" and a place where they could capitalize on the growth and many opportunities.

As a result, they founded a software design company to develop collaborative applications for the Internet. The software allows two or more people to access the same application simultaneously from different parts of the world. Each person can see what the other is doing because it is a collaborative applicationa, which is an area of the Internet that they feel is still relatively new and has tremendous potential.

The name for their company, Avanteer, represents a combination of avant-garde and pioneer and their showcase product is a three-dimensional software engine that allows multiple users to access the Internet simultaneously. The software can be used for games or for business applications and Bean and Rochon are hopeful that it will ignite interest in the corporate world.

To get a better feel for the software, Bean gives an example. The software would enable an automobile dealership to create a sales floor. It would be a three-dimensional layout with cars on display and salespeople walking around. The customer could log on, meet the salesperson, and walk around to see the different cars.

To demonstrate their software, Avanteer has developed a game called Funtopia that allows it to showcase its capabilities; however, the founders emphasize that the software can have business applications as well and that they can meet any virtual need.

Avanteer is in the hunt for funding that will help them develop their product. In the meantime, the company survives by providing clients with computer training and software design. They feel that this is good exposure for the product side of the business as well. "It's all exposure and that generates interest." They do recognize when to say no and are not going to accept any offer that comes along. They had an offer for $1 million that they rejected because "there were too many strings attached."

Rochon's motivation stems from the freedom, the independence to be able to do what he wants when he wants. Additionally, it is the ability to make as much money as he'd like to make. But, he also indicates that "success isn't just money, it's a lot of things. It's the balance of life, the free time, the flexibility, you're doing it yourself and the sky's the limit."

Bean has a different purpose for the company. He views the world as getting smaller and smaller because of the Internet, and their software allows more and more people to come together who otherwise would not have been able to do so. That, he feels is the purpose of the company, to facilitate interaction among people.

Harvest or lifestyle

Building to sell or for a lifelong income?

For entrepreneurs, harvest means the act of liquidating their stake in their business. Whether it be selling or going public, it is taking the appreciation that has been built and transferring it to the founder. The entrepreneur must know when to exit the business.

The opposite of that is a lifestyle business that you plan to keep and run throughout your life. In a lifestyle business, you are building a business that will give you a handsome, substantial income. But in the end, it may not have any stand-alone, intrinsic value. It may be difficult to sell or to realize any appreciation. Some firms are passed down from generation to generation, and others are kept going just long enough to be purchased by someone else.

You must decide if you are building a business to harvest or if you are building a business for your lifestyle.

Recognized market

Do customers know or is education involved?

Is there a segment of the population already willing and able to buy your prospective product? If so, your advertising and publicity tasks may be less complex, but you may also face strong competition. On the other hand, if your product is innovative and new, you probably won't have the same level of competition. However, you will have to devote significant resources to convincing the public that it needs what you have to sell.

In the early 1980s desktop computer manufacturers had a lot more to prove to the general population than the makers of traditional appliances like refrigerators and ovens. Historically, entrepreneurs have gravitated to unrecognized markets so that they can build a niche and solidify their position before the competition arrives. But, you must choose whether or not you prefer to work with a recognized market or not.

Worthy challenge

Does it make sense and cents?

A business is a worthy challenge if it makes sense, including cents, for you for the future. A new business will require all of your energy and dedication. You need to ask yourself if your business idea will justify and reward that sort of commitment. There is a saying in the banking industry that it takes as much work to do a small deal as it does to do a big one—you just don't make as much money on a small one. Likewise, you might make a pile of money opening a store that sells rubber tires and nothing else, but will you be happy spending your days there? Simply put, is this business worth your while? In all aspects?

Frequency of purchase

Repeat customers or single, long-term customer?

Some businesses offer products that will be bought only once by each consumer. The entrepreneur may spend considerable time counseling the client and building a relationship before a purchase is made. Afterward, the two parties have little contact. This often happens in residential real estate.

On the other hand, some businesses count on repeat customers, and it is this pattern of repetition that creates the relationship. This is true in many service-oriented businesses like hair cutting or dry cleaning. Are you more comfortable cultivating a relationship and building up to one large sale or do you prefer to nurture many relationships and create a large number of repeat customers?

Perceived need

Do customers know they need it?

Whether or not there is a perceived need for your product or service is another distinguishing aspect of the model business. Is yours a product that is seeking a home or are you really a solution looking for a problem? You may have the perfect product that no one needs. Or, a recognized market may exist for your product, but that does not mean that there is necessarily a perceived need. For example, a recognized market exists for laundry detergent, but is there really a need for another brand? On the other hand, if the new brand represents a technological or performance breakthrough, then the answer may change. What area are you more comfortable exploring—a recognized market or a perceived need?

Credit and collections

What is the essence of your business?

Considering that entrepreneurship is truly about doing what you love, you must understand that the nature of some businesses is not about the business itself, but about related secondary issues like credit and collections. There are many businesses where the essence of the business—the vital area—is in handling the collections. An example is the lumber industry in which 2x4s are standard and quality has been defined by numbers. People must compete on price, and the people that succeed spend most of their time collecting. Will you be satisfied in a business where most of your energy is spent collecting receivables as opposed to enjoying the product and the industry?

Liability

Challenging to maintain compliance or frustrating?

If your business deals with dangerous equipment and raw materials, produces a potentially toxic substance, or targets certain segments of the market, you will have to pay extra attention to liability issues. You could be in the cleaning business dealing with toxic substances or dealing with the public and exposing them to perilous situations. These businesses, by their very nature, carry a large potential liability. How would you like to release a line of children's toys, only to turn on your television set at the beginning of the Christmas season and find the evening news warning parents away from your product for safety reasons? While no industry is free of these issues, some are more prone to them than others. Do you see this as a dagger hanging over your head or does this challenge of maintaining compliance excite you?

Technical obsolescence

There are entrepreneurs in the high-technology sector that absolutely thrive on the fact that their products will be obsolete in two years or less. Computers and other such high-tech items change rapidly, and if you want to sell these items you'll need to work extra hard to keep up-to-date with industry standards. On the other hand,

Infinite life, or obsolete in 6 months-what is best for you?

there are entrepreneurs who are more comfortable with something that has an extended life and is without the threat of obsolescence. For example, a nursery or day-care business offers a chance to have an infinite life. You must decide what makes sense for you.

Regulation

How much control do you want?

Many entrepreneurs begin their journey because they want to have control over their working lives. There are many industries, such as healthcare and telecommunications that are heavily regulated by the government. This diminishes your ability to control pricing or may even limit what and to whom you can sell. Many an entrepreneur has died at the hands of a legislature's pen. Which environment is more comfortable for you?

Summary of model business

It's time to start your journey - what business is right for you?

It is essential to remember that these issues have no objective right or wrong answers. In each case, you need to figure out which end of the spectrum is more suitable for you. What does your nature dictate? Regardless of the business that you choose, it must be one that is compatible with your own needs, strengths, desires and abilities. That is the essence of the concept of a model business—a model that works for you and enables you to embark on your own entrepreneurial journey.

It is time for you to decide about your model business and to start your journey. Use the exercise on the next page to help you get started. You can change your mind as you progress, however, you must choose an industry to begin to explore. For example, if you are interested in the restaurant business, start learning about that industry. Read every trade journal that is published, go to every association and market meeting that you find, and visit other restaurants. In this exploration, you should be looking for keys to success, what is it that makes that restaurant successful? Discover its vital areas, what is the value being created. Take note of what you are now seeing that you may not have observed before you began to understand the entrepreneurial mindset.

It is time to embark on your entrepreneurial journey.

Challenge: Are You Ready?

Entrepreneurs anticipate. They are always ready.

You are at a cocktail party. You meet someone who asks you what you do. Are you prepared to answer in an intelligent, brief manner that causes the listener to go—WOW—and wants to be involved? The classic test of whether you can articulate your concept and show its value is if you can do that by the time an elevator goes from the top to the bottom floor. If it takes longer than that, you probably are not ready.

Or if someone were to say to you—"what would you do if I gave you a million dollars?"— would you know how to answer?

Entrepreneurial Exercise

Model Business Evaluation Scale

Review the following criteria of the model business and circle the number that corresponds to how closely you match that side of the model business. There is no right score. Do not add the numbers, they merely give you a sense for what direction to pursue in your model business.

Hunter ——————————————————————————————— Fisher
1   3   5   7   9

Labor to Manage ———————————————————— Little Labor
1   3   5   7   9

High Investment Required ———————— Low Investment Required
1   3   5   7   9

Risk Taker ————————————————————————— Risk Averse
1   3   5   7   9

Harvest ——————————————————————————————— Lifestyle
1   3   5   7   9

New Market ————————————————————— Recognized Market
1   3   5   7   9

Worthy Challenge ————————————————————— Easy Entry
1   3   5   7   9

High Frequency of Purchase ———— Low Frequency of Purchase
1   3   5   7   9

Education Required ————————————————— Perceived Need
1   3   5   7   9

Collections are Vital ———————————— Collections not an Issue
1   3   5   7   9

A Lot of Liability ——————————————————— Limited Liability
1   3   5   7   9

Technical Obsolescence ————————————— Lifelong Product
1   3   5   7   9

Limited Regulation ——————————————— Highly Regulated
1   3   5   7   9

⇒   **Tear out and move to your entrepreneurial road map binder.**

Chapter Summary

- Entrepreneurship is a journey filled with passion, hard work, and a great deal of dedication.
- Entrepreneurship is unique to each and every individual and your journey will be different.
- Defining entrepreneurship has been met with much controversy.
- Entrepreneurship is a phenomenon driven by one's attitudes, skill sets, and personal characteristics and traits.
- Accept the entrepreneurial mindset and learn to embrace outside the box thinking.
- Learning to live in an ambiguous world, recognizing that the market is your only judge, and learning through trial and error are imperative for a successful journey.
- Networking and seeking a mentor are critical parts of the entrepreneur's world.
- The model business is a tool that should be used to assess what type of business is most suitable for you and your lifestyle.
- At the end of this chapter, you will meet the "Hot Tamales" of the Border Grill and read about the characteristics and skill sets that have helped to make them successful.

> *I can sleep as late as I want, I can take days off that I want and the lifestyle really fits me becuase I work by obsession."*
> - Jerry Teisan, Founder, Trick R/C

Chapter One Exercises/Discussion Questions

1. What are your thoughts on the entrepreneurial revolution and how do you see it playing a part in your life?
2. Are you prepared to face the many issues that entrepreneurs must deal with?
3. Think of an entrepreneur whom you know and identify what issues were most difficult for them to face.
4. Identify the primary differences between a small business and an entrepreneurial venture. Which is more appropriate for you?
5. Can you identify your passion? What gets you really excited?
6. Can you identify the industry in which you are interested? Make a list of all the facts and information you know about that industry. Find two to three trade journals in the industry and seek out more information.
7. What do you believe is the definition of an entrepreneur? How does that differ from the classic and descriptive definitions presented in this chapter?
8. Think of three instances in which you have been faced with an ambiguous situation. How did you cope with the ambiguity? Why is this important in the world of entrepreneurship?
9. Come up with three instances in your own life where a failure led to eventual success, or when failure provided the knowledge to make some other goal possible.
10. Identify a time when you offered assistance to another student, friend or family member in the form of giving advice or tutoring. How did helping someone in need make you feel?
11. What did you, as a mentor, get out of the experience? What does this tell you about how to recruit a mentor for yourself?
12. What is the difference between a perceived need and a recognized market? How does this affect entrepreneurial thinking?

Project One: Entrepreneur Interview

Project One is aimed at being able to understand an entrepreneur's mindset, characteristics, and skill sets. Your goal is to become intimately acquainted with his or her persona—try to find out what makes he or she tick.

For this project, you must conduct an **IN-PERSON** interview with an entrepreneur whom **YOU DO NOT KNOW.** Make sure that this person or team's venture is innovative, growth oriented and creates value. It is better not to choose a small, lifestyle venture and/or small business owner for this project. Ideally, you'll want to choose someone **in an industry in which you are interested.** That way, you will have the opportunity to investigate this area further with project #2, the Value Chain. Your written paper should be succinct, clear, and informative. It should **NOT contain a verbatim transcript of the interview.**

Instead, explain what you learned, in your own words, with rich, thick description. In your paper, be sure to addresss topics that reveal the characteristics of the entrepreneur. Your goal should be to leave the interview and the experience with a better understanding of what it takes to be an entrepreneur. This will enable you to help determine your capability in the entrepreneurial world. Feel free to deal with any issues that seem relevant and important to both your learning experience and to the entrepreneur.

You should also be prepared to present your findings to the rest of the class. Just as you should always be prepared to present yourself and your business concept, you should be ready for your professor to call on you. Keep in mind that an oral presentation should not be a mere reiteration of your paper, rather it should highlight the important lessons learned from the entrepreneur and show how the entrepreneur's story relates to what has been learned in the course.

Can this person be a mentor for you?

> *"Entrepreneurs are alchemists. They add value to existence-turning iron into gold-through strength of will, intelligence, and a determination to succeed."*
> -Lloyd Greif, President & CEO, Greif & Co.

Welcome to Border Grill!

Journey One: Border Grill

Susan Feniger and Mary Sue Milliken began their 17-year entrepreneurial journey with a passion for cooking and took it to new kind of restaurant in Los Angeles, California that catapulted them from a hot plate to the national spotlight. They are among the many entrepreneurs you will meet in this book who prove that the entrepreneurial journey can begin anytime and/or anywhere.

Background

Feniger and Milliken first met in Chicago in 1978 when they were both apprenticing at a fine French restaurant. They found themselves together again at a cooking school in France, and it was then that they decided to work together. They shook on it, and "in the Midwest, when you shake on it, it means something." They were drawn together because of similar interests and an abundance of energy. Milliken even said "I think what was really great was that she had the same passion, the same commitment to our craft that I had and I hadn't met any body, male or female, up to that point, who was quite as similar to me as she was." While in France, they worked together, studied together, and were completely obsessed with learning the industry. Separately, they recorded everything, each keeping a logbook so that they would not forget anything and then comparing notes at the end of every day. To this day, they both still have their logs.

In 1981, Feniger was back in the States working for a soon to be household name, restaurateur Wolfgang Puck. She also took a second job at a tiny start-up café that was so small she did her cooking on a hot plate, City Café. As Milliken recalls, Feniger called her and said "why don't you move to California, I've got two hot plates, one for you and one for me." As a result, it was at City Café that they developed their signature cuisine, an eclectic mix of Indian, Asian, and Latin Marketplace cooking. Due to the small size and autonomy that they had while working at City Café, they were able to experiment with their culinary abilities as well as learn the business sense needed to run a successful restaurant, all without great expense. As do all individuals learning and experimenting, they made mistakes, but in such a way that was not costly and that became part of their learning curve. And, they were "having a blast," doing what they loved to do.

Restaurant # 1

Feniger and Milliken were having such a good time, they decided to open their own restaurant, City. Their first challenge was raising capital, which turned out to be the simplest of the many tasks that lay ahead of them. They relied on family, friends and loyal customers for the $660,000 that was needed to start the business. They had built a track record and were putting it to good use.

Once they had the financial support, it was quite an exciting and rocky road to opening night. Admittedly, they had no idea how large an undertaking they had begun. But, as Milliken stated, "When you're that passionate about something, it's almost like you don't have a choice. It's almost like you have to pursue it whether you fail or succeed because you have to have tried."

The Challenges

The first major hurdle that they had to overcome was a general contractor who thought of them as just a couple of "cute girls." They had to fire him, which they did not realize until about six months after they should have fired him. However, they were responsible and did what was needed.

Their second challenge was dealing with bureaucrats at the Department of Water and Power who almost would not turn on their utilities. With opening night less than two weeks away, they learned that DWP was refusing to turn on their power for two more weeks. Always thinking on their feet, Feniger and Milliken managed to work with the system and get the date moved up.

Acquiring a liquor license proved to be quite difficult as well. Milliken even stated that "had we not been able to get it, we wouldn't have been able to make a go of it, it would have been a total disaster."

The final hurdle was obtaining a permit from the Department of Health. Unable to put any food in the kitchen until they had the permit, they had to wait to stock the place until two days before opening, when they were finally presented with the appropriate permit.

But, they persevered in the face of these many challenges and did not let anything stand in the way of opening night. They had the drive and the eagerness to make it work and having the hunger for success enabled them to overcome all obstacles. At times, they had to do things that were perhaps "a little bit outside the lines, something a little bit wacky, a little more gutsy than someone else might do."

Border Grill

Opening night came and City Restaurant was a huge success. Before long, they opened a second restaurant, Border Grill and were soon LA's hot new chefs.

But as fate would sometimes have it, both Mother Nature and a recession intervened. In a two-year period, the Los Angeles economy experienced a downturn, the LA riots occurred, there was a massive earthquake, and there were fires and floods in the area. All of this was happening at a time when both Feniger and Milliken were feeling a bit tired and burnt out. They had been through a lot, had experienced success, and were now faced with fierce challenges. But, an entrepreneur's job is never done and it was not in their nature to give up. They needed to dig deep inside and find a solution.

The Bleak Days

Like every entrepreneur, they do remember their bleakest moment. "Going to the bankruptcy attorney was pretty bleak." They hadn't been taking salaries and were putting all of their money into keeping the restaurants alive. "That was something we would commonly do during periods when things weren't that good. The first thing to go is the owner's salary; they just don't get paid. You do whatever it takes to keep the business going."

It was during this time that they were faced with one of the hardest decisions they would ever have to make. Closing City Restaurant, which was "definitely like our child" left them both in tears.

Hope

During this time of turbulence, they were forced to tap all available resources. They did the smartest thing anyone in their position could do: they started calling people and asking for help. Amazed at the positive and helpful responses from their friends and associates in the industry, they received some much needed advice and assistance. One of their greatest supporters is their former mentor and nationally known Wolfgang Puck, who "has for years always been an amazing support for us, for whatever we've needed." Admitting to trouble and seeking advice is not always easy, but clearly the right thing to do. With the new found emotional and directional support, they would not only survive, but would prosper.

Today, Feniger and Milliken are back on top with two restaurants, cooking shows on radio and television, four cookbooks, and their own product line. They have leveraged their knowledge and expanded the business into every avenue that makes sense for them. Getting involved and getting their names out in the community has improved business in all areas. They have not lost sight of their core business, however, and are always concerned with the entire restaurant operation, not just the cooking. "The cooking is really important to us, but at the same time, if the bathroom is really dirty or the refrigerator needs to be scrubbed out, or whatever, we'll do it, we're really interested in the entire picture."

The Why

Feniger wouldn't have dreamed of getting into any other job, "this is what I love to do, I love being in the restaurant, it's got a great energy. It's what I'm passionate about, it was natural to think about doing it, and I always thought of myself as being my own boss."

Milliken had her own reasons, "I always knew I wanted a big family and I also knew that I wanted to be in control of my finances, I wanted to make my own money. I also love the fact that this industry has allowed me to change my role so many times and in so many ways."

Feniger and Milliken are successful entrepreneurs for many reasons: they never take no for an answer, they persevered in the face of many challenges, they never accepted failure, they experimented with new things that did not always work and never let anything stop them. Most importantly, they took something that they would do for free and turned it into a successful enterprise that accommodated their lifestyles and their families.

They started with their passion, learned the industry from the inside out, and built a team of mentors as well as a support circle. When they started it was in the most modest way possible and when successful, they leveraged their accomplishments to start a "real" restaurant.

Today, they continue to build upon their experience as they prepare to open two, possibly three new restaurants, which could be viewed by some as being quite risky. But, in many ways, it is not risky because they know the business extremely well and have developed an instinct over time to guide them. They are well prepared for any and all challenges ahead as they continue their entrepreneurial journey.

Journey One Case Questions

1. What does Feniger and Milliken's experience say about the entrepreneur's journey?
2. Do successful people ever fail?
3. Does failure mean you have no potential for success?
4. Why were they willing to continue in the face of failure?
5. What are the characteristics that they exhibited?
6. What skill sets did they develop?
7. Who did they turn to for support and why?
8. Why was this their model business?

Entrepreneurship is a Phenomenon

- By definition, has no definition
- Comprised of attitudes, skill sets and personal traits

"I think the most important characteristic of an entrepreneur is to understand the process of entrepreneurship. To understand that it is a systematic, purposeful process that can be learned, developed, and managed. It's not some seat of the pants gut feeling that you have, it's a professional discipline that can be learned and practiced and developed."
-Mike Singer, Chairman & CEO, Strategic Partners

Chapter Two
Myths & Characteristics

Chapter Two Major Concepts

- What an entrepreneur is not: myths of entrepreneurship
- Entrepreneurial characteristics
- Entrepreneurs vs. managers

Journey Two: Kinko's Inc.

Up Front & Personal: Colby Care Home Health

Up Front & Personal: Zotos & Stein

What is an Entrepreneur?

In the previous chapter we explored the entrepreneurial mindset and how to discover what type of business is right for you, personally. In our journey, we have already met two entrepreneurs—the Hot Tamales of Border Grill—who displayed their entrepreneurial mindset and type of business.

This chapter.

Continuing our journey leads to the exploration of the question: what is an entrepreneur? To arrive at an answer, our approach will be twofold. First is an examination of what entrepreneurs are not, or the myths that are commonly held about entrepreneurs. Second, we will learn about entrepreneurs by comparing and contrasting their mindsets with those of managers.

Entrepreneurship is a phenomenon.

We have already established that perhaps there is no single definition of an entrepreneur and the very fact that entrepreneurship is a phenomenon, means it has no true definition. However, it is apparent that this phenomenon is comprised of attitudes, skill sets, and personal traits and there is no one set of attitudes or skill sets or traits that are common to all entrepreneurs. Each entrepreneur is different.

What an Entrepreneur is Not: The Myths of Entrepreneurship

Myth 1: Entrepreneurs are born, not made

Myth 1: born, not made.

If entrepreneurs were born then there would be no need for this book or for the academic discipline of entrepreneurship. The belief that you either have the "e" gene or you do not is not supported by any research whatsoever. Furthermore, if this were true, then all who have this mythical "e" gene would be both destined and limited to entrepreneurship and would think and act in a common manner. However, there is nothing further from the truth.

The reality is that the argument of "born, not made" is said to be true of almost all skill sets. Is someone born a baseball player or a musician? Or are those skills developed over time? It is true that certain individuals have special gifts, such as good hand eye coordination, a great voice, or an ear for music. But, it is also true that an artist or a musician needs to train and develop technique. An artist does not simply become an artist because of the ability to sketch. Likewise, a baseball player does not enter the Hall of Fame because he can catch. Success comes from the time and effort put into the development of skills and will be dependent on one's attitude toward working on and improving his or her skill.

Are salesman born?

Think about salesmanship. Forty to fifty years ago, this same myth revolved around sales personnel. Salesmanship was believed to be a born talent and yet many large corporations quickly proved that myth false by training individuals to be successful at this trade. Selling is not about personality, just as entrepreneurship is not about personality.

> *"I have not seen any evidence that there is such a thing as an entrepreneurial personality. Entrepreneurs look like the general population of individuals, and they have the same kind of motivations."*
> -Dr. William Gartner, Entrepreneur Research Scholar

Role of environment.

There are, however, some researchers who argue that although entrepreneurs are not born, being born into the right "e" environment is critical. While there is no empirical evidence to support these observations, many who study the entrepreneurial journey believe that if you grew up in an environment that created a sense of support, fostered an attitude to try new things, and treated mistakes as necessary parts of learning, then you have a higher propensity to embark on an entrepreneurial journey of your own.

Childhood patterns.

For example, being brought up in a family in which financial security was a priority may have led a child to seek employment that offered security, benefits, and a history of life-long employment. On the other hand, a childhood full of entrepreneurs and exposure to entrepreneurial endeavors may provide a child with a different type of role model.

> *"The thought never entered my mind to interview for a job after college. Of my parents friends and acquaintances, I never knew any that ever had a job; everybody had their own businesses. And so the way my mother raised us was with the idea that we were going to have our own business one day. All my life I knew I was going to have my own business."*
> -Paul Orfalea, Founder, Kinko's, Inc.

What is typical of entrepreneurs is that successful ventures often do not occur on the first try. Research suggests that it takes 2.7 to 4 ventures before meaningful success is achieved and that ventures are not a great bang or single event, but are usually evolutionary with 89% occurring in areas/industries in which an entrepreneur is already involved. As such, becoming an entrepreneur is not an event, it does not just happen. It evolves and changes with age, experience, and perspective.

Learn by doing.

The final reality of this myth is that most successful entrepreneurs will tell you that what they are doing is something they learned, often in the middle of doing it.

Myth 2: Entrepreneurs are risk takers

Myth 2: Risk taker or risk manager?

Risk is a relative word and is in the eye of the beholder. What is risky for some is considered the norm for others and vice versa. Risk is proportionate to the perception of control over the outcome, as well as the potential downside if the event is not completed or successful.

Ask yourself if you think rock climbers take risk. Do you think they perceive climbing as risky? Why do they hang from cliffs at 5,000 feet? Are they stupid? To the ignorant observer, rock climbing may seem like an extremely risky thing to do and potentially even borders on suicide.

Risky to climb Half Dome?

However, in reality, climbers are not taking risk. When asked about the inordinate amount of risk they seem to take every day, rock climbers brush off the danger and risk involved because they know how to climb without jeopardizing their safety. They point out that they prepare, are in the proper physical and mental condition, and have trained in mountaineering before attempting a climb such as Half Dome in Yosemite National Park. With the proper training and a plan to attack the mountain, there is no real risk. They are in charge, are prepared, and have control over the outcome. A climber would not attempt an ascent without being properly trained and knowledgeable of the potential consequences and how to handle them.

Rock climbers: risk managers.

Individuals such as these mountain climbers are better described as risk managers. They have minimal exposure. They control the circumstance through preparation and planning and build safety into their plan by using harnesses, ropes, and other appropriate equipment. Teaming up with similarly trained individuals also minimizes the risk involved and is part of the planning process. As a result, a misstep need not be fatal.

The same analogy is true for entrepreneurs. If properly prepared with a solid team and with contingency plans in place, then the entrepreneur is managing risk and controlling the variables. Entrepreneurs carefully weigh the possible outcomes, do their homework, and are fully prepared for all scenarios before they will do something that may be perceived as risky. Therefore, they are properly managing what might happen and not just blindly stepping into a risky situation.

> *"Always think strategically, what's the opportunity? How do I address it? What can go wrong? What can go wrong internally, which means in your company, whether or not you capitalize it properly, and your team, whether or not it is properly in place. And what can go wrong externally, which means the environment and what's going on in the industry and in the competitive situation."*
>
> -Lloyd Greif, President and CEO, Greif & Co

Entrepreneur controls all variables.

The ultimate risk management strategy of an entrepreneurial start up is one that puts all the variables in the control of the entrepreneur. For this reason, ventures that can attract a <u>customer-in-hand</u>—having an order before starting—will minimize the risk. If a customer already wants what you have promised to deliver, the risk then becomes your ability to deliver it, which is completely within your control.

There is a certain amount of risk involved in any profession, but if you are properly prepared, trained and know what the worst possible outcome could be, and if you have contingency plans in place, then it is a properly managed risk.

Myth 3: You need a lot of money to be successful

Myth 3: money is a necessity.

Money is the great excuse for not starting a business and is the "ultimate in the box" thinking. In surveys of "would-be entrepreneurs" (those who want to be but have not even tried to start the process) the top two reasons given for not trying are money related. First, they claim they do not have enough money to start. Second, they cannot afford a cut in salary or a change in life style. Such is the attitude of those who do not embark on a journey of their own. In reality, what they are seeking is to be the owner of a company that has a large checking account. They want someone to pay them to do the job of a president. It just does not happen.

> *"At the time we started, we didn't have a computer, it was just a desk, a telephone, a paper, and a pen. And that's what we had and that's what we worked with."*
> -Carolyn Colby, Owner, Colby Care Home Health

Apple Computer, Inc. began when two teenagers sold their van and calculator and raised $1600 to begin their journey. Five years later sales crossed $500 million.

Money is an enabler.

Most entrepreneurial ventures start with little or no funds. The classic start up in a garage or game room is the norm, especially for first ventures. Once started and initial value is created (first customer, prototype), then money will find the entrepreneur. In this context money should be looked at as an enabler, not as a cause. Money cannot create a business, it can only allow a business that is started to continue in motion.

Money = booster rocket.

As such, money is analogous to a booster rocket because it carries no benefit or payload by itself, it cannot start the journey. It is the entrepreneur who has prepared, has learned the industry, has defined and positioned his or her niche, and has already received feedback from initial customers. The entrepreneur is the primary first mover. Money, on the other hand, is a booster. When the rocket is in motion, the booster propels it into orbit. Likewise, when the entrepreneur is in motion, money propels the business into action. Money cannot give birth, its role is to give strength and support to the newborn.

Myth 4: All you need is a great idea

Myth 4: great ideas can start the business.

Surveys reveal that not having a great idea is the third most frequently cited excuse for not starting a business. In reality, there are very few great ideas that start businesses. Being "great" typically means the idea is unique and protect-able (through a patent for example), which is often the domain of researchers and inventors and takes decades before that idea actually reaches a point when opportunities exist for entrepreneurs.

Famous Amos

Wally Amos is the founder of *Famous Amos* Chocolate Chip Cookies—a brand that started in the 80's and has survived long after the entrepreneur has gone. When addressing an entrepreneur class, Amos told of his passion for baking cookies and his struggle to commercialize his hobby. It was his perseverance and sacrifice that enabled him to begin by selling out of his kitchen and later to open a retail store, which was unheard of at that time.

During his story, a student interrupted him and said that he, the student, could be as successful as Amos if he had a cookie that tasted as good as Amos'. Amos politely said to the student that the challenge was the execution, not the product, and continued. As Amos discussed his entrepreneurial journey and his efforts at increasing sales at his marginal retail stores and getting shelf space in grocery stores, the student again interrupted and reiterated that Amos' success was largely due to his magic recipe. Undaunted, Amos again emphasized execution and spoke of trying to get distribution both nationally and internationally. The student interrupted a third time and said that this was all verbiage, the secret was the recipe. With dignity, but without patience, Wally Amos looked at the student and said, "I got my recipe off of the back of Nestle's Chocolate Chips. Now let's see how good you are."

The student was obviously quieted, but the message was not. It was loud and clear. It is not about a great idea or a great product. It is about execution—what you do with that idea and that product.

Popcorn heads.

Observations of nascent entrepreneurs suggest that there is not a lack of ideas. Many claim that they have multiple new ideas daily. One young student described himself as having so many new ideas that they popped out of his head like popcorn.

A hamburger was not a new idea.

In reality, entrepreneurship is rarely about a new idea. It is about taking someone's idea to a new level. Ray Kroc, one of the original founders of McDonald's Corporation, did not invent the hamburger. It had been around for a long time. While on his rounds as a milkshake hardware salesman, he observed the three McDonald brothers and their three hamburger stands in California. The McDonald boys did not invent the hamburger either. They simply changed the way it was served. Instead of sitting down and ordering, walking up to a window resulted in quick service. Thus, the term "fast food" was coined. But, in actuality, hamburgers and hot dogs had been served fast food style from corner vendors and at fairs for hundreds of years.

Execution counts, not the idea.

In retrospect, it is hard to find a new idea in any part of the McDonald's story. What becomes evident is that an old idea of selling hamburgers was executed more efficiently by a certain entrepreneur. The critical variable in this equation is execution, not the idea itself. Very rarely are entrepreneurial journeys started because of a great idea. It is great execution of an idea that leads to success.

Solutions looking for problems?

The search for a new idea can become even more complicated when individuals limit themselves to seeking new products. In effect, they are often focused on finding solutions to problems that do not exist. Forcing a vision on customers and trying to create a product for which there may not be a market is not a successful start up model. These businesses fail because the entrepreneur is in love with his or her product and does not take the time to learn whether or not anyone else, i.e., the market, is in love with the product. Again, this supports the research that suggests it is not the idea or product but rather the execution that is critical to success.

Myth 5: Entrepreneurs are lone wolves

Myth 5: entrepreneurs are lone wolves.

Again, nothing is further from the truth. Entrepreneurs often need to create solutions because they lack the resources to buy them. They are totally dependent on their network of contacts to accomplish tasks. Without these contacts, sales cannot be achieved, products cannot be developed, and money cannot be raised. The old adage, "who you know is more important than what you know" is certainly true in this environment. Many scholars of Apple Computer, Inc. attribute its birth to the influence of the 1970's Home Brew Computer Club meetings that Jobs and Wozniak attended. This club was comprised of individuals interested in computers who met to discuss and analyze trends in the industry. Without this network and exchange of ideas, Apple would likely not have happened.

Networks play a critical role.

Entrepreneurs often come in pairs.

While it is typically one founder that is highlighted and accredited with getting a venture off the ground, the number of companies that have multiple initial founders represents the majority of all start ups. Certainly the just cited Apple Computer had multiple founders. Microsoft Corporation, the grand daddy of all entrepreneurial ventures, was not the result of a solo effort, but rather the works of both Paul Allen and Bill Gates. Even the history books attest to this fact as is evidenced by Hewlett Packard and Sears Roebuck.

> *"You have to realize that there is very little that you can do alone. You have to build a team around you, whether it's a team to run the company or a team to help you acquire a company. A lot of different players are involved."*
>
> - Mike Singer, Chairman and CEO, Strategic Partners

Complementary talents.

A network to support and help mold new ideas and strategies, introduce new contacts, and guide entrepreneurs on their journey is a crucial ingredient. Additionally, because no single individual has all of the types of skill sets needed to succeed, the joining of complementary talents to form a winning team is part of the profile of success.

Myth 6: Entrepreneurs work long, hard hours

Myth 6: lots of work involved.

This certainly by most standards is true. The amount of time and dedication needed to give birth to your business is incredible. Even when you are not working—when you are in the shower, eating dinner, or trying to sleep—your mind is totally engaged in your business. You are constantly reliving every conversation, thinking about every detail.

However, when discussing the amount of time and number of hours spent consumed in their passion of starting a venture, entrepreneurs will tell you that it is not work. It is what they love to do.

It isn't work if you would do it for free.

An entrepreneur's wise mentor once made the point evident. He said that to those absorbed in starting a venture, the people on the golf course may look very inviting. However, the professional golfer spends as much time at his craft—practicing, playing, traveling—as any entrepreneur does in his business. In response, you might say, yes, but the golfer loves golf. Therein lies the point, entrepreneurs are entrepreneurs because they do what they love to do: start ventures, exploit opportunities, and control their destiny. The mentor was absolutely right because it is not work if it is doing what you would do for free if you had your choice.

Involve your family.

That same wise mentor also speaks of one of the most important pieces of advice for any entrepreneur. That advice is to include your family in all aspects of your venture, to go out of your way to involve the kids. This may be contrary to your experiences as a child if the family business was never discussed at home. You may have had no idea how Pop spent his day.

The mentor's advice was not just about scheduling time with your family. His advice is about having your family involved in the emotion of your business. They need to be a part of the ups and downs, to celebrate when the big order is won, and be saddened when a system fails. Having your kids stuff mailers or build sales books while your spouse is in the office cleaning up the paper work or being part of a month end "get the product out" all nighter is important.

Share the journey.

Without having your family involved, you may end up a successful lone wolf. The journey is too exciting to keep to yourself—share it at all levels.

> *"They talk about entrepreneurs being workaholics and there is a time when you have to put in the effort; however, you have to enjoy life, there definitely is a balance."*
>
> -Tony Rochon, Co-Founder, Avanteer, Inc.

Entrepreneurial Exercise

This is your opportunity to debunk your own entrepreneurial myths. On the lines below, make a list of all the associations you have about entrepreneurs and why you think they are true. Then, exchange lists with a classmate, evaluate his or her list, and write down whether you think they are myths or reality. Likewise, your classmate will write on your sheet why he or she thinks the myths you have written down are in fact myths and if so, what the reality is. Discuss your findings.

Myths:

1. _____

2. _____

3. _____

4. _____

5. _____

Reaction to classmates myths:

1. _____

2. _____

3. _____

4. _____

5. _____

⇒   **Tear out and move to your entrepreneurial road map binder.**

Entrepreneurial Characteristics

Entrepreneurs vs. leaders.

When researchers seek to define the "person" part of entrepreneurship, their studies usually prove to be inconclusive as to the characteristics of entrepreneurs. They do find that the profiles that best match successful entrepreneurs correlate with the characteristics of leaders. The connection between the two is to some degree obvious, but only to a point. Entrepreneurs are leaders and leaders are able to be entrepreneurial in that they creatively find solutions that others might miss; however, not all leaders are entrepreneurs and not all entrepreneurs are leaders.

When entrepreneurs are asked why they are successful, they do not find it as inconclusive as academics. Most entrepreneurs have strong feelings for the causality underlying their success. While there is no one characteristic for success, the ones that appear to be most often cited as the cause of success by entrepreneurs are examined below.

Passion

It is a journey of passion.

Doing what you love to do and doing it with determination and commitment is almost always cited as being critical to success. Although most believe their passion is equivalent to a love of their product or service and this may be the case for some entrepreneurs, it is really a very limiting description.

Entrepreneurs are usually more passionate about starting the business than about the product or service they provide. It is the excitement of birth—of creatively bringing together all of the components for the journey—which creates the passion. Assembling a team, even if it is a team of one or two, attracting mentors and advisors to guide and give balance to the journey, exploring customer needs, and designing benefits to fulfill them are the true passion of entrepreneurs. When brought together, these elements give you the answer to what you would do if you could work for free.

Perseverance

Perseverance is critical.

Entrepreneurship is a journey full of exhilaration. Coupled with that are ups and downs, surprises, and changes in direction. At the moment when all seems bleak and nearly impossible, the entrepreneur needs to make a decision: Do I have it in me to keep going? Do I have the mental toughness to say go on? To not give up?

A Fish Out of Water

When a fish finds itself on the bank, it is in obvious peril. At that point, the fish has two choices. It can remain still and face certain death. Or, it can continue to flop back and forth. If it perseveres and keeps flopping, one of two things can happen. It may flop itself right back into the water. Or, if that does not happen, it may flop long enough for the tide to come in and pull the fish back to sea. In either case, if the fish perseveres, two positive things could happen. If the fish gives up, the worst outcome is guaranteed.

-Dr. Richard Buskirk, Entrepreneur Professor

Strain is also placed on the entrepreneur's physical being. Long hours, always behind schedule, and people and markets not moving fast enough will test everyone's metal. There is a significant difference between giving up and making a conscious decision not to pursue the opportunity.

Not every venture will be successful.

It is important to realize that not every venture will be successful. Just as diligence is necessary to determine what is needed to start, there is an equally great responsibility if you decide not to pursue your venture. You owe it to everybody that has supported you—customers, suppliers, advisors, partners, associates, and family—to inform them of a decision to terminate. Do it honestly and truthfully. One young entrepreneur followed this advice. When he called his largest customer to inform him of financial problems and his plan to close the business, he was pleasantly surprised when his customers said that they did not realize they were creating a problem and found a way to prepay orders to keep the company alive. Instead of an unhappy customer and a defunct business, a successful entrepreneur and a satisfied customer resulted.

Never, ever give up.

It pays to persevere. As Stefan Bean of Avanteer, Inc. puts it, "Man, you just never give up." If you stay in the game, you will outlast your competition.

Many also believe that perseverance will even beat talent.

Credibility/integrity

Credibility is like virginity, you only lose it once.

As the road curves and you travel on your journey, you will be challenged. When problems arise and the wisdom of your decisions is in question, you will need the support of all those around you. As those turbulent times occur and as you are challenged and turn to your associates, the single most important thing that you need to survive will be your integrity. How you have treated your shareholders up to this point will pay dividends. If you have built a culture of honesty, you will receive very positive dividends. However, if you have walked the edge of honesty or have even crossed over the line ever so slightly, then your dividends will be negative. When support is needed the most, it will not be available.

> *"Whatever we are deep down, in our core values, in our personal principles, our ethical standards, our integrity. Whatever we are in our personal values, our company is going to become. It is unavoidable, it is irrevocable, if we are SOBs, so are our companies, so are our people, so is our reputation. If we are driven by human values, by long term consideration for other people, respect for diverse opinions, the ability to help other people to be the best that they can be, our companies will reflect those values and every one of our customers will feel it."*
> -Ann Graham Ehringer, Entrepreneur Professor

One lie can be a deathblow.

Your personal sense of integrity must be reflected in all transactions—large and small—of your company and it is more important than you may imagine. A lie told to one customer, one supplier, or one shareholder can be a deathblow to a start up company.

In the final analysis, credibility is like virginity, you only lose it once and you can never get it back.

Enthusiasm and optimism

Entrepreneur must be the positive, excited, optimistic parent.

Entrepreneurship can be compared to a ride on an emotional roller coaster. There are highs and everyone is naturally excited and enthusiastic about the outcome. But, then there are lows and the world seems to want to stop. Everyone around you will begin to question you and the future. Is it still possible?

Nothing is as contagious as enthusiasm. Others need to see it while entrepreneurs need to generate and exude it.

The entrepreneur does not have the luxury of questioning whether or not it is possible. He must enjoy the highs without letting them get too high. Likewise, he must endure the lows without letting them get too low. As the leader, everyone will be looking at him for direction, just as children look to their parents for reassurance that everything will be all right.

Low support needs

Being able to accomplish a great deal with little or no money is the entrepreneurial way.

There is a finite amount of money available for an entrepreneurial start up. It is necessary to be frugal in every possible way. Entrepreneurs do not have the luxury of a vast staff to do their work; they do most of it themselves. If their former employer believed they should travel first class, their new employer—him or herself—does not agree.

In addition to the obvious value of not being extravagant, the real value is that entrepreneurship is in many ways a time game. Regardless of what is laid out in the plan, things will take longer to develop, customers will be slower to commit, and investors with deep pockets will have shorter arms than you perceived. Time will become your greatest enemy and it will not be measured in days or weeks, but rather in dollars saved and spent.

The burn rate.

In the entrepreneurial world it is called the burn rate, the rate at which your firm spends money in excess of income collected. Obviously, the lower the burn rate, the better chance the company will stay in business. Likewise, the longer you are in business, the better your chances are of succeeding.

Low support needs is also beneficial because of the perception it gives potential investors. In the early stages, people invest in you. If their money is going into a fancy office or a big car, they will be tentative in their funding. They want their investment spent wisely in a new marketing plan or completion of a prototype, for example.

Fosters environment of creativity.

Finally, low support needs fosters an environment of creativity. Ingenuity and outside the box thinking will find solutions to problems. If, however, money is freely available, then money will be thrown at issues and problems thinking they will then disappear. But they won't.

Therefore, keeping a lean and mean firm buys time, gives investors a feeling of value, and fosters the creative process.

Customer driven

Knowing your customers and what they want is imperative.

Entrepreneurial success results when there is a customer who is satisfied by the benefits of a product or service. The operative word is customer.

Some entrepreneurs perceive opportunity as a unique product and a small percentage of them are able to successfully complete an entrepreneurial journey with that as their basis. However, entrepreneurs who instead perceive opportunity in a customer have a higher rate of success. As entrepreneurs learn about their customers and their customer's needs, they determine how to develop the benefits that have the highest value for the customer.

Seek solutions to existing problems.

When Ray Kroc was asked why he started McDonalds, he said it was because he saw a line of people outside the hamburger stand. When they are customer-driven, entrepreneurs are usually seeking solutions to problems that customers already have. They seek to answer the question: what can I do to make your task easier? They are looking to deliver benefits that are needed.

When they are product-driven, entrepreneurs almost always want to showcase their product and what it does, how fast it is, how light it is, and so forth. They never take the time to ask the customer what he or she needs because they are certain that every customer needs at least one of what they have. As one entrepreneur told me, let your customer lead you to success.

> *"The success of QAD has been one of being very close to our customer. We came up from the manufacturing floor and really analyzed what their needs are instead of coming from the software technology side and trying to push the solutions down."*
> -Pam Lopker, Founder, QAD

Perceptive/sense of priorities

Perception of the moment can be learned.

Successful entrepreneurs and successful leaders seem to develop a sense of the moment. They are perceptive of their environment and all that transpires within it and are able to sense actions before anyone else. They always seem to know what will happen next, whether it is in a sales call or in a meeting with an investor.

In questioning entrepreneurs about this ability, one would expect them to cite experience as the primary reason for this characteristic. While a few acknowledge experience as a factor, many indicate that it is something they practice. They always ask themselves what is next, where are things? One entrepreneur said that after

What is next?

every meeting or phone call he asks himself what was the best part of that meeting and what was the worst. After answering those two questions, he asks himself what he would change if he could do it all over again. This enables him to fine-tune his sense for what is occurring during the meeting. He then senses how to react before the meeting is finished instead of waiting to see what may transpire after the meeting.

Entrepreneurs keep a macro view.

To some this may sound like entrepreneurs have a micro sense and manage details to the nth degree. In fact, this may be true for some, but not for most. Entrepreneurs anticipate the future and think about many details, but they also perceive a macro view of their world.

Perception is complimented with a strong sense of priorities. Entrepreneurs strive to know what the critical issues are that need to be addressed. Not all tasks are created equal and not all tasks can be done. Some minor tasks may even be on the "to do" list, but are never addressed.

It takes great discipline and practice to order your priorities and allocate time to them in proper proportion. If you own a restaurant, are passionate about food, and spend your entire day on that aspect of the business, it is likely that your service will go down. A computer-based entrepreneur who spends his day programming is apt not to be listening to the marketplace. How do you allocate your time?

There are no excuses.

Being perceptive and having a sense of priorities are challenges met by entrepreneurs. This notion takes us back to the issue of responsibility and no excuses. Entrepreneurs are responsible for their venture and can blame no one but themselves if events take a turn for the worse. Using their sense of perception and being able to prioritize helps entrepreneurs to execute that responsibility.

Up Front & Personal: Zotos & Stein*

One of Tom Zotos' daily rituals was to have breakfast at one of LA's local delis. On a muggy morning, during the summer of 1990, Tom entered the eatery and as he was approaching the counter he heard his friend from many years call him over to his booth.

Tom, You look like hell. What's going on?

His friend Bob Stein was genuinely concerned about Tom's apparent distress. Tom sat down and just shook his head.

Bob, the Disney people have decided not to renew their license. The company I work for is completely dependent upon that license, after ten years of hard work, I am back at the beginning. The new owner is 60 and he doesn't have the energy to do it again, I still see a big market for our product. I just don't know what to do...

Tom Zotos

Tom was born in Southbridge, Massachusetts, the middle of three sons of parents who had emigrated from Albania. His father worked in Southbridge's optical glass mill before W.W.II, then learned barbering in the army. After the war, he went into business for himself as a one-chair barbershop in this same town. Tom's Mother was a home-maker, and the home was filled with exuberance, music, and love in an old fashioned Eastern European traditional way.

Tom remembers that his first entrepreneurial experience was to make $5 shoveling snow for a neighbor. He grew in pride and stature when he gave the money to his Mom. He fondly remembers the feeling of satisfaction he got from doing something on his own. Several years later, Tom loaned his Dad money to open a successful custom glass scientific apparatus business in the garage. Tom, the teenager, financed his Dad's dream. He felt he was being trained to be an entrepreneur from early childhood.

Tom's parents exposed their young boys to culture—primarily art and music. Tom's art was music; he played guitar, formed a band and did gigs for high school dances featuring many of the songs he had written himself. He got pretty good at this music making business and on some weekends netted $400. He finished high school and went on to Quinsigamond Community College to study business. From this base, Tom made as much as $1000 per week on the college concert circuit.

Tom's life was music, but after 250 music gigs his interest was waning. His first exposure to printed art was when, as a teenager, he was given a book of illustrated art by Allen Aldridge. This book and its contents made quite an impression on Tom. As Tom's interest in art grew, he moved his young family, now a wife and eight-year-old daughter, to Los Angeles, a better scene for art than New England. By chance, he met his teenage idol and began an association with Aldridge that would help form his future.

Aldridge's work had featured a number of super-star musicians including the Beatles, Elton John and others. Their meeting and friendship began shortly after the unfortunate death of John Lennon. A musician at heart, Tom did an art piece on Lennon and decided to sell it commercially as a memorial. With Aldridge as lead blocker, Tom was able to meet Yoko Ono and convince her to let him go forward with the project. The piece was successful and got the recognition Tom needed to begin his new career.

These serendipitous events—the gift of the book, meeting with Aldridge, his Lennon poster—combined with Tom's networking and the mentoring of his new friend, led to his first formal job. Tom had never worked for a company before, he always had worked for himself. This first LA job at OSP (One Stop Posters) was really an informal loose partnership where Tom ran the art arm of the company. This firm designed, printed and distributed posters, buttons and high-end gallery art.

In 1986, Tom tried to get the Disney organization, in Burbank, interested in upscale art designed for adults. Trying a direct approach, Tom had been pestering the licensing agents at Disney to take a chance on stocking art posters and showed his designs based on pictures of Walt Disney. The agents would have none of this departure from the low-end art items which they sold to tourists. Tom felt that the market was ripe for a more classier image in poster art and who better to buy a picture of Walt than Disneyland visitors?

The licensing people could not figure into which category of merchandise this type of art might fall. After several attempts to get rid of him, the licensing managers told Tom to meet the head legal person at Disney. Tom asked if this person would negotiate a license with him. No, they said, he just likes art, and maybe he will understand you; we can't.

…They simply didn't know what to do with me because they didn't know what I was talking about. They always had two-dollar posters in their stores. I told them I wanted something I could hang in my office. They asked, "Why?"

Tom describes the meeting with the head legal person as a "godsend." He walked into an office where a Dali and a Picasso hung on the wall along with other art prints. He asked the attorney if a Disney shouldn't be on the wall as well. Sure he was told, but what kind of Disney? Tom explained his idea for a four part series. The man said go ahead and show him some rough paste-ups. They were done without all the formalities of a contract, but with a handshake from the head lawyer and a big dose of hope from Tom.

Tom developed the pieces that featured a young Walt Disney standing in a doorway with a cartoon shadow of Mickey Mouse cast on the open door. The head of legal loved the artwork, gave Tom a license, and OSP had their first significant success. The Walt/Mickey poster remains a classic.

The success with the Lennon and Disney posters gave Tom the nucleus of his new career. He was secure at his position with OSP. Then changes occurred. In 1989, the company went through a transition that forced a buyout from an individual within the firm. The buyer and new owner regarded Tom as just an employee. His boss was approaching 60 and Tom was approaching 40. "My career could have been funded by this person in the company, but we were on different wavelengths. I have a family and monthly expenses and I was at an age and time when I had to be careful with my decisions."

Bob Stein

Bob was born and raised on Long Island, another middle of three sons. His Father, who emigrated from Austria, worked for a stock brokerage firm in New York City as a market maker for several stocks. Family conversations allowed Bob to share in the basics of his Father's career. His parents were very supportive of any of his endeavors. Through high school, Bob wrote music and played tournament tennis.

He attended two years (1974-76) at the University of Rhode Island on a tennis scholarship, but left school because he felt he was not getting enough out of it. "Business School let me down, I didn't respect my professors." After a short break, Bob came back for one year of liberal arts study—philosophy, art, and history—that was much more to his liking; but he never finished college.

The music bug eventually drew him to New York City where he was determined to become a songwriter. He admits he never read a note of music in his life; he just heard it in his head. Using his tennis background, at age 20, he started working at the Gramercy Racquet Club where his responsibility was to open the club at 7:00 am each morning. One day, one of the tennis pros was sick, and Bob took over one of his lessons. In the waiting area, Walter Cronkite watched Bob give this lesson and was impressed with his patience and teaching style. He asked Bob to give him a lesson, so Bob, the new employee, told the head pro, "Mr. Cronkite would like a lesson with me." The pro was a bit intimidated, Cronkite intervened and Bob was promoted to instructor on the spot.

Bob continued to work on his music while paying his way with the tennis lessons. His music writing was doing well, but his efforts to market his music ran into conflicts with the record companies.

On his twenty-first birthday, Bob flew to Los Angeles.

> It seems that lawyers controlled how music was made and if I wanted to be involved in promoting my music, then I had to think like they did.

As a result of his earlier networking, and apparent good tennis teaching, Mr. Cronkite wrote a recommendation letter for Bob to the Southwestern School of Law. This letter, Bob's glibness and his high LSAT score persuaded admissions and he was accepted, without a Bachelor's degree, to law school.

Bob had an internship experience at ABC Records, during his final year in law school. The job was to prepare "fair use" letters, which let licensees use bits of songs for other uses. In effect, the letter grants a specific license. This became boring work. ABC had lost $40 million that year and was being acquired by MCA. With lawyers leaving ABC, Bob got the opportunity to handle option contracts.

Bob got his J.D. degree in 1980. In 1985, he wrote and produced a record with Rudy Vallee, the old time crooner. It was Bob's type of music. His passion for it was without measurement. He loved his product, but the record companies did not share his passion. Music would have to take a back seat.

> You can only be different and successful if you can find a market that is totally discontent. You will be totally successful or completely rejected. It's all or nothing if you are different. I don't want to be like anyone else.

Within the next year, Bob took a job with a small legal firm and studied for the bar, which he passed in Hawaii in 1987.

His law career continued through 1990. Most of the work dealt with taking firms public. He attributed his skill, in part, to his exposure to Wall Street through his Dad. What he liked most was the chance to see many firms try to develop new ideas, He loved the creative part of expanding the scope of the client's offerings and accepted the legal mechanics as a necessary evil. He knew his creative talents were being underutilized and he was growing restless.

One of his friends throughout this time was Tom Zotos. Tom's brother was part of the band that Bob had formed in the mid-eighties and was part of the Rudy Vallee record deal. Bob and Tom often met and talked for hours on end about, music, art and their future. The meeting at the deli this morning was typical of their frequent sessions:

At the deli, Bob was concerned as he looked at his friend:

Stein: Tom, what are your choices? What can this company do over the next decade?

Zotos: Bob, you know what I believe. The world is changing. The time for merchandising is coming. The product that sells the movies and the records and the movies and records that sell the products are integrating. You can't separate the two anymore.

Stein: If you stay at the company, what are you going to work on next?

Zotos: I hear that Warner Brothers is finally ready to talk about licensing Looney Tunes and Batman. That's going to be a big part of the next years for someone. I just don't know.

Stein: Do you believe in this?

Zotos: Of course I do. I've got eleven years in this industry. It will happen!

Stein: How much will it take?

Zotos: Probably a hundred grand. A little more, a little less.

Stein: That's a lot, but if you believe in it...all things are possible.

Zotos: It doesn't matter if you don't have any money. All I've got is $20,000 in an account for my daughter's college and that's just not negotiable. And I need funds to live. But, yes, I believe having the rights to Bugs Bunny on an art poster is the most exciting thing that could happen to us. I just don't know if this is the time to go after it.

Stein: If you wait for a hundred percent thing, it will never happen.

The two exchanged pros and cons for the next hour. What's Next? What makes sense? Bob and Tom were exhausted. The conversation ended with the two friends leaving and promising to meet in two days.

Please review the entrepreneur profile on the next page and rate yourself, Tom, and Bob on your characteristics on a scale of 1 to 10.

*This case was researched and written by Professors William H. Crookston and Thomas J. O'Malia. This case is intended to be an introduction into the People Side of Entrepreneurship. Some details have been changed to protect the confidence of actual individuals and companies involved. Copyright © 1995.

Entrepreneurial Exercise: Entrepreneur Profile

B
E
0
5
10

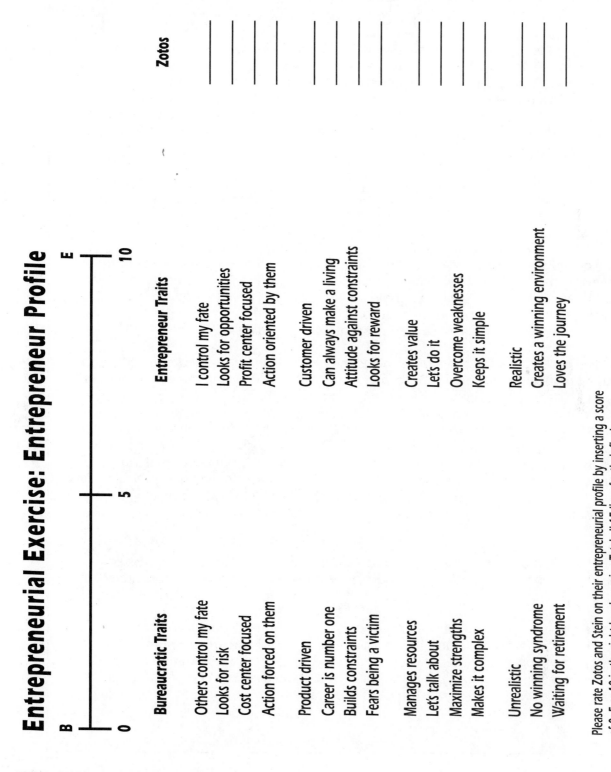

Bureaucratic Traits	Entrepreneur Traits	Zotos	Stein
Others control my fate	I control my fate		
Looks for risk	Looks for opportunities		
Cost center focused	Profit center focused		
Action forced on them	Action oriented by them		
Product driven	Customer driven		
Career is number one	Can always make a living		
Builds constraints	Attitude against constraints		
Fears being a victim	Looks for reward		
Manages resources	Creates value		
Let's talk about	Let's do it		
Maximize strengths	Overcome weaknesses		
Makes it complex	Keeps it simple		
Unrealistic	Realistic		
No winning syndrome	Creates a winning environment		
Waiting for retirement	Loves the journey		

Please rate Zotos and Stein on their entrepreneurial profile by inserting a score of 0, 5 or 10 in the right hand margin. Total all 15 lines for their final scores

⇑ **Tear out and move to your entrepreneurial road map binder.**

Up Front & Personal: Colby Home Health

Carolyn Colby started her career in health care as a manager at what was then Kimberly QualityCare, a large health-care company. She was quickly promoted, moving up the ladder from highly productive assistant branch manager to corporate vice president. Colby's focus was building a new business line for Kimberly in the home-nursing field. She became an expert in home-care and hospital staffing, Medicare regulations, opening offices, and troubleshooting in the 45 branches she was managing. "I don't think there was a person that was more corporate than me," Colby recalls, "but then I decided that if I could start the business for Kimberly, I could also do it for myself."

Colby went back to school to get an MBA. She then took out a $25,000 loan and began what would become two agencies, Colby Care Home Health and Spirit Home Health Care. By the end of her first year, she had generated $1 million worth of business from her clients—HMOs, hospitals, doctors, and clinics.

Colby has successfully carved out two distinct niches in the home-health industry that set her apart from her competition. First, she works with minority populations that other agencies do not want to handle. "Our nurses will go into areas that other nurses will not," she explains. The second focus of her business is on pediatrics and the company cares for a lot of developmentally disabled children.

Colby has had her fair share of struggles throughout the birth and growth of her company and money was at the center of most of her problems. Payroll, overhead, and tax liability kept growing every week, faster than her clients were paying her. Soon she couldn't meet payroll. She tried to get a bank loan but learned a painful lesson instead. "I went to all these banks," Colby recalls, "and I said, 'You know, I've got this business. It's a wonderful business. Would you give us a loan?' And they looked at me like I was crazy...I didn't have any equity in a home or anything like that." Other problems cropped up. Colby found she didn't have enough time to keep track of what all her employees were doing. One result was that some employees even stole money from the company.

She has learned while doing and has traveled far on her journey. "I've grown a lot," Colby says today. "I'm stronger. I'm wiser...I've dealt with things I never would have had to deal with, types of people that I probably would never have encountered. That's growth and I really enjoy that."

However, what makes Colby really feel good is helping the patients in their own home. Unlike the sterile hospital environment where all you are is a number, someone's home is a better environment for healthcare. "If I can bring a nurse in there and make someone feel more comfortable with a disease, that certainly does enhance their quality of life. And that's the most important thing."

Entrepreneurs vs. Managers

Entrepreneurs vs. managers: fundamentally different.

So far, we have tried to explain the entrepreneur by discussing what he is not. There are many myths surrounding the entrepreneur and looking beyond those myths gives a better understanding as to what the entrepreneur truly is, regardless of what the popular press professes.

The review of characteristics as defined by both research of entrepreneurs and the direct antidotal introspection by entrepreneurs themselves suggests a set of traits that has given further insight into the persona of the entrepreneur.

A comparison of how managers and entrepreneurs differ is the final insight into this special individual and completes the broad view of what an entrepreneur is.

The criteria of comparison used to explore this difference between entrepreneurs and managers is threefold. We will examine the difference between:

Who they are—what profile and propensity for action is demonstrated by each.

Compare and contrast the two.

What they do—how do their actions differ. Do they lead in the same way or is that a chief differentiation?

Why they do it—what are the underlying motives of their actions.

Through these three perspectives, the definition of an entrepreneur is brought into greater clarity.

Who you are:

Entrepreneurs	Managers
Seek new areas to exploit, find and develop new ways of doing things. Innovation is the battle cry.	Stay within the existing areas of expertise. Work within core competencies. Optimization of the known is the driver.
Go outside the box. Challenge conventional thinking and accepted rules. Deviate from the norms.	Bound by what works-constrained to the process and procedures by which they are governed. Deviation is unacceptable.
Opportunity dependent. Their future comes from what does not exist or is not fulfilled today. Defining, researching, and delivering new benefits are the yardsticks.	Resource dependent. They are judged, rewarded, and promoted by how well they use the resources assigned to them. The returns on people, plants, and dollars are the yardsticks.

How they view the world.

Opportunity or resource dependent?

What you do:

	Entrepreneurs	Managers
How they execute.	Driven by the uncertainty of their journey and confined by their non-dependency on resources, entrepreneurs move in short stages, managing risk at each stage and defining the structure as they proceed.	Driven by the resources available to them, they design the project in a single large stage. Adjustments along the way are minimal. Their best probability of success comes from overwhelming the project with resources.
Effective or efficient?	Their goal is to be effective. Use flat organizational structures with an entire team on the same level, in constant communication and all with a common knowledge of the goal and the plan to get there. Communication is by joint sessions in social surroundings such as a beer bust or pizza Fridays.	Their goal is to be efficient. Use a pyramid structure based on ranks, power, and authority wherein information is shared on a need-to-know basis with decisions made by consensus through committees and communicated by memo.

Why you do it:

	Entrepreneurs	Managers
What drives them?	Seek to control their destiny and enjoy the lifestyle-either hectic or slow-as they desire it. They find great joy from doing it their way. They thrive on the excitement and challenge of their journey.	Seek to manage their career and will do anything and everything not to jeopardize it. The closer they do it "the company's way" or "by the book," the safer they feel. They deplore the unexpected and live by the CYA creed (cover your butt).
Adventure or survival?	Every day is an adventure. Seek to create a lifestyle satisfaction and, if possible, personal wealth.	Everyday you survive is a good day. Seek to build security and count the days to retirement.

"One of the things you'll get when you call Superior Bankcard Services that you won't get when you call one of our competitors is a live person on the phone. It drives me crazy when you get an answering machine and your estimated time to be answered is 10 minutes and once you go to the department you want, you're put on hold again. That will not happen at SBS."
-Joe Kaplan, President & CEO, Superior Bankcard Services

Chapter Summary

- There are many myths associated with entrepreneurs that are in fact just that—myths. To travel on a successful journey, you must realize that these myths are not reality and that reality is what you make of your journey.
- The most commonly held myth is that you need a lot of money to be successful, which has been proven false by many successful entrepreneurs.
- Another commonly held myth is that a great idea will lead you to success. In reality, the execution of the idea is far more important than the idea itself.
- While there are no defining characteristics that one must possess in order to be an entrepreneur, research has shown that most successful entrepreneurs possess some similar characteristics.
- Among the most common characteristics are passion, perseverance, credibility, enthusiasm, low support needs, customer-driven, and perception.
- A brief history of Zotos and Stein is given, which portrays two individuals discussing a potential venture.
- There are fundamental differences in the way entrepreneurs and managers think and act. One primary difference is that entrepreneurs are opportunity dependent while managers are resource dependent.
- Carolyn Colby was introduced as an example of an individual who transformed herself from a manager in the corporate world to an entrepreneur in the start up world.
- At the end of the chapter, you will meet Paul Orfalea, who started Kinko's Inc. and grew it to become a leading copy and printing shop.

Chapter Two Exercises/Discussion Questions

1. What characteristics do you feel an entrepreneur should possess? Are they different from what is presented here? How? Why?
2. What are the job skills and career concerns of middle managers in large corporations? How do they differ from those of the entrepreneur?
3. Identify and discuss five of the most commonly cited characteristics found in successful entrepreneurs.
4. Consider how your current work attitudes, skill sets, and reward system—how you judge yourself to be a success or failure—match up with Carolyn Colby.
5. List any changes you think you might need to make in your thinking and attitude to become a successful entrepreneur.
6. Think of three instances when you have been told that it is impossible to do something that you have subsequently found a way to do. How has your perseverance paid off?
7. Make a list of reasons as to why you are passionate about your business idea.
8. Identify five things that could go wrong in your new business. List what you could learn from these foul-ups and why the foul-ups will not deter your efforts.
9. List four of the myths of entrepreneurs and what the reality actually is.

Journey Two: Kinko's Inc.

Entrepreneurs come in all shapes and sizes. Paul Orfalea, founder of Kinko's, Inc. the photocopy chain, is certainly an odd-sized entrepreneur and seems an unlikely person to have succeeded in any venture. He admits it himself, "I have absolutely no mechanical ability. None. And, I'm a horrible reader."

Orfalea's Beginning

While in second grade, Orfalea's parents and teachers realized that he could not read and subjected him to a battery of specialist examinations including eye doctors and many others. His parents even offered his brother and sister $50 if they could teach him the alphabet. Eventually, they discovered that he is dyslexic and suffers from Attention Deficit Disorder. Even after the diagnosis though, it was a tough road in the world of academia. As he states, "I flunked second grade, and finally graduated from high school as a wood-shop major, but I finished eighth from the bottom of my class of 1,200."

The gift of a silver tongue enabled him to persuade an admissions officer to let him into the University of Southern California where he received his undergraduate degree. Orfalea remembers thinking that his professor was speaking a foreign language in his first college class. He attributes his ability to graduate from USC to figuring out how to get into the classes with the football players who always lowered the curve. Even still, he only scraped by, receiving C's and D's throughout his four years. He also made deals with his fellow students: They would help with his class papers in exchange for his acting as their gopher, making copies on the photocopy machines that were then still relatively new on the market.

Orfalea's early environment also played a role in his choice of an entrepreneurial lifestyle. Throughout his childhood, he never knew anyone who had a job or who worked for someone else; everyone had their own businesses. He was raised with the assumption that he too would have his own business some day and never even considered any other opportunities. When asked what type of companies he interviewed with for a job after college, he said that the thought *never* crossed his mind. He knew he would never work for anyone else.

Kinko's Beginning

Orfalea's idea for his model business stemmed from the deal he had made with fellow students to act as gopher for them as well as a marketing class that introduced him to the product lifecycle. The copy machine seemed to be in the very beginning of the product lifecycle and he saw enormous potential for it in the future.

This fascination with the copy machine led him to rent a store in Santa Barbara, California that ran through the main artery of the university campus. A loan of $5,000 was all he needed and he was in business. The name for his business came from his nickname, "Kinky O," inspired by his curly hair.

Notebooks and pens lined the sidewalk in front of his store on the first day of classes and he sold over $2000 worth of goods. He began to develop the business tactics that would make Kinko's a success. His salesmen were college students who he sent to the dorms knocking on doors. The boys would visit the girl's dorms and vice versa. "I just basically started as a peddler," he remembers.

Orfalea has been a big fan of "wandering" since the opening of his first store. He claims it is where he gets his best ideas and how he is able to anticipate the needs of his customers. For example, the idea to offer students the same study material at Kinko's that professors typically only left "on reserve" in the library originated during one of his late night wanderings around the reserve book room. After observing many students vying for the same material the night before an exam, Orfalea posted a flyer telling the professors to leave materials on file with Kinko's in addition to at the library. This is just one of many tactics that Orfalea used to stay abreast of his customer's needs and desires.

People

However, Orfalea does not claim to be passionate about making copies. "There is nothing special to me about the services Kinko's provides. I don't like reading. I don't like technology. I have no love for the printed page." His passion is for his people and, in reality, he is in the people business to a much greater extent than he is in the copy business. If his people, both customers and co-workers, are not content, then he truly believes that there would be no business. As a result, Orfalea is certain that if it were not Kinko's that he started, it would have been some other business.

Kinko's has had many competitors, but from the beginning Orfalea set his company apart by giving his co-workers better training and by taking pains to make them happy. He also never refers to his co-workers as employees because he feels that it is degrading and "makes it sound like indentured servitude." Orfalea feels that "the word 'employees' comes from the steel mill where you 'employ' steel, meaning that you bend it to your will." He does not want to refer to his co-workers as having to bend to his will, rather, he works with people, nobody works for him.

With so many competitors in the market, the only advantage he has is his people and the attitude of his people. Orfalea's motto is "anybody else can do it better" and he questions "doesn't it make more sense that happy fingers will ring happy registers?" At Kinko's the co-worker is the number one priority because Orfalea does not think it would be possible to take care of his customers if he did not have "happy fingers" ringing the registers. As a manifestation of his respect for his co-workers, Orfalea chose not to franchise his business. Instead, he entered into partnerships with people who wanted to open Kinko's stores. His philosophy is that he would rather make money with people than make money on them. Orfalea chose to operate on a collaborative basis because he has always been more successful when making investments in people as opposed to places.

Trial and Error

Orfalea has both failed and succeeded at several other ventures including frozen yogurt shops, print shops, a vegetable stand, and a string of cappuccino stores. He places a tremendous amount of value on the process of trial and error and feels that too many young people have excuses in today's world. Instead of saying "but" after the mention of a potential new business, students should embrace the idea and look for the opportunity, not the problem.

Similarly, he encourages his co-workers to take chances. At Kinko's, mistakes cost relatively nothing, so Orfalea instills the philosophy that people should "go out there and take a chance." He recognizes that if he were running a nuclear power plant, his philosophy might be different and he would not want a lot of risk takers in the company, but Kinko's is the type of business where more benefits than setbacks are reaped from trial and error.

Customer Needs

Orfalea has determined that his customers have two very basic needs: "they don't know what they want and they want it yesterday." Similarly, they have two distinct characteristics: "they are uptight and confused." As a result, Orfalea has tried to make the customer experience as pleasant as possible and this begins with the moment the customer walks in the door. For an uptight, confused customer who does not know what he or she wants, the first thing Orfalea wants to do is calm the individual down. Thus, he painted the inside of his stores blue, a symbol of calmness and serenity. He also stresses the importance of keeping the stores impeccably neat and clean in every aspect so that customers will naturally relax and leave some of their stress at the door. Being in touch with his customers and understanding and anticipating their needs has been critical to the success of Kinko's.

Integrity

Admittedly, Orfalea did not recognize the importance of honesty when he first started Kinko's. However, he has since learned and sincerely believes that in order to be a good leader, one must be impeccably honest. "People will not follow you if you have bad integrity in any way, shape, or form." In any business dealings, it is critical to be honest and fair because "you want to live a life that allows you to live with yourself."

Societal Benefits

Orfalea feels that more businesses should be cognizant of the contributions they make to society. He is proud that much of the work done at Kinko's has real meaning and that his co-workers are keenly aware of the importance of their work to their communities. For example, when a little girl was abducted in Spokane, Washington, the parents called the police first and Kinko's second to print the "wanted" posters. Similarly, if someone has lost their precious cat or dog, he or she will come to Kinko's to make flyers. Both Orfalea and his co-workers feel good about the service they are providing for people.

Management

Orfalea feels that the role of management is to remove obstacles and solve problems on a macro level. Everything done in his office is for his co-workers so that they can better serve customers. He defines his job as "to make Kinko's better, not just to take care of business." Throughout his career at Kinko's, Orfalea has never spent more than eight hours a week in his office. He is the visionary of the company and chooses to spend time in the field learning where the opportunities are. Additionally, he believes that people work better if they are forced to solve problems for themselves. As such, he does not have an open door policy and tries to make himself unavailable so that people must make decisions for themselves. He trusts that he works with very bright, capable people who are able to take care of the day-to-day business.

Going Forward

Kinko's' modest beginning has led to phenomenal success. With over 900 outlets worldwide, Kinko's is synonymous with copies and Orfalea is confident that the company will be in business a century from now. He feels that "we've got the best trademark in the industry" and that Kinko's is perfectly positioned to capitalize on a lot of the macroeconomic trends occurring in society today.

As advice for young, budding entrepreneurs, Orfalea offers: "Everything is difficult when you get older. In your 20s, try it all. In your 30s, figure out what you do best. In your 40s, make a lot of money at what you do best."

"I got intrigued by the xerox machine."
-Paul Orfalea, Kinko's Inc.

Journey Two Case Questions

1. What myths surrounding entrepreneurs did Paul Orfalea prove false in his journey?
2. What characteristics typical of entrepreneurs does Orfalea possess? How have they helped him?
3. How did Orfalea get his idea to start Kinko's and why was that a good entry strategy?
4. Did Orfalea's early environment play a role in his path to success? If so, how?

Challenge: Stranger Diary

Start a log. One that you will keep for the rest of the semester at a minimum and the rest of your life as a maximum.

Go out and meet ten new people a week and record the following information for each one:

- Name & date of meeting
- Contact information
- Expertise
- What you learned from that person in the course of your conversation

Be prepared to share this with associates or friends when asked. Perhaps one of your associates has met someone from whom you might benefit and vice versa?

I think an entrepreneur is someone that is really willing to commit to something. Someone that has a tenacity, a sticktuitiveness, that just won't say no and continues to work thier idea and their dream."
-Bill Sanderson, Founder, Popcorn Palace

Chapter Three
Finding Your Idea

Chapter Three Major Concepts

- Customer vs. product driven
- Four stages of an entrepreneurial company
- Role of the idea and recognizing opportunity
- Protecting your idea

Journey Three: Kiyonna Klothing

Up Front & Personal: Food from the 'Hood

Finding Your Idea

Where do ideas come from? How do we recognize them when seen? How do we exploit them when recognized?

The search for the idea that is right for you.

These are the questions that, when answered, start the entrepreneurial journey. But before we begin the search for ideas, let's recall two very important points we have already explored:

- Entrepreneurs think differently, they are willing to go past conventional wisdom and look at ways to find the opportunity, not the problem.
- Lack of a good idea is the second most cited excuse (after money) for not starting a business. It is the great rationalization.

Both of these points need to be kept in mind as we explore opportunity recognition and the search for the idea that is right for you.

Entrepreneurial Thinking

In the discussion of entrepreneurs vs. managers in Chapter Two, we shared at great length that the two do not think alike. Nowhere is this more prevalent than in how they view a company start up.

Different approaches to starting a new project.

For illustration, assume a manager and an entrepreneur both begin the task of starting a new company. Managers immediately seek to learn how many resources will be available—how much money, how many people, and what manufacturing and distribution are at their disposal. They want the largest army and most materials, as they perceive they are about to wage war on the marketplace to secure ground for their product or service. Almost always, they will start with reviewing how this venture fits into their company's mission statement and within its core competencies. Before beginning their campaign, managers will also spend a great deal of time discerning how this project will affect their promotion timeline and career.

Entrepreneurs on the other hand, desire to explore this new opportunity. Their interest and passion in the project drives them. Since they usually have limited resources, and because they are the company, little time is spent on the issues of career management and resources available that are of concern to managers.

Managers: start with vast resources.

When managers and entrepreneurs begin to explore an opportunity, their initial approaches are almost always in opposite directions. Managers will usually start with a project plan showing the efficient expenditure of resources and answering budget questions dealing with internal rates of return (how much the project will earn on funds invested) and hurdle rates (volume needed to get corporate approval). In almost every case, the first principal expenditure is a preliminary market study, which often costs upwards of $250,000.

Entrepreneurs: alternatives to resources.

If entrepreneurs were to start by spending $250,000, their journey would immediately end. It is not because managers' approaches are wrong, it is just that managers "assume" (makes an <u>ass</u> out of <u>u</u> and <u>me</u>) that core competencies and resources exist. For entrepreneurs, they do not. They have to create value based on their knowledge of the industry. They must seek alternatives to resources.

> *"Why do some people and not others discover particular entrepreneurial opportunities? Although the null hypothesis is blind luck, research has suggested two broad categories of factors that influence the probability that particular people will discover particular opportunities: The possession of the prior information necessary to identify an opportunity and the cognitive properties necessary to value it."*
>
> - Scott Shane, Entrepreneur Research Scholar

Customer vs. product driven

Start with a customer.

If you do not have resources, then you need an "entrepreneur's" approach, which almost always begins with the recognition that you start with a customer.

Without resources, entrepreneurs are dependent on having their potential customers guide them to success. They listen to the needs and desires of their customers and build their start up around those specifications. Managers, on the other hand, know what their company does well (core competency) and already have existing product lines on which to build future products. Having such resources available facilitates the process for the manager, enabling him to move forward building products with relative ease. This difference between product-based companies and customer-based start ups clearly shows how a manager's project plan and an entrepreneur's journey differ.

Four Stages of an Entrepreneurial Company

Journeys undertaken in stages.

In creating their customer driven venture, entrepreneurs recognize that their journey is usually undertaken in stages. By understanding these stages they can focus on a manageable set of tasks with minimal and sometimes no resources.

There are usually four stages of an entrepreneurial company as is illustrated in the diagram below.

Four primary stages.

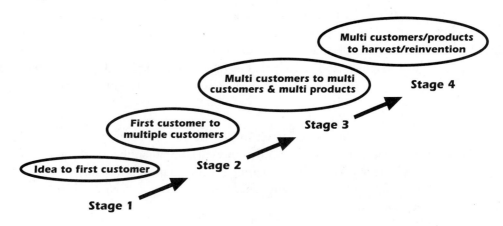

Stage 1 - Idea to first customer

Single goal.

The first stage is when the entrepreneur's focus is exact—it is on the customer. He or she is all consumed with finding a customer, the single goal of this stage. This not only keeps entrepreneurs moving toward a known target, but it also enhances the probability that when their idea for a good or service is completed, there will be a sale because a customer already exists who wants to buy.

The opposite of concentrating on individual customers is a focus on a market or on a product.

Never assume you are the customer.

If your journey starts with a product, you often find yourself with a solution looking for a problem. Just because you think it is neat, cute, and that everyone needs one does not make it so. Starting with a product does not tell you what is needed. You only know your desire, your need, and your solution. What counts is that some and many others need it as well and you do not know that unless you have asked your potential customers. Never, never assume you are the customer.

In searching for the first customer, you will find others who would purchase it if you were to change one or two aspects of it, something you can decide to do or not. But if you have a finished product that is not what the customer wants, then all of your time and cost to build it are wasted because you could have learned this in advance. If you are customer driven and ask constantly—what can I do to help you and your firm, what is your biggest problem, and how can I help solve it—then you will learn your customer's needs and by fulfilling them, you will create your new venture.

Your market is not your customer.

Another important consideration in the first stage of idea to first customer is to be certain not to confuse your first customer with your market. A market is the sum total of all customers. To reach all potential customers requires a large organization with existing distribution and sales resources not available to a start up. Production and sales materials can not be bought or created overnight even if money were available, which it is not. This should be the long-term goal of your company, not the focus in the beginning stage.

Big guys fail 99% of the time.

A critical lesson can be learned by studying the results of market and product based company introductions. They start with dollars, often millions of dollars, vast budgets, and talented, experienced and innovative people, and often end in failure. Firms such as Procter & Gamble, Nabisco, and General Mills, Inc. fit this profile. Of all the thousands of products introduced each year, less than 1% reach the market place and are put on shelves for customers to buy. If this process with resources and personnel available is wrong 99% of the time, why would entrepreneurs try to emulate it? They don't. That is why entrepreneurs start with a customer.

First customer for a restaurant?

Not all businesses appear to have the capability to sell to a single customer. Certainly you can not serve your first meal in a restaurant before the great expense of building the physical shell and staffing the restaurant. But restaurants often fail because they are product driven and, once built, they can not change their location or even their motif.

"ShopTrac, a bar code based tracking system, started when we spent $19.61 on a brochure defining what we were proposing to do and then visited companies that fit our profile. With our $20 and countless hours on the phone, we landed three accounts that understood our background, our knowledge of the industry, and the software we were going to build. They believed in us and knew the value we would provide. With the help of some price concessions, we landed three accounts that put up 50% deposits. We had $250,000 in orders, $125,000 in cash and our company was born, all from starting with a customer."
-Mark MacWhirter, Co-Founder, ShopTrac

So what does someone do who has a passion for food and wants to be in the restaurant business?

All businesses can start with a first customer.

Many successful chefs or restaurateurs started by getting into the private meal business. They would go to a personal home and, for a fee, prepare an elaborate meal from soup to nuts for their client's dinner party. Alternatively, they would use their home or rent facilities to cater parties. When their reputation and clientele were in place, they would open their restaurant and use their prior clients to spread the word of the quality offerings. They found a way to get a customer first.

If you work hard enough to think outside the box, you will find that almost every business can be designed to find a first customer.

Stage 2 - From first customer to multiple customers

From one to many.

This second stage of the entrepreneurial journey can be misleading. Having a first customer creates great momentum, but getting to multiple customers is not a simple progression.

Initial customer provides credibility.

The greatest advantage of having an initial customer is the credibility it creates. It is a sign to future customers that you can do what you promise and propose. It is now your reference account, a place and benefit you can direct other potential customers toward when answering their questions and allaying their fears. It is the crucial first step in the journey.

Initial customer provides value.

The second major advantage is that a first customer creates value that you can leverage with potential investors. Before the first customer, you are viewed as a bright person with a great idea and the passion to deliver. The value of your idea and passion is next to nothing. It is a floating promise. With a customer in hand, you have created initial value for the company, and have effectively launched the company.

"What's the most important word in business? Some say profit, others equity and others satisfaction. They're all wrong. The most important word in business is customer. You are not in business until you have one."
-Dr. Richard Buskirk, Entrepreneur Professor

The challenge after the initial customer then becomes growing from one to many customers. This is a challenge many underestimate and journeys often end as this abyss is crossed. The reason is simple.

Entrepreneurs are selling themselves.

The first sale, especially one done prior to a finalized product (discussed at length in a later chapter), is achieved because entrepreneurs are selling themselves—their integrity, their experience, and their skill sets. In growing a company, multiple customers must be obtained, but you, the entrepreneur, must understand that you can not do it all. It is impossible for you to make an infinite amount of sales calls while also guiding the development of your new product, seeking funding, and building a staff. You are one person and, no matter how special you are, you are finite.

From "I" to "We."

With this realization, the first of many transitions begins. You adjust and learn to build a team. You attract bright people who can make sales calls, create the products and services for which you have customers, and take over the tasks you need accomplished. You are one person with one customer, and if you wish to get to multiple customers, it will require multiple people. You will always be the driving force, the one who makes it happen, but you will begin to transition from I to We. This is a challenge worthy of your energy and talent.

Stage 3: From multiple customers to multiple customers and multiple products

Establish needs and fulfill them.

Your existing customers will continue to educate you about their needs. They will tell you of their problems and you will grow by expanding your goods and services to solve these problems. They will tell you what their customers need and you will satisfy both the end consumer and your customer's needs. It will not be unlike your first sale, your road to success is based upon establishing needs and then fulfilling them.

Remember the lessons of birthing.

At this stage some entrepreneurs will forget the lessons of their own birthing (with a customer focus) and begin to push their ideas, perceptions, and notions of customer needs (product-driven) on potential and existing customers. They will take all of the resources they have accumulated from initial success and gamble them on new product offerings for which they believe a customer exists, but may not.

In effect, they will become product or market driven (resource managers) and will attempt to do what they so successfully avoided in the first stage of their journey, but with a limited amount of resources. As a result, success to date will cause them to act like managers instead of entrepreneurs.

Don't revert to management.

Do not let yourself fall into this trap. Always maintain a customer focus as you travel on your journey, particularly from multiple customers to multiple products and multiple customers.

Stage 4: Multiple customers and multiple products to harvest or reinvention

Policies and procedures are necessary evil.

When entrepreneurs reach the final stage of their journey, they have built a company. Just as in any successful company, people, customers, and products exist. To communicate with and manage all of these various interests, policies and procedures need to be formulated.

The form of these policies is not important, but they must be developed. Set holidays, sick leaves, and personnel review processes become a necessity. Likewise, written procedures on how to receive inventory, what papers need to be filled out and distributed, guidelines on who can spend how much on what, and yes, even designated private parking spots may be allotted.

Some will suffocate.

It is at this stage that most entrepreneurs feel like they have awoken in the middle of a bad dream. Everything they have worked to avoid is closing in on them and they are the managers who created the procedures and have to run the processes. They are suffocating.

At this point one of two things will happen. Entrepreneurs may recognize that they have taken this leg of their journey as far as it can go. They no longer feel like the driving force or that the value they personally contribute is needed. The fun and excitement of the start up is gone. The hunt is over. The destination has been reached. They have replaced themselves, or so they believe.

Sell the company?

Once at this stage, many entrepreneurs consider selling their company, which is not a selfish decision but rather a value decision. They can sell it to a well-established firm with a larger sales and production force thereby assuring future employment for their associates and employees who have traveled the journey alongside them. Selling the company enables them to take the wealth created and return it in liquid form (cash) to shareholders, associates, and themselves.

If an acquisition solution is not available or desired, entrepreneurs may seek an initial public offering, IPO. That topic will be discussed in a later chapter.

Reinvent and reposition.

Reorganize and rebuild.

Entrepreneurs must consider completely reinventing themselves if they choose not to harvest, but to continue. Often this requires spinning off parts of the company and building the next generation, usually with ample funds and greater experience. Others may elect to change their roles and position themselves away from any and all operational tasks, acting as the visionary for the next generation. Still others will reorganize and split the company into separate teams. Often these new teams will be kept away from the company's main operation and will function almost in secrecy to avoid the crippling burden of a bureaucracy. When successful, these teams and their new businesses are used as a model to rebuild the company.

Consider all alternatives.

The point here is simple. Entrepreneurs enjoy starting and building companies. Most do not enjoy managing them. When it reaches the point of managing, it is time to consider all of the alternatives available.

Recognizing the four stages of an entrepreneurial company will focus and position you for success.

The Idea

Where are ideas? With an understanding of how entrepreneurs (as opposed to managers) view projects and in particular how they are dependent on customers for their opportunity recognition, we can continue our journey with the question—*where do we find the ideas to start our company?*

Get physical fast. First you must become sensitive to the search. Start by looking, not just thinking, and by recognizing that it is time "to get physical fast," which means you need to get out there and meet and talk to people. This may seem overly simplistic, but it is a necessary first step because if you are not looking, you will not see what may be right in front of you.

> *"Entrepreneurs are the people that are walking down the street and have the ability to notice the $20 bill lying on the road. They're the people that actually stop, pay attention, and pick the bill up. Most people are too busy in what they are doing to take any kind of time to look down on the ground and find the $20 bill. So, entrepreneurship fundamentally begins with paying attention—looking around you and trying to discover opportunities and notice the $20 bills that are already laying on the ground."*
> -William Gartner, Entrepreneur Research Scholar

Be sensitive to your surroundings. Being sensitive to your surroundings and not only understanding, but also diagnosing what you see is critical. Most people have not trained themselves to recognize opportunities.

There is a successful ice cream store in Princeton, New Jersey that is privately held, with only one location that does not advertise. It is almost equidistant between Baskin-Robbins, four blocks south, and Haagen-Dazs, three blocks east. On a given Saturday night the usual six or seven customers can be found at 31 flavors and a smaller, more discrete group is at Haagen-Dazs. A line of 20 to 40 people is often overflowing on the sidewalks in front of this Mom and Pop shop.

Always investigate. If your first reaction is why, then you are on the right track and have promise. 99 out of 100 people that pass this store don't even notice the line and certainly don't investigate. They are not looking for that $20 bill. They walk right past it.

What this company does is somewhat unique but not proprietary. After all, there are only so many ways to sell ice cream. What is more important is to stop in and ask, "How did you come up with this? What led you to this point?" Learning how others see and exploit opportunity so that you may see it is a critical part of your entrepreneurial training. Be sure that you are always looking for that $20 bill. You never know where or when it may appear.

Failure provides lessons too.

Opportunity recognition lessons are by no means limited to success. Modern medicine owes most of its growth and innovation to examining failures. Only by doing an autopsy can we know why someone died and what, if any, effect the prescribed treatment had on his or her illness. Don't overlook failures in an industry as a potential learning tool and a means by which to recognize an opportunity.

So, how do entrepreneurs think? How do they find their ideas? How do they see the things that launch companies? How do they see the things that others miss? They do it in a variety of ways.

> *"Ideas in the end are about people's problems and what solutions you can offer that people are willing to pay for."*
> -William Gartner, Entrepreneur Research Scholar

Don't only look for a new idea

Very few pure, new ideas.

As strange as this may sound, only looking for a new idea is the least successful way to start your venture. All too often entrepreneurs seem to spend their time looking for the perfect idea, something so new, so different, and so special that it becomes all consuming. The reality is that there are very few pure, new ideas that turn into ventures.

Everyday thousands of new companies start without a new idea. Pizza shops were everywhere when Pizza Hut opened. Tacos and bagels existed for many years before there were retail outlets selling them.

Execution counts, not the idea.

The message is simple—ideas are not the key drivers, execution is. The search for the great idea is a pipe dream, it may feel good but it does not get you started. It probably even postpones any action. Execution is action and execution started when you did the model business, when you said I want this or that type of a business. If you like retail, then start your search there. If you prefer direct sales, then assess and grow your skill sets as you learn that business.

> *"I didn't invent popcorn, I didn't even invent flavored popcorn. People had done it for many years before. My grandmother made strawberry popcorn bars for us when I was a kid. But, it was the packaging of all of that. The bundling of the product with the merchandising and the marketing in a mall environment with the brand. And all of that was unique and then being able to execute that, actually getting the leases, and hiring the people and having them share the dream. Then being able to convey all of that to the customer in a positive, value-added way. That's what it's all about and that's what made it so successful."*
> -Bill Sanderson, Founder, Popcorn Palace

Start your journey in your own backyard

Entrepreneurs more successful in areas they know.

A very high percentage of entrepreneurs achieve their success in an area that they already know. It is rare for an entrepreneur to successfully enter a foreign industry, an area that may require skill sets that are unique to that industry; skills sets and knowledge they do not have.

In a research study done by Lumpkin, Hills, and Singh at the University of Chicago at Illinois, 1,400 entrepreneurs who started information technology consulting firms were surveyed. 73% of respondents indicated that their new venture idea came from prior experience and 32.8% reported business associates as the source for their new venture idea.

New industry requires more time, greater commitment.

It is obvious that the probability of success is greatly enhanced when an individual already possesses skill sets and industry knowledge. Understanding the customers and the competition is critical to success, especially with the limited resources available to a start up. Entry into a new area will take more time and a greater commitment.

If you do not have a backyard, or if you have one you do not like, your initial challenge is to choose one. This is best done by first understanding what you do not like to do or are not very good at. By a process of elimination you will begin to develop a list of things that you are good at and that you do like.

Can recognize niches.

When you are inside the industry, you will have the insight and opportunity to recognize niches to explore.

> *"I'm a bit of a product of my environment frankly. I love boating, I was raised boating, it's always been in my life and I started sailing when I was six years old and I was in the Yacht Club when I was younger and was the commodore of the Yacht Club. I've just always been in boating and currently, I race sail boats. At the time I was looking for a way to mix my business with my love of boating."*
> -David LaMontagne, Founder, Vessel Assist Association

Up Front & Personal: Food from the 'Hood

Tammy Bird, a biology teacher at Crenshaw High in South Central Los Angeles did not have to travel far to recognize an opportunity. Her own backyard, which happened to be a class gardening project, was where her journey began and then blossomed to success.

How it Started

In 1992, Los Angeles was torn apart by race riots ignited by the Rodney King verdict and Crenshaw High was in the thick of it. After the smoke settled, Bird sensed that her students wanted to do something to take charge of their lives. As one student re-called, "we were trying to show everybody that not only bad things like drive-by shootings happen in South Central, there are also good things happening with people trying to help and give back to the community."

Bird felt that "this was my chance to get them out there and to create a green spot in this charred and cement area." In order to make it work, however, she knew the students would have to have a sense of ownership and feel like they were making a difference in society. Realistically, with high school students, projects like this typically only last two to three months before students would get bored, lose interest, or start thinking about the prom or a next project to tackle.

To give the project that little extra edge, Bird and the students went out into the community. After the riots were over, many of the looted grocery stores in the neighborhood failed to reopen, so the students decided to do their part in the recovery by selling their produce at a local farmer's market and by donating some of it to local residents. From there, Food from the 'Hood really began to grow.

From Produce to Salad Dressing

The students took their produce outside of South Central and sold the organic vegetables at other farmer's markets. While at the one in Santa Monica, California, the students really listened to what the consumers were saying. Some suggested that they make their own salad dressing and thought they could effectively compete with Paul Newman's line.

When they returned from this selling venture, the students discussed the potential of creating a salad dressing. It was their idea and they were interested in making it happen, "which is really cool because you can't give students a project and say, hey, you're going to do this because then they don't have ownership and they don't buy into it. But if they think they came up with the idea and started developing it, then they have complete ownership," says Bird.

It was a natural progression to go from growing the vegetables to producing the salad dressing and with Bird's and other helpful adults' assistance, the students began to make and market their own salad dressing. Their first real task was to get the dressing ready for mass production.

They turned the production into a pizza party in the science lab where they played with different combinations using the basil, parsley, and other vegetables from the garden. They took specimen bottles, mixed and matched different vegetables, blended them and finally created a dressing they liked.

They then had to get the dressing ready for mass production and so enlisted the assistance of a food chemist. The students were exacting about their product. Several tastings later and after changing the sodium content, the oil, the color, and other chemicals six or seven times, they finally were satisfied with the product.

Next, they needed a label for the product and together came up with the original label of two hands coming together with a sprout in the middle. An artistic student then photocopied that label, took it home one day, and with crayons designed the label that is used today.

How

The students did not know any of the rules of business, they made them up as they progressed from idea to concept. As Bird states, "people go to school and get their masters and they say, you have to do this in business, you have to write a business plan, but nobody knew any of those rules, so I was telling the kids, yea that's o.k., go ahead, and everybody was supporting each other."

They created a network of support that encouraged and motivated the whole group to collectively make the vision a reality. It was not until after the first bottle of salad dressing was sold that someone sat back and said "man, I didn't think that was ever going to happen," and someone else said "you either?" They all laughed and realized that they had been feeding off of each other thereby creating a true foundation of people and support.

One original student owner commented "I just thought it would be a little tiny thing in school, I was surprised when the salad dressing came out, I never thought it would go that far."

Why

Currently, Food from the 'Hood's Creamy Italian and Honey Mustard salad dressings are sold in major supermarkets across the United States. It is a non-profit corporation and proceeds fund student scholarships for the student owners who work for a point system and accrue a certain number of points for performing various tasks in the garden and in the office.

Bird attributes the success to the student ownership, "it's not about the adults running a program. It's about the students owning a business."

The students enjoy the experience it gives them and recognize that it will benefit them in the future in terms of lending credibility on college applications and ultimately having control over their lives. As one student owner said, "I think handling your own business is pretty hard and that's what we do here, handle our own business and it's hard. Close deals, meetings, paperwork, and people calling all the time, you get stressed out. Of course, I want to have my own business some day, and the experience I get here is worth it."

For Bird, the reward for starting a business is not stock, it's not millions, and it isn't an impressive title, it is the intangible satisfaction that entrepreneurs value above all else. "I guess I would do anything to teach students and I'm a science teacher so I do hands on things and I guess I was in the right place at the right time. So, if I can help create an educational process along with it, I think that's my goal in life."

Consider the organizational entrepreneur

Are you an organizational entrepreneur?

Many successful entrepreneurs will tell you they never had a great idea, or even a mediocre one. What they did have was the ability to listen to others who had ideas and organize them into ventures. Their skill set was to facilitate the process.

Recognize, research, and exploit ideas.

Organizational entrepreneurs are not managers. Rather, they are very much entrepreneurs but their skill and their contribution to a venture is that they can recognize, research, and exploit ideas brought to them by others. They usually have a high degree of industry knowledge and a keen awareness of customer needs and competitive pressures. But other entrepreneurs who could not take the project forward had the original idea and perhaps even built prototypes. These early stage entrepreneurs (often inventors) are well served by joining with organizational entrepreneurs who are able to execute the project.

A classic example of an organizational entrepreneur taking the helm is the marvelous journey of Mike Markula at Apple Computer. Steve Jobs and Steve Wozniak exemplify the "garage" entrepreneurs who toyed with various projects, exploring the potential of the personal computer. Their efforts and accomplishments are well documented and they deserve credit for bringing the computer to the masses.

Apple brought in organizational entrepreneur.

However, while experimenting with the computer, but struggling in the garage, they were introduced to Markula, an organizational entrepreneur. He was a gentleman 15 years their senior whose background was in the semi conductor industry. He knew the patterns of change in electronics and knew where the computer market was heading. He had no "new idea" but that came from the Steve's. What he did was to recognize the value he could bring to their idea. The story of Steve, Steve, and Mike is now entrepreneurial history.

By being knowledgeable in an industry, you will not only recognize opportunities, but many opportunities will also be brought to you when you have developed the skill sets of an entrepreneur.

> *I think I've always had a pretty good sense for looking at what other people in the industry are doing, at what other industries are doing. Reading, business magazines or publications, the paper, and picking things up that way, really without a formal business education.*
>
> -Michael Garvey, Founder, The Dumbell Man

New vs. need – think in terms of need

Focus on known needs.

Let others look to new ideas, your focus should be on known needs, which have many outward signs. The first is usually a line of customers or difficulty finding or buying something. Paul Orfalea, founder of Kinko's, observed a group of students walking across campus to the bookstore. He was and is sensitive to opportunity and he chose not to walk by that $20 bill. He stopped, investigated, examined, and asked.

Learning that they were on their way to buy school supplies and use a copy machine prompted him to put a copier and a rack of supplies outside their dorms. Today, Kinko's serves the needs of students by offering school supplies, the use of copy machines, and, more recently, the use of computer peripherals and Internet access. Most Kinko's are located in the main artery of a school campus where students walk from their dorms to classes. This was a simple observation of a need that has yielded a long and successful journey.

Dissatisfied customers = opportunity.

Many businesses also begin as a result of hassle and dissatisfaction by consumers. Mothers who can't find adequate baby care start day care centers. Secretaries and administrators attempting to serve their boss' needs to purchase corporate or personal gifts start gift-buying companies. Young ladies frustrated by the coordination of a wedding including the selection of a gown, flowers, photographers, invitations, etc., start wedding coordination services.

What is your unfulfilled need? There may be a business there.

Make a long-term commitment

Commit for the long haul.

Your goal is to start a new company. Your goal is not to set the record for starting it faster than anyone ever started a company. You need to recognize that this is not just a game of speed. What is critical is that you start now and commit to seeing it through to the end. There will be many mistakes and disappointments, but you must persevere.

2.7 venture attempts and 5-7 years before success.

A successful entrepreneur suggested that it takes an average of 2.7 venture attempts and 5 to 7 years to get to success. That is not to say that you will fail on your first try. Rather, a more common result of a first venture is that you spend time and energy learning an industry and your first concept is either short-lived or just does not pass your feasibility test for a variety of reasons and you elect not to go forward. When this happens you do not loose, especially if it is in an industry of your choice.

With each step your knowledge base becomes broader. Your experience is cumulative. Learning more about the nuances of the area in which you compete can be compared to growing from the rookie leagues to the majors and is a necessary progression.

Become bankable.

However, at every level, you must seek to make yourself more credible, or as entrepreneurs like to say, more bankable. This means that it can be to your benefit to work in the industry of your choice for a period of time before striking out on your own. Learn the industry on someone else's dime, not your own. By learning the business you gather more contacts, more knowledge of customer needs, and information about the customer buying process. Just as you would not want your first swing of a bat to be in a major league situation, you would not want to have your first customer or investor pitch be without practice.

Choose your industry, commit to it, and increase your bankability every step along the way.

Record your observations

It takes discipline.

All too often we find excuses not to do things. How many of us have promised to go to the gym, but have not? It takes discipline. This same discipline is needed when searching for new ideas. You need to set goals, learn at each step of the journey, and leave a trail of the messages gained.

Talk to strangers.

One such challenge for new entrepreneurs is to set a goal of talking to five strangers a day. Ask them any and all questions related to your area of interest, questions such as what is the biggest hassle you have had this week, what did you have a hard time finding or buying, or what broke.

Making a commitment to do these types of things and to record your findings is a good first test of your real desire to be an entrepreneur.

Structure your search

Never be caught unprepared.

Have a somewhat defined approach to how you view and explore all opportunities. For example, sales personnel are trained to prepare for a meeting by coming up with all possible questions that may be asked of them. They record all questions and prepare answers for each. By doing this, they should never be caught unprepared. What kinds of questions will your potential customers, suppliers, and investors ask you? Are you ready with a well thought out answer or will you try to ad lib and thus appear glib. Only with discipline and structure will you improve.

Following that same meeting, these sales personnel reanalyze the entire meeting in order to refine and improve upon their presentations. They ask themselves what the best and worst part of the meeting was and what they would do differently if given a second chance.

With a structured set of anticipated questions, you are prepared for the unknown. With self-analysis after every encounter, you will improve.

Prepare for potential ideas.

The same level of preparation and follow-up is needed when you see a potential idea. You can not just say you like it or you don't. If you don't know the industry well, then there is no basis for any such statement. Always remember, your vote does not count, only the customer's vote does.

First question: who is the customer?

So what is your structure when you see a new opportunity. Your first action should be to ask the question **"Who is the customer?"** Who wants to benefit from what is being proposed? Be careful as you analyze this question. Too often the first response describes the market or the consumer, not the customer. Be sure you know who the customer is, that is, the one who will write you a check.

Second question: who are the competitors?

The second question should be **"Who are the competitors?"** Assessing the competition in a market enables you to understand the pros and cons of entering that market. An industry without competition probably lacks customers. An industry with excess competition may have reduced price points, which may prohibit a start up from succeeding. Analyzing the competition is the easiest and most effective way to learn.

Structure your search to know the questions you may encounter and to become intimately knowledgeable about your customers and your competitors.

Be wary of fads

Fads are generally defined as changes that occur without warning and without reason. They seem to appear from nowhere, are usually short-lived, and then disappear. When they do appear, hundreds of imitators typically emerge rapidly.

Shooting stars burn out.

Fads should not catch you off guard. You need to be in an industry and know everything about the workings of new products, distribution methods, and other happenings so that you are never surprised. Even a fad will give some early warning signals that will enable you to prepare. If a fad does catch you by surprise (verses a major change in product needs), remind yourself that it is not wise to try to start a business by trying to catch up with a shooting star that burns out.

Skate to where the puck will be, not is.

Perhaps an analogy to the philosophy of the hockey great Wayne Gretzky gives the best advice. When asked the secret of his success he answered, "I skate to where the puck will be, not to where it is." This is good advice in both hockey and business.

Be wary of new inventions

Long time to market.

The opposite of a fad is a technological break through. However, for many truly significant inventions, the time from the lab to the marketplace is usually decades. For example, the transistor was invented by Bell Laboratories, Inc., but did not appear in commercial products until 17 years later in a television set. Another 17 years after that, the microchip replaced the transistor and the personal computer industry was born. Historically, and generally speaking, the domain for new inventions, new medicines, and new technology belongs to the highly capitalized larger firms.

Wait until the technology is marketable.

Instead, entrepreneurs seek to build their domains on applications of technology when the technology itself and market acceptance are close at hand. Creating a product based on an invention, i.e., building software on the chips, is when technology and the entrepreneur are in harmony, not when the technology is still a new invention.

Look for the innovation

Find a new way of doing an old thing.

As opposed to doing new things, consider the alternative of doing known things in a new way. Take the old, time tested approach and change something about it. Domino's Pizza, Inc. was based on an old business, pizza, but the company decided to bring it to you instead of you having to pick it up. Mountain bikes were based on an old product, the road bike, but companies made them lighter, with fatter tires, and more durability, effectively repackaging an old product.

> *"There were other copy shops when we opened up. I saw them all and I saw what they did, but I also added to them. The best way to go into business is to be the second one on the block, not the first, because the first one is already advertising what they've done."*
> -Paul Orfalea, Founder, Kinko's, Inc.

Nature of new products and services

Many ways to come up with new products and services.

	Characteristics	Examples
True Invention	Creating something that doesn't exist. Long-term. Often resource dependent.	Light bulb, vacuum tube, transistor.
Combination	Conjunctive creativity. Taking a known and applying in new situation.	Vessel Assist - combining AAA and stalled boats. Henry Ford - seeing slaughterhouse and applying to manufacturing.
Innovation - Based On	Changing what is. Copy cat, made better.	Dominoes delivering pizza. Gateway custom building computers.

Entrepreneurial Exercise

The following exercise is designed to get you started in structuring your search and recording your observations. Take a moment to write down three things you have observed in the market place and begin to record your observations about those opportunities.

New opportunities observed:

1. _____

2. _____

3. _____

Who is the customer?

1. _____

2. _____

3. _____

Who are the competitors?

1. _____

2. _____

3. _____

Are they successful? Why or why not?

1. _____

2. _____

3. _____

⇒ **Tear out and move to your entrepreneurial road map binder.**

Sources of New Ideas

Sources are abundant.

There are several differing opinions among researchers on how ideas are generated. What really works is not absolutely clear and most studies tend to support the notion that each person learns and thinks differently. Thus, entrepreneurs will find their own unique way to innovate and exploit opportunities.

However, to assist in your approach of generating new thoughts and new ideas in your industry, three action initiatives are explored.

Creativity

Freedom fosters creativity.

Creativity needs an environment of freedom to exist where it is believed that anything is possible. If this is not the case and if new ideas are challenged, or worse ridiculed, then new thoughts and/or the flow of ideas are inhibited, which leads to an environment that is not conducive to creativity or to entrepreneurship.

Start a creativity lab.

A helpful exercise to enhance creativity is to set up a creativity lab. Start by gathering a group of friends and associates together and place a marked coffee can in the center of the room. One person should throw out an idea and everyone else is encouraged (if need be, required) to make suggestions about that new idea. If a participant begins his or her comment by saying the **problem** with what you are suggesting is xyz, then that person is fined $1. The word problem is not acceptable. If anyone demonstrates body language or utters a sound that suggests "problem" then a fine is incurred. Using the word challenge in a constructive way is acceptable provided a positive directional thought is forthcoming. If the presenter is attacked by a participant who says something like "that's a stupid idea" or "I've seen that tried and it doesn't work" or "someone is already doing that" then there is a $5 fine.

Maintaining a positive environment will be easy after a few dollars in fines are paid.

Develop the ideas.

The next challenge is getting participants to develop and grow the basic ideas. Participants feel a sense of excitement and progress by making suggestions that they perceive add value and enhance the idea or concept being explored. Having individuals put their original idea on a poster board and then having everyone make written comments on that board is a good icebreaker.

Cross-pollinate for new ideas.

As ideas begin to flow, cross-pollinate and expand the ideas by mixing and matching. Take an idea about pizza delivered to the house and ask what else can be delivered with it, a movie rental, ice cream, and a six pack? Or what is not delivered to a home that could be?

Let creativity flow.

The goal is not to come up with the perfect idea. The goal is to enhance the ability to seek and recognize ideas and to twist and turn them into viable ideas and concepts—to let creativity flow.

Entrepreneurial Exercise

In the world of entrepreneurship, cross-pollination of ideas occurs all the time. For example, someone who wants to start a coffee shop might team up with someone who wants to start a bookstore. The result is a place to read, relax, and enjoy a cup of coffee. Barnes & Noble, Inc. and Starbucks Corporation have effectively done this in many of their sites. For this exercise, you should first pick a partner. Then, individually write down six ideas, products, or services that come to mind.

1. _____

2. _____

3. _____

4. _____

5. _____

6. _____

Next, compare your list with your partners' and try to come up with as many business ideas as you can by combining different items on each of your lists. Record your observations below and decide if any of these concepts make sense for you to explore as your model business.

1. _____

2. _____

3. _____

4. _____

5. _____

6. _____

⇒   **Tear out and move to your entrepreneurial road map binder.**

Meet strangers

Record your conversations.

An excellent exercise introduced by a fellow entrepreneur is to require students to meet, converse with, and then record conversations with strangers. For example, walk up to people in a retail store and ask them why they shop there. When you see someone with a new car license plate, ask him or her where and why they bought the plate. Or, reverse the scenario and ask a storeowner who his or her competitors are and what the competitor does better than he or she does.

As you become comfortable doing this you will also be at ease calling on experts in your industry, even presidents of companies. You will be capable of professionally asking them what types of changes they see in their industry and how they are preparing for them.

Form a round-table of experts.

If you have a group of associates also meeting strangers, you can compare notes and leverage your knowledge. If they have made contact with experts, bring the experts together and form a panel or round table discussion. The results will astound you.

Exploring through a round table with potential customers and suppliers will also increase your bankability and your knowledge level. Sprinkle in a few outside experts and you are learning about your industry, building a potential customer and supplier base, and preparing yourself to notice and grab the first $20 bill you see.

Remember that the customer you want tomorrow is a stranger today. Get physical fast.

Sources of strangers

What other strangers are there?

Primary Strangers	Secondary Strangers
Successful entrepreneurs, especially in your industry Potential customers Employees of competitive firms Suppliers to industry Business brokers Franchisers	Trade boards, associations, magazines Chambers of commerce Bankers, lawyers, accountants, professors

Create opportunities for yourself

Won't happen if you sit on your butt.

You will not find new ideas and you will not start your journey by sitting on your butt. You need positive environments and many strangers. But in addition, you can also create individual opportunities for yourself.

Visit every booth.

Go to a trade show. Even if it is not in your industry, you will be exposed to multiple ideas. Walk up and down every aisle and visit every booth. Prepare questions in advance that show your credibility and solicit insightful answers.

If the trade show is in your industry, you will be amazed by the preview of the future you will see. It may even scare you, but forewarned is forearmed.

Ask questions of competitors.

Analyze a potential competitor. When you get close to your niche, learn all about those already there. What do they sell? How do they sell? How many bodies work there? Run a Dun and Bradstreet report (a business credit report including a history of the company) on them.

Count customers.

If you are analyzing a retail store, count customers. How many enter and leave is a measure of success or failure. Enter the store, act like a customer, and analyze the services. Examine the nature of the customers and talk to the hired help. One successful entrepreneur enhanced his competitive advantage by looking in a dumpster at discarded invoices to find where his competitors bought their supplies.

Why are businesses for sale?

Read the classifieds and yellow pages. Find businesses for sale and explore why. Look for companies hiring and interviewing to learn why this niche is growing. As Paul Orfalea of Kinko's states, the yellow pages serve as "a list of successful businesses."

You can never know enough about your competitors. The more you learn, the more you know about your industry and eventually your niche.

Get physical fast

Who else can you talk to?

Primary	Secondary
Competitors (if you want to catch a mouse, make a sound like a cheese)	Trade Journals Want ads Yellow pages Businesses for sale

Protecting Your Idea

How to protect yourself?

No study of the tools used to create new ideas and to recognize opportunities would be complete without a similar review of how to protect those ideas and the intellectual property being created. However, protecting ideas is extremely difficult, always expensive, and at times of questionable value.

Legal vs. tactical approach.

There are two basic approaches to protecting ideas. The first is legal and involves the filing of patents, trademarks, and copyrights. The second is tactical and involves what you do in practice to protect yourself without following a formal legal process.

The first challenge before determining which approach is best is to prioritize. Given that you probably have a limited amount of resources, do you want expenditures going to your legal team or to your hunt for a customer?

What is legal protection?

Secondly, an analysis of the actual protection you receive should you choose a legal course is necessary. To properly understand the different types, a definition of each of the legal remedies available is shown on the next page.

Three types of patents.

Patents are defined as the grant of a property right to an inventor and are issued by the U.S. Patent and Trademark Office. The statute states specifically that a patent gives "the right to exclude others from making, using, offering for sale, or selling" the invention in the United States or "importing" the invention into the United States. International patents are also available, but appropriate legal council is advised if you feel this is necessary. The three types of patents are described below.

The three types of patents

Utility patent is most common.

Utility Patent	Design Patent	Plant Patent
Machines such as computers or engines; Manufactured articles; Compositions of matter such as pharmaceutical or chemical; Processes such as to manufacture pharmaceuticals and chemicals; 20 year term.	Ornamental design for article of manufacture; Protects appearance of article, not its structural or functional features; 14-year term.	Discovery of or asexually reproduced distinct and new variety of plant, including cultivated sprouts, mutants, hybrids, and newly found seedlings, other than a tuber-propogated plant or plant found in an uncultivated state; 20 year term.

Source: United States Patent and Trademark Office Web Site

Patents are costly.

Patents are designed to prevent others from duplicating your product, for a limited time. These are not often used by entrepreneurs in the early stages of a venture because they are quite costly to receive.

Other forms of legal protection are outlined in the table below.

Trademarks, copyrights, and trade secrets: usually easier and less costly.

Trademarks	Copyrights	Trade Secrets
Protect your name, logo, words, and symbols. Entrepreneurs need to defend rights from the beginning.	Protect expression of written and/or graphic material, but not ideas or inventions. Include literary, musical, graphical, and sculputral works, computer programs, and audio visual works.	Recipe for "magic sauce" or secret manufacturing process or data. Not patented, simply kept secret.

Legal protection is not always clear cut.

Some believe a patent, copyright, or trademark is a legal device that stops others cold from copying what they are doing. They see it as a glass wall that is impenetrable. The competition simply can not get in.

Nothing is further from the truth. Legal protection would more properly be described as a line in the sand. It is your public statement of what you believe is your right. It means that if someone steps over that line, you will seek to protect your property on the basis of the disclosure.

Often not about who is right or wrong.

Therein lies the catch. The people who challenge your legal filings are often large corporations with full-time legal staffs who will quickly make this a game of who has the most time and money and not who is right or wrong. Some patent and copyright suits have gone on for decades costing literally tens of millions of dollars. It is a battle entrepreneurs seek to avoid.

Legal review and battle sometimes inevitable.

A more difficult situation is when an entrepreneur learns that a large company has legally protected a basic idea that the entrepreneur created and is currently using. It is even more discouraging in a case where an entrepreneur can prove they have used this concept for a long time. At this point a legal review and possibly a legal battle must be undertaken. The strength of the case will be your proof of your original concept development and whether or not you treated it as intellectual property.

Tactics used are critical.

It is this latter point, the tactics used to protect your property, that is most critical. The legal tools will not stand the test unless backed by your actions and practices. Furthermore, if the actions are properly undertaken, perhaps the legal process need not be started.

The basic tactics used to protect your intellectual property on your own are:

Tactics often more effective than legal process.

- Do not disclose intellectual property. If you have a trade secret on how you do something, keep it a trade secret. Do not share your secret. Do not file a patent and tell the world how you do it. You may be providing education instead of securing protection. The formula for Coca-Cola is a trade secret that is best protected by not telling anyone.
- When you do feel it necessary to send confidential information that you want to remain proprietary, clearly mark all documents with a legend that it is company confidential and not to be used by or disclosed to anyone other than for internal use.
- Keep detailed notes in your journal of how you saw and exploited your ideas, with whom you share them, and under what conditions.
- When entering a serious discussion, have the other party sign a non-disclosure or confidentiality agreement. But be careful, some companies have policies that they will not sign such a document and requiring them to sign may mean that you lose that potential customer.

Don't throw away money on attorney's fees.

- Give away the technology. By offering it as part of the service you provide you will get the client to recognize that it is not the formula or recipe that is important, but rather the preparation and execution.

In the end, keep in mind that you are working and raising money to start a business, not to pay attorneys fees.

> *Classic example of a trade secret which has not been patented or copyrighted is the Coca-Cola formula. It is well known that that particular formula is limited to the number of people that have a chance to understand it and see it—supposedly only three."*
> -Gene Miller, Entrepreneur Professor

Chapter Summary

We have approached the question of finding ideas to start your business from four major vantages, which are:

- Knowing how entrepreneurs start firms versus how managers start projects by understanding the four stages of an entrepreneurial company.
- Understanding the role of ideas in a new venture. It is not the idea, it is the execution that counts.
- Recognizing that there are many actions you can take to start the process of creativity and opportunity recognition.
- Realizing that there is value in your ideas and that your intellectual property may be protectable.

It's now time to "get physical fast" and enter the ambiguous world of generating new ideas. Go talk to a stranger.

> *Then an idea popped into my head that instead of them coming to the store, I should go to them."*
> -Miguel DeLeon, DeLeon Enterprises

Chapter Three Exercises/Discussion Questions

1. Write down two ideas that you think could make a successful new business. Consider how these ideas occurred to you and think about what you might do to increase the intensity of your idea search.
2. Think of a successful business that you are familiar with and try to identify the four stages that it has gone through in its journey.
3. Are you an organizational entrepreneur? Would you be able to execute an idea if a friend came to you with one?
4. Make a list of five things that you do not like to do or that are difficult for you to do. Can you think of any products or services that would make these tasks easier for you?
5. List three weaknesses in your industry of interest. How can you turn those weaknesses into venture opportunities?
6. Create an idea lab with friends and strangers and collectively see what ideas you can come up with.
7. How do you plan to get physical fast? What opportunities can you create for yourself?
8. Study a competitor of your future business. Describe what the competitor does right and what it does wrong. How would you do things differently?

Journey Three: Kiyonna Klothing

The fashion industry is one of the most competitive and difficult to enter, but Kim Camarella and Yvonne Buonauro identified an untapped and eager customer, effectively designing themselves a niche in the garment industry. In this highly competitive landscape, survival of the fittest is the only rule and these two entrepreneurs have successfully satisfied an overlooked customer.

The Beginning

Kim Camarella was a business major in college when she had to write a business plan for a course project. Struggling to choose a concept to develop and considering a variety of different ideas, Kim stumbled upon the notion of designer clothing for plus-sized women from the media. She noticed the idealistic nature of the fashion industry and that there was a lack of advertisements for full-figured women. Commercials in this industry neglected the majority of women and modeled women with perfect, size six bodies to display fashions.

Recognizing this, Camarella began to further explore the validity and potential of this concept. She noticed that plus size women's needs are continually disregarded and rarely are the means to satisfy their demands offered. Research indicated that many plus size young women are forced to sew their own clothing because the cultural stigma placed upon size steered companies away from this industry toward the more acceptable petite market.

As a result, Camarella decided to pursue her idea of designing a line of clothing to meet the needs of full-figured women. "It wasn't necessarily that I wanted to do fashion, I just wanted to do something for which there was a real genuine need. And within the fashion industry, there's a genuine need for women over the size of 12 to have something decent to wear."

At the same time, Yvonne Buonauro was attempting to pursue her own dream—fashion design. Ever since she was a little girl, she had always loved fashion and design. "I've always, in high school, even in elementary school, wanted to do something in the fashion world. I drew when I was in junior high, I sketched, I made my own prom dress, I just knew how to put clothes together, it just came natural to me."

Camarella and Buonauro were good friends and after many discussions about this unmet need in the fashion industry, determined that they made a perfect combination. Camarella provided the business expertise and knew how to sell the line while Buonauro had the eye for fashion and merchandising. "We just clicked," Buonauro recalls.

The Research

Despite their belief in the concept, the two wanted to make sure their idea would sell before putting the scissors to any fabric. They set out on a market research effort and, among other things, went into malls to survey plus sized women. They asked these women where they shopped, where they wanted to shop, and if they liked the styles that were on the market.

The responses were the same ninety-nine percent of the time—women were not satisfied. Camarella and Buonauro were told that the clothes were not stylish, there were limited options, and nothing was available that made someone "feel good." The concept was also reinforced by a friend of Camarella's who said she had to make all of her own clothes because the selection was so awful.

The Business

After graduating, Camarella went to work full-time thereby postponing the initial launch of the company. However, she never lost sight of the vision and continued to research and learn about the fashion industry. After a period of time, she and Buonauro were ready and felt confident that they could satisfy this unmet need.

Having confirmed their belief through industry research and knowledge, the two each inves-ted $6,000 and blended their names into Kiyonna Klothing. Camarella worked to refine and complete the business plan in order to seek the necessary funding while Buonauro focused on developing the line of clothing.

While diligently working on the business plan, Camarella used her available resources to the fullest extent possible. She sought advice and support from her parents, whose backgrounds were in the financial industry and in teaching English, as well as other trusted associates. After much work, she felt conformable with and convinced that it was a superior business plan, one that would enable Kiyonna Klothing to secure financing.

However, despite her diligence, they did have difficulty securing the necessary funding in the beginning, but persistence was their ally and eventually paid off. After being rejected by two banks, they turned to the Small Business Administration Women's Pre-Qualification Program from which they received a loan in only three days, which happened to be one of the fastest approvals in history. They were on their way to success.

First Customer

It was in the very early stages that they took their line to the Las Vegas Big & Tall trade show where they got their first customer, Great Changes, a North Hollywood, California-based retailer that sells to famous clientele and has a great reputation in the industry. "They ordered probably a few pieces out of each of our groups and it made us feel really great that they believed in us," recalls Camarella.

Having obtained a customer-in-hand, they felt confident in continuing their efforts. It lended credibility to their venture and enabled them to leverage that one customer into many more. Great Changes became their reference, the customer to which they could point when potential customers would ask where their line was being sold. It gave them great confidence and the wherewithal to move forward.

Success

Currently, 45 boutiques in 22 states carry the Kiyonna Klothing line and every month, a half-dozen new customers place orders. "It's so rewarding when we see girls try on our clothes and say 'oh my gosh, it's so pretty, we love it,' so rewarding. Sometimes it really does bring tears to my eyes, it's very touching," says Buonauro.

Their busiest time is in the spring and summer when their signature line of sheer dresses sells quite well. They have built an image of contemporary, stylish clothing that appeals to the majority of plus size women. Customers also indicate that their sheer dresses are "sexy and romantic" looking and allow for a feeling of comfort and content in what they wear.

Camarella and Buonauro recognized a need in the market and sought a first customer before launching their product. They were diligent in their research and ensured that the niche existed.

Fashion is one of the worlds toughest industries with its constant change and unpredictable trends, but these women have a dream, they have made a commitment to the industry, and they are finding a way to build a niche.

"We asked women of all ages. Where do you want to shop, where do you shop now, what styles do you like. A series of questions. Every single person had the same answer: they weren't truly satisfied with their options."

Kim Camarella, Founder, Kiyonna Klothing

Journey Three Case Questions

1. How did Camarella and Buonauro decide on their business idea?
2. How did they create opportunities for themselves?
3. What efforts did they undertake to prove their concept?
4. Does this business make sense for the two founders? Why or why not?
5. At what stage of an entrepreneurial company are they and how have they gotten there?

Chapter Four
Lifecycles & Entry Strategies

Chapter Four Major Concepts

- Lifecycles and entrepreneurial lifecycles
- Personal skill sets
- Entry strategies—customer, product, and money

Journey Four: Pamela Lopker

Up Front & Personal: Strategic Partners

Up Front & Personal: Trick R/C

Up Front & Personal: Subway

Entry Strategies

Ready to jump?

You've picked your industry. You've gotten physical fast by attending trade shows, reading trade journals and most importantly, by talking to strangers. You are learning new things and acquiring new skills on a daily basis. But even though your knowledge base is rising, you're not sure how to dive off that diving board. What's going to prompt you to say—"go!"? How do you get started?

First, always remember that when talking to strangers, the first thing out of your mouth should be: "How did you get started? What did you see that indicated this was a feasible project? What was your inflection point? What pushed you off that diving board?"

What leads entrepreneurs to jump?

Having had the pleasure of asking these questions over three decades has yielded many interesting, albeit very different, answers. It should not be surprising that no two answers are the same because we have learned that the journey is unique to each individual.

Myriad of variables.

The underlying cause behind differing entrepreneurial journeys is that no two entrepreneurs think alike, or have the same skill sets, or enter their journey at the same point in time, which represent three defining variables that produce a myriad of different final outcomes.

This chapter.

Thus, the challenge to starting is simple. Hopefully, you have already assessed what you like to do (your model business). This chapter will focus on helping you determine your strengths (skill sets) and where your industry's maturity point (lifecycle) lies.

Lifecycles

Companies like people.

Products, companies, and industries are very much like people in that they go through a fairly predictable lifecycle. Babies are born, they grow to adolescence, to adulthood, and into their senior years and each stage along the continuum is filled with different activities and interests. In the beginning, there is a strong need for care and support. A great deal of experimentation occurs during adolescence, which not only includes periods of growth and maturity, but also typically brings many unwelcome setbacks, failures, and disappointments.

Predictable stages of growth.

With adulthood comes a period of mellowing and wisdom. We move slower but with greater knowledge and deliberation. At this point our life path is usually set and we become accustomed to fewer changes and growth spurts, allowing outside interests to take over. In our senior years, growth seems to all but disappear and we revert back to the need for greater assistance and care.

In many ways products and entrepreneurial companies resemble this lifecycle. They need great care in the beginning, grow in spurts as different versions and features are introduced, settle in as they become commodities later in life, and are eventually replaced by newer entries into the market place.

Classic product lifecycle.

Below is a classic product lifecycle curve. It reflects the life of a product from introduction to maturity.

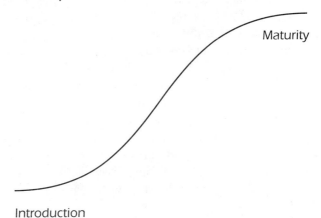

Maturity

Products move from introduc- tion to maturity.

Introduction

Product stage

The first stage of the lifecycle is known as the product stage. It is often the domain of technoids, individuals whose passion and skill set lead them to develop new products and new ways of doing things.

Domain of technoids.

It is important to note that even though this is the product stage, it does not necessarily mean that it is product-driven, especially for entrepreneurs. Rather, entrepreneurs involve their current and potential customers in every phase of development within this stage. As always, customer needs and desires should drive product definition.

Customer involvement at all levels.

The lifecycle curve portrays that new products have little volume and limited market share when they are introduced. First customers are often early adapters or innova- tors because entrepreneurs seek to find and sell to individuals who like change and are not afraid to experiment. Often early sales volume drops as either a product shortcoming or the failure to fulfill a real need is discovered. During this infant stage the product is constantly changed, either significantly, such as a new operating system or superficially like a new packaging design, to reflect what is learned.

First customers are early adapters.

This first stage is the birthing stage of your company.

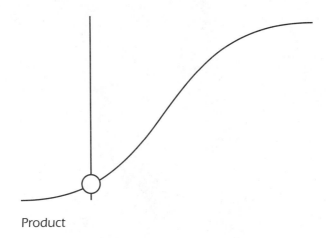

First stage is birthing stage.

Product

Market stage

Shift to marketing emphasis.

As customer acceptance and knowledge of the product or service increase and as the base product becomes stable and standardized, then the marketing phase of the lifecycle is entered. Emphasis is placed on marketing the products and services and shifts away from the products produced and customers tested.

Formation of army.

With the market phase comes the formation of an army that will sell the package to customers. The army often starts with members of the founding team selling themselves and their company. After initial success, they are able to attract experienced associates who have credibility and sales skills and the journey picks up momentum. As the army grows, more efficient means to support selling are introduced, including marketing and advertising. New distribution and sales channels are introduced in the later period of this stage in an effort to reach additional potential customers.

Marketing and advertising are introduced.

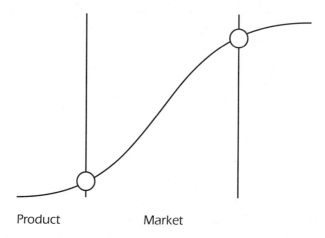

Product   Market

Management stage

Mature stage of life.

All products have a finite life and all markets have a point of saturation. As the latter happens and as individual efforts at reaching new customers approaches the point of diminishing returns, the cycle moves to its last phase—management. The excitement of new products and expanding markets has gone and the nature of the business is about managing how to sell and what to charge. It is the maturing part of life and the domain of those who seek the highest financial return or the most efficient process. The creativity of the original players is long forgotten.

Reach the point of diminishing returns.

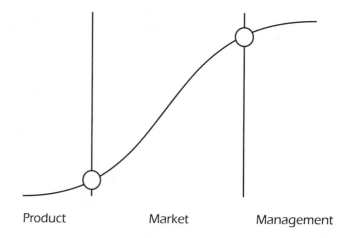

Product   Market   Management

Time to leverage accomplishments.

In today's better managed companies this is a time for reinvention and discovering how to leverage accomplishments, return to the roots, and start all over again. For companies with strong sales and distribution systems it is time to introduce new products into the pipeline. However, for companies that cannot reinvent themselves or do not have a leveragable strength, the only alternative may be to manage into liquidation.

Entrepreneurial Lifecycle

Product life is road map for industry.

Entrepreneurs use this product lifecycle as the road map for what occurs in their own industry and firm; they recognize that the changes from product to market to management really apply to the entire firm, not just the products.

Entrepreneurs also realize that when an industry grows from one stage to another, i.e. from product to market to management, chaos and confusion often mark the periods of transition. The early innovators and named leaders of emerging niches will often find that more significantly established companies are entering the competition.

Transitions are greatest opportunity.

However, entrepreneurs are uniquely positioned to recognize these periods of transition as the points of greatest opportunity. At this time, the larger firms are beginning to consider entry into a market, while the entrepreneur is already firmly entrenched. As others are installing systems or exploring new opportunities, the entrepreneurs are already satisfying customer needs.

Entrepreneurs firmly entrenched.

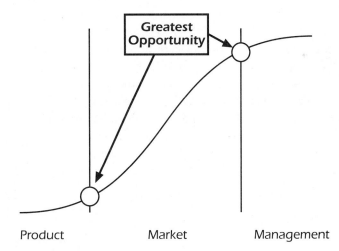

Product   Market   Management

Operate in a niche.

In the product stage of the cycle entrepreneurs operate in a niche, knowing that it is too small for the larger firms and that the hurdle rate of these large companies won't allow them to enter. By being customer driven, entrepreneurs listen more intently to the needs of the early adapters and join with these customers to define needs and even pre-sell benefits. In an established company, this phase is typically handled by the "new product" division, often with little input from outside the hallowed corporate walls. Limited to that input, classic product development will often yield

Benefit develop-ment does not equal product development.

new inventions or add features that may not address customer needs. Because entrepreneurs involve the customer, they label this period of development "benefit development" as opposed to product development.

Product to market

The first point of chaos and confusion occurs as the industry, and therefore the entrepreneurial company, transitions from product to market. At this stage, we must be in the business of satisfying customer needs; therefore, if the transition to a customer driven company has not yet been made, then now is the time to do so.

Celebrate smallness.

Entrepreneurs are able to celebrate their smallness during this transition. They can move faster and quicker. The team is close knit, shares the same vision, and is nimble and can change a brochure or design in minutes or days. The larger competi-tion is an elephant capable of crushing all in its path, but slow to adjust because changes require committee approval and sign off on design. This difference in timing and ability to act immediately enables the fast paced entrepreneurial gazelle to get off to a head start.

Customers want a knowledgeable sales force.

A second dynamic is at play during this initial transition from product to market. The nature of early adapters is that they are very knowledgeable about their industry as well as the product development activities of many companies. They want and need sales people who are equally as knowledgeable. Larger companies fail in this regard because they often divide sales and product development into different departments with little interaction between the two. Thus, it is impossible to provide effective customer service because the sales person does not have first hand product knowledge and cannot intelligently answer questions regarding product development or release dates.

Team includes experts in each area.

On the other hand, benefit development personnel, or the founders themselves, are typically responsible for initial sales in the entrepreneurial company. These teams are comprised of experts in both product and sales thereby enabling them to be knowl-edgeable in both areas. There are many examples of these teams, such as Jerry Yang and David Filo, founders of Yahoo! Inc. or Bill Gates and Paul Allen of Microsoft Corporation. The combination of talents provides the critical juncture and when both are present, success is imminent.

Market to management

Transitioning from market to management marks the second period of chaos and confusion. At this point, the market is mature, the total market size is stable, and price becomes the focal point of competition because there is little difference in offered benefits.

Different breed of entrepreneurs emerge.

While classic managers begin to review their career options at this stage, a different breed of entrepreneurs recognize the potential. Inside the box thinking would indicate that this is a sinking ship, it is time to jump off. However, entrepreneurial minds, such as Wayne Huizenga, who brought credibility to the world of used car sales with AutoNation, Inc., see the opportunity. As a result, the well-established

Entrepreneurship takes on a new form.

world of car sales will never be the same. The outsider, the entrepreneur, moved into the mature world of auto sales and changed distribution channels, didn't accept the norm. Other examples include Lee Iacocca who took an ailing company, Chrysler Corporation, and employed his financial skills to restructure and revitalize it. These are both outstanding examples of entrepreneurs recognizing opportunity in industries that were clearly in the mature management stage of operation. The nature of entrepreneurship is very different at this stage, but equally as possible and as effective.

Who Qualifies as an Entrepreneur?

Chapter Two focused on the characteristics and attitudes of entrepreneurs. But this is a different question. Do you have to start a company to be an entrepreneur?

Was Ray Kroc an entrepreneur?

When asked this question, a surprisingly high number of respondents answer yes. However, if that is the case, then the question arises as to whether an individual such as Ray Kroc, always referred to as the founder of McDonald's, is really an entrepreneur? Kroc was a milk shake machine salesman soliciting orders from restaurants (he knew the industry) and was amazed when he saw the new "quick service" format at the McDonald brother's restaurant. Kroc recognized the opportunity and acted on it. He bought their three fast food sites and turned it into the 12,000 that it is today. But he was not the founder. It was not his original idea. He was an entrepreneur who saw a line of people and explored and exploited the idea. A simple case of opportunity seen, opportunity seized.

It's not about starting or even owning.

If an individual acquires a Subway franchise, is he or she an entrepreneur? If you have a small wedding consulting business run out of your home, are you an entrepreneur? Can an entrepreneur exist inside of a large corporation? Can a large corporation be entrepreneurial? There are many different answers to these questions and everyone will answer in his or her own way. However, most agree that entrepreneurship is not about starting or even about owning, it's about who you are, what you do, and why you do it. If you have an attitude of self-dependence, creativity, and seek reward for your efforts, most believe you are an entrepreneur.

Different skill sets at different stages.

But how do we recognize the differences between the skill sets of a Wayne Huizenga, Ray Kroc, or Lee Iacocca and those of other entrepreneurs? How does it all fit together? It works because each stage of the entrepreneurial journey requires a different type of entrepreneurial skill set.

> *It's exciting, it's varied, it's different every day with the different clients we have, the different products we have. If I didn't like it, I would have found something else."*
> -Tony Rochon, Founder, Avanteer, Inc.

Product stage

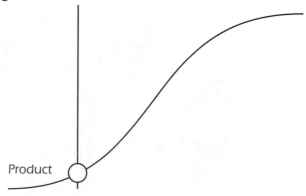

Product

Creator Promoter Organizer

Different types of entrepreneurs.

In the early product stage there are often three different types of entrepreneurs. The first is the <u>creator</u>, usually a product or service creator who knows the patterns of change in an industry and is positioning his or her belief of the next generation service to the needs of a customer. While some of these entrepreneurs are inventors, the majority of them are innovators, but they all possess a product creation mindset.

Creator creates products or services.

The second type is the <u>promoter</u>; someone who also knows the industry but is more focused on transferring the value initially created. These people have a sales mindset and their skills enable them to excite potential customers, regardless of the development stage of the product. They represent the hype and charisma of the company and are the ones who breathe life into the startup.

Promoter breathes life into start up.

The third type is the <u>organizer</u>, the organizational entrepreneur introduced in Chapter Three, who coordinates the efforts of the creator and promoter and gives structure at this early phase.

Company begins.

These three different attitudes and unique skill sets intertwine to create the beginning of the company.

Market stage

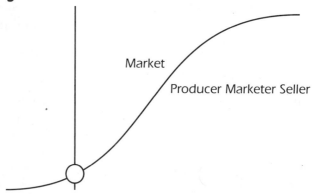

Market

Producer Marketer Seller

New skills needed in market stage.

A reliance on the skill sets of the original team may prohibit an effective transition from the product to market stage. The market stage requires larger production of

Consistent delivery becomes key.

working goods by a <u>producer</u> as opposed to creation of prototypes and sale of benefits by a golden-tongued promoter. The organizer has supplied the tools to blend the skills together while the early adapter customers have remained flexible, growing with the firm through early schedule and delivery issues. Now the time has come to deliver consistent, quality products and services. Building one doesn't count—building many on a consistent basis does.

Apple Computer delivered when others did not.

This skill to deliver a repeatable product or service represents the first type of entrepreneur as the market stage of the lifecycle is entered. It is thus not surprising to note that Apple Computer's next team member was a production whiz who produced at this critical stage. There were 12 firms ranked ahead of Apple at that time (the infant years of the personal computer industry), but Apple delivered consistent quality and won the race while others struggled to get from prototype to production.

Need for sales force emerges.

With consistent quality as their bedrock, firms then start to position themselves in the industry. This positioning requires a need for additional tough, driven, and production-oriented personalities. Sales on a one-on-one basis to the early adapter customer base is no longer enough, a sales force is needed. Additionally, for a larger sales force to be effective, a marketing campaign must also be planned. As for Apple, it too required a different mindset.

Marketing campaign becomes critical.

Image creation, advertising (on a creative basis), and package development are among the many components needed at this stage. Apple recognized this need and brought in the high-tech communications agency, Regis McKenna, Inc. which is usually given credit for Apple's image: the bright, multicolored apple with a "bite taken out of the forbidden fruit."

With a solid foundation including an image, identity, and sales force, the lifecycle continues and the market positioning is accelerated. This phase of the cycle is about selling many, many units and thus requires the mindset of a <u>marketer</u> and a <u>seller</u>. The skills to position the product (marketing) and the skills to deliver the sale (seller) are necessary, which inevitably leads to a tremendous need for process, procedure, and the resulting politics. In the beginning, the founder controlled everything with first hand knowledge. This stage of growth requires a different set of rules and the beginning of a structure.

Jobs' challenge to Scully.

In the world of Apple, this stage belonged to John Scully, a very successful executive recruited from the Pepsi-Cola Company. John's background was selling thousands of units to a youth oriented soda market. Founder of Apple, Steve Jobs challenged Scully to "do something more valuable than sell sugar water to kids," which is what prompted Scully to join Apple. Ironically, it also marked the beginning of the politics that drove Jobs out of the business. Scully's efforts at promoting Apple Computers to schools and catching the generation on the way up (just as Pepsi did) placed Apple in a strong market position for a decade.

Management Stage

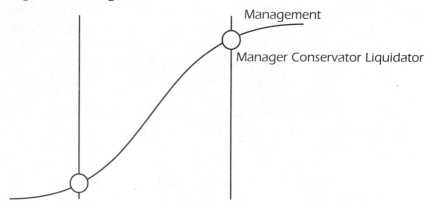

Administrative focus begins to emerge.

Grown from effective to efficient.

This final part of the lifecycle deals with management. As the sales drive reaches full throttle, the need to control the flow of goods (and therefore cash flow) increases. The demand from outsiders for earnings replaces the demand for satisfaction by the founders. It is a company. It is administrative. It needs an administrator, a <u>manager,</u> complete with organization charts and personnel manuals. The company has gone from a metric of how effective to how efficient.

Different attitude and skill set is needed.

Somewhere during the growth of Apple, the company went from an entrepreneurial to an administrative focus. Even if this can be done creatively, this transition represents the need for an attitude and skill set that most entrepreneurs don't want and probably aren't able to embrace. As one entrepreneur remarked, "I started my company to get away from forms and procedures. Why do I want to stay when it has grown to a company based on the forms and procedures I hate." Once again, this takes us back to what you would do if you could work for free for the rest of your life and finding the business model that is right for you.

Possible to reengineer into a manager.

However, this is not to suggest that all entrepreneurs reach a point where they cannot or, more importantly, do not want to reengineer themselves into managers. Numerous examples provide evidence to the contrary and inside of these success stories are many examples of how entrepreneurs had to change from being a driving force to serving as a visionary—a change from an entrepreneur to an entrepreneurial company. Certainly Andy Grove, who was part of a team of three that started Intel Corporation and took it from birth to world dominance without giving up an entrepreneurial culture, is a prime example. There are many others. For most it is not a question of can they change but rather, do they want to change.

Growth curve starts downward.

As the firm matures and when growth at acceptable rates is no longer possible, a new phase begins—the phase of the <u>conservator</u>. The growth curve starts moving down and although entrepreneurship is still possible, it is hard to see. If you are not going forward, then by definition, going backwards is appropriate. Even though management exists to hold on and hopefully milk the cash cow, there will be a loss of market share. It is a period of little vitality and of controlled expenditures.

Liquidation may be inevitable.

The final phase of the management stage is <u>liquidation</u>. When there is no value being created, it is time to end. Ideally, this will occur in such a way as to protect jobs and increase shareholder's value, potentially through a sale of the company. Examining these final phases is probably best left to the more classic study of business.

However, the point is simple. The company changes as it progresses in life. Entrepreneurs start businesses because of a certain attitude and set of skills, which may be in conflict at a later stage of the firm. Recognizing these personal changes and determining the best course of action for you personally is necessary for success.

Different needs at different times.

Understanding the need for different skill sets at the various stages allows entrepreneurs to recognize the critical issues that they will face in starting and growing their firm and be prepared to attract individuals with complementary skill sets at the appropriate times.

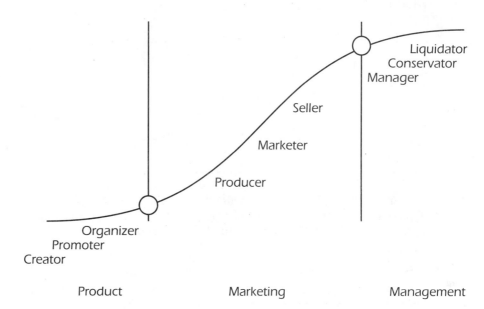

"Ask yourself what you would do if you could work for free for the rest of your life. The answer will help you determine the best business for you. Try to imagine yourself 10 years from now at a cocktail party. When chatting with friends, new and old, what do you want to be able to say that you do? About your personal life as well as your business life."
-Ann Graham Ehringer, Entrepreneur Professor

Entrepreneurial Exercise

For this exercise, you will first need to pick a partner. Together choose an entrepreneurial business that you both feel has progressed through the product, market, and management life cycles, but do not discuss the business cycles. Next, in the space below, separately write down your observations of this business and how it has handled the transitions from product to market and market to management. Has it celebrated its smallness and acted nimbly in response to customer demand? Has it been able to reinvent itself into a well-managed company? What has happened to the original entrepreneur(s)?

Business: _____

Observations: _____

_____

_____

_____

_____

Now, exchange your observations with your partner and read through his or her comments. Discuss your findings. Do you agree or disagree with each other? Can you see each other's points? Record your findings below.

_____

_____

_____

_____

_____

_____

$\Rightarrow$ **Tear out and move to your entrepreneurial road map binder.**

Skill Sets

In the introductory stages of this journey, we defined entrepreneurship as a combination of who you are, what you do, and why you do it: your attitude, skill set and reward system. We have also learned that different skill sets are needed throughout the lifecycle of an industry.

Do you know your model business?

Thus the picture at this point should be clear. You need to know yourself, know what you like to do (model business), and know where your strengths lie in order to determine the most effective way for you, personally, to start a business. Many believe that your attitude and the attributes of integrity, passion, and perseverance are most important. But, perhaps even more important are your skill sets—what you can do.

> *While watching a boxing match with his father, a little boy noticed that the fighter had knelt in the corner to pray before the fight started. The boy quickly asked his father if he felt the prayer would help the fighter, to which his dad replied – yes, if he knows how to fight.*
>
> -Anonymous

To put the different skill sets in context, it is necessary to understand that there are three primary foci of business—a customer, a product (benefit to entrepreneurs), and money—which are best perceived as the cornerstones of an entrepreneurial triangle as shown below.

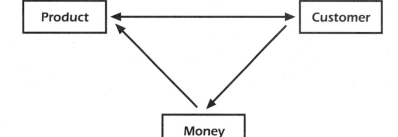

Three foci of business.

The role of the entrepreneur is to integrate these components. In order to successfully do that, the entrepreneur must recognize that two different, but complementary skill sets fall under each of these three foci and that a myriad of subcategories, such as advertising and public relations under marketing, also exist. The primary categories are:

Different skill sets match focus of business.

Focus	Skill Sets
Customer	Sales, Marketing
Product	Development, Production
Money	Accounting, Finance

What is your entry strategy?

Every entrepreneur does not possess equal expertise in each area; thus, the challenge is to determine where you best fit. That is, what should your entry strategy be?

Entry Strategies – Customer Focus

An individual who is able to recognize and position a customer (marketing) and an individual who is able to deliver a customer (sales) have historically had a higher level of entry success.

Customer is most important word in business.

As we know, the most important word in business is customer and nothing will happen without one. By focusing on a customer you are being driven by a need, not by a solution for which a problem may not exist. The individual who can sell to the first customer has this critical skill set. That person must sell themselves and their knowledge of the industry thereby convincing the buyer that the solution can be delivered. The marketing side of a customer focus is equally important, but typically not a skill that is added to the team until the second stage of the start up.

Customer in hand

You are the only wild card.

As has been discussed, the entry strategy that is most favored is to start your firm with a customer in hand. The theory is simple. You can exist with little or no money, on a full or part time basis, and avoid dilution of ownership if your starting point is the signing of an initial order. With a customer in hand, there are no variables or unknowns—except your ability to deliver, which is something you control. Only you are the wild card. If you worked your model business in advance and if the result of talking to strangers is closing a first order, then you are in business, not just conceiving a business.

Leveragable into multiple customers?

The questions of whether this business can be grown to a size that meets your needs (worthy opponent) and if it will have value for a third party to acquire or a public offering (harvest) will remain. Too often the theory of customer in hand is perceived to be about small business start ups and certainly a carpenter who contracted work with a friend (customer) was in business as a contractor. Whether the or she is able to leverage that into multiple customers (by referrals perhaps from having a show room or small ads in local newspapers) is up to the attitude and skill set of the individual. The initial challenge of starting was met. The next challenge is growing to multiple customers.

Customer in hand is not only for small business start ups.

But having a customer in hand is not limited to small business. The journey of one woman who started with a customer in hand and grew her company to the point of an initial public offering, at which time she was defined by *Forbes* Magazine as "the most successful women in the history of commerce," is testament to the strength of this entry strategy. The woman is Pamela Lopker, the company is QAD, and her marvelous journey is featured at the end of the chapter.

Observation of a market

This second customer based entry strategy occurs even before a customer is in focus. It stems from observing the next wave of change in an industry. Sales people are ideally positioned to capitalize on this method because they are in onstant contact with people in the industry and aware of the evolution of technology and patterns of

Sales people ideally positioned.

change in that industry. Thus, sales people can see the hazy outline of potential customers, can recognize the initial idea, and can then progress to the primary strategy of customer in hand.

> *The Internet was becoming somewhat popular at the tail end of my years at USC. So, it was new to me. I knew nothing about the Internet and neither did Stefan."*
> -Tony Rochon, Co-Founder, Avanteer

Join an emerging company

Joining does not equal copping out.

To some nascent entrepreneurs this may seem like the ultimate cop out. If you have a strong desire to start your own firm and someone says, "don't start a firm yet, join an emerging organization," it seems like the antithesis. But, it may not be. Whether this meets your needs again comes back to the model business and your goals for your journey.

Reward can be exciting journey with low risk.

In reality, very few entrepreneurs today want or expect to have a 100% ownership of their business. They want to be the driving force and to have a significant equity position, but they realize that to reach their goal requires attracting others into the company—that other might be you. If you have knowledge of a market and contact with customers, you can be a critical component of a primary team. The reward is an exciting journey in an industry of your choice with strong financial upside and low risk. This is especially true if you are just starting to explore the entrepreneurial trail. The number of associates who have become millionaires in Apple, Microsoft, Intel and other fast growing firms is extremely high. More importantly, they all got there doing what they love to do.

> *"In the newspaper in the LA Times it said: we need a consultant in home health, a registered nurse. So, I called this number, and it was this 67-year-old lady. She was a wonderful person, and she was sitting behind this desk, and she said, I'll never forget it, she said, 'well, I'm gonna start a home health agency.' And I thought to myself, hmmm. And she said, 'but I don't know anything about the business.' So I said you are and you don't? And she said, 'yeah.' And I said Oh, I see. And she said, 'and we really need someone to help us run the business, could you help us run the business?'"*
> -Carolyn Colby, Colby Home Health

Entry Strategies – Product Focus

Don't lose sight of customer needs.

An individual who is able to develop a product or benefit (inventor, innovator, adapter) and/or an individual who is able to deliver it (producer) have a product focus. Individuals with a product focus, provided it is in the context of developing the product with a focus on a first customer, have also enjoyed tremendous success.

The skill here is twofold. First, it is developing a focused benefit with customer input, leaving the sales and positioning of the product to someone with a customer focus. Second, an equally great skill is to produce a consistent benefit/product, a task typically performed in the second stage of the start up.

Invention as an entry strategy

Repositioning of existing component, or invention.

For some entrepreneurs, the journey begins with the design of a product, which can come in one of two forms: an innovation from the repositioning of existing components to make something new, or something truly new, that didn't exist before, which would be classified as an invention.

Education is needed with inventions.

While many successful ventures have been started with a product, the warning relating to product-based companies is worth repeating. Starting with a product typically means that you are creating a solution and then seeking the problem for which there may not be a customer. A pure invention is even more complicated because you are dealing with an unrecognized need. Your market will need to be educated, which will take a long time and thus, it may be difficult to reach commercial application.

Regardless of the starting point—new way or new thing—you will quickly find that at some point, your focus will have to be on the customer and market. The skills of selling yourself will always be critical to success.

Do customers know what they need?

It is important to note that some successful entrepreneurs believe that giving a customer what they want can be limiting because the customers don't always know what they need. While this is valid point, the journeys of these entrepreneurial travelers have been difficult. For example, the videodisc was developed in the labs at Phillips Magnavox in the mid 70's. It provided a more efficient means of delivering higher quality, lower cost video programs than the conventional VCR. But the VCR won the battle because it offered viewing, recording, and playback as opposed to viewing only with the videodisc. As the market becomes more educated and as technology improves (CD Roms now being standard), the final solution will probably be the videodisc, but it was a solution 20+ years in coming.

Innovation

Make changes, instead of create new things.

The alternative to invention is innovation. Broadly defined, innovation is "to make changes" in existing things as opposed to "create" new things. The "make changes" is usually classified under the product skill set but is intended to be considered in a broader context of all changes, i.e., changes in production methods, to packaging, or to distribution of products. The classic examples of innovations are the change in distribution methods from firms like Dell Computer Corporation selling computers

Dell, Domino's, Gateway, etc.

direct and Domino's delivering pizza. Gateway and Levi Strauss & Co. have also made significant changes in terms of mass customization—individually assembling or building to custom specifications.

Just as with an invention, these changes are better done when a customer is in sight and best done with one in hand.

Reposition a product: Starbucks.

Innovation also includes the repositioning of a product. Clearly Starbucks Corporation has repositioned coffee by making it the center of the social world—replacing bars as a primary meeting place. Innovation by positioning is also accomplished by branding an aura of excellence as Orville Redenbacher did with popcorn.

> "Orville Redenbacher for instance. I mean, popcorn is popcorn. But he really truly believed that if you dedicated your life to one thing and did one thing better than anyone else, which he did, this is a true person with popcorn, he dedicated his life to coming up with the best popcorn, then you can differentiate it from all other products in the marketplace which were really commodities."
> -Bill Sanderson, Founder, Popcorn Palace

Trade technical expertise for equity

Join with customer focused entrepreneurs.

In today's world this is the number one route to entrepreneurship. As is true with the other skill sets, bringing your product talents to a firm with an entrepreneurial culture enables the firm to share the risk. It can offer a reasonable salary with a large upside through stock options. This gives you exposure to the entrepreneurial company and allows you to share ownership. Thus, being an entrepreneur by joining should be considered, especially in first ventures.

> You know Larry is probably one of the most outstanding, intelligent Java developers in the world and we have him. How did we get him? Well, we gave him ownership in the company."
> -Stefan Bean, Co-Founder, Avanteer

Turning a hobby into a business

What's your passion? Can it be a business?

If it is true that entrepreneurs do what they love—what they would do if they could work for free—then it is logical that their hobbies are their passion and provide an industry in which where they want to spend their times.

If your model business suggests pursuing your hobby as your journey, then it is worth exploring. It is common, however, for hobbyists to be in love with their product and you should be careful of this trap. Being in love with your product could mean that you are blind to all else, which has caused many an entrepreneurial failure.

Hobby may equal lifestyle business.

Be sure that you recognize both the potential as well as the limitations of your hobby as hobbies often provide a lifestyle business and personal income, but may not have a harvest capability.

"I've always heard that turning your hobby into a business was losing both of them, losing both your hobby and your business. But, it certainly hasn't worked that way for me. I thoroughly enjoy each one of them and I maintain my life, I still go fishing, I still take pictures. And I still fly model airplanes as a hobby, but I can do it as a business too and I do not find it a distraction. I have not lost both."

-Jerry Teisan, Founder, Trick R/C

Up Front & Personal: Trick R/C

Jerry Teisan had no idea that there were as many model airplane hobbyists in the world as he discovered. Nor did he even remotely consider the notion that these hobbyists would be interested in the model airplanes that he had been building and racing since he was a child. However, this man with a hobby is now an entrepreneur with a business, Trick R/C, which designs and manufactures model airplanes.

His mother notes, "He was always building, airplanes came first, then photography and then fishing and now its back to airplanes."

One day he took a newly built model to a race and was "really surprised when I got up there and everyone wanted one of my airplanes." After just a few hours of work, he supplied 10 people with their own planes and felt that it was the easiest $400 he had ever made.

Teisan possessed the three essentials for starting a business: a bright idea, career know-how, and customer demand. After quickly selling the 10 planes, he felt he was being very ambitious, but made 50 more, which also sold immediately. The run of 50 increased to 100 and the "next thing that happened, I made a run of 600 and thought it was about the dumbest thing I had ever done." But, yet again, they all sold at which point he began to have confidence that he could turn his hobby into a business.

With an investment of less than $10,000 from his brother, Jerry moved Trick R/C from his garage and living room to a larger shop. With just this small investment, Teisan has reached every part of the entrepreneurial life cycle—product, marketing, and management. He started with his passion and now has a business.

Hobbies can be turned into businesses and they are the kind of businesses that people love to run. What is your hobby? Can it be turned into a business?

Entry Strategies – Money Focus

Individuals who are able to raise money (finance) or oversee the management of money (accounting) represent the third, and equally as necessary, focus.

Money is an enabler.

However, as we have learned, the role of money in an entrepreneurial venture is greatly overstated. Money is an enabler. It allows the plans of the driving force to be executed. It *enables* but it cannot *create* value. If someone gives you $1,000,000, it doesn't mean you can start a successful business.

Money skills are critical.

Of the two money skill sets, raising or managing money, raising it is of greater value. When an infusion of funds is needed, having a member of the primary team skilled in raising money, coupled with having an active network of first round investors (known as angels or cocktail circuit money), is critical.

In reality, when entrepreneurs are at the entry point, money will usually find them, which will be discussed in greater detail when we review funding a start up. Since money cannot start a deal, while plentiful, ways to enter a business with a money focus usually occur as a result of someone else's idea.

Trading money skills for equity

Can you find a worthy opponent?

It is always possible to join an emerging firm if you possess money skills. The bright-eyed sales people and innovative product types with customers need your skill to enable the process. Finding the worthy opponent, the right company to join is your challenge.

Buying an existing business

Entrepreneurs do buy businesses.

Sometimes purists react strongly and claim that it is not possible to be an entrepreneur by purchasing a company. Nothing could be further from the truth. Was Ray Kroc an entrepreneur? Certainly. Did he start his own company? No, he bought it. Did Bill Gates write DOS? No, he bought it. Is he an entrepreneur? Clearly. Once again, it is about who you are, what you do, and how you execute that makes you an entrepreneur.

Buying customers in hand.

In success of entry strategies, buying a business ranks second to customer in hand. What are you doing when you buy a business? You are buying customers in hand and a track record. You are taking over a momentum that already exists and hopefully raising the accomplishments to a new level.

Leveraged buy out is one alternative.

Buying a business is money-based and has two major advantages. If the company being acquired is successful, it has leverage capability thereby enabling you to raise money or borrow funds for the acquisition. Second, if you are in a management position of a company ad have proper industry background, experience, and credibility, you can borrow funds to acquire the business or a division of it, otherwise known as a leveraged buy out ("LBO"). In either case, both investors and banks can see the existing cash flow and therefore, the risk is more quantifiable.

Maybe an entrepreneur who owns will finance an acquisition?

Or, in your search, you may find an entrepreneur who has a life style business that has no successors and no chance of harvest. You could negotiate a deal to first become an employee of the business and then acquire the company over time. In effect, the entrepreneur is then financing your acquisition. He or she (the seller) becomes the investor and you provide an attractive exit strategy for that entrepreneur who otherwise would have had to close instead of being able to sell to harvest.

Breathe life into a dying entity.

Another alternative is to acquire a failing business. Entrepreneurs are always looking "outside the box" to find an opportunity and exploit it, for example, a company with problems. Investors in and lenders to such a company are stuck. In order to liquidate, they need someone to breathe life back into the entity, someone to be a driving force. As a result, with little or no funding, you can revitalize the firm while also building the right to buy out other investors when the firm is healthy. This strategy has provided many a money entrepreneur with his or her dream.

Up Front & Personal: Strategic Partners

Mike Singer is an entrepreneur who seizes opportunities when and where he finds them. While in college, he created a calendar based on Frank Zappa's classic song parody Valley Girl. Subsequent to that, he published a national collegiate newspaper. In 1989, he became sales administrator for a large apparel company, Cherokee. While traveling these many journeys, Singer discovered that there are different paths to entrepreneurship. The one that he has pursued for the past ten years stemmed from an opportunity he recognized and then executed while at Cherokee.

After about a year as sales administrator for Cherokee, Singer was given the opportunity to take over a small division for the company, making uniforms. Over the next five years, the company experienced many difficulties, including two bankruptcies. But at the same time, the uniform division that Singer had taken over grew very rapidly.

Having been in the business for six years, Singer was confident he could continue the growth of this division, without Cherokee. Thus, he decided to buy the uniform division out from under Cherokee, a process known as a leveraged buy out ("LBO"). He had built a strong management team who collectively felt as though they could successfully run the business outside of Cherokee and that their prospects for growth would be greater as an independent company.

Once the decision to buy the division was made, Singer had to walk a very careful line, as the potential for conflict of interest was vast. As he recalls, "A number of people running the division might take the tact of slowing the growth down to be able to buy it cheaper. We wanted to continue to build the company and make it a very strong company so we still had a very rapid growth right up to the purchase of the company."

Singer and the acquisition team knew the asking price, weighed the value of the assets, determined the size of the note Cherokee would accept, and calculated the equity needed from investors as well as from themselves in order to make it work.

To raise the required money, they first pooled their own resources. Singer believes very strongly that entrepreneurs must "put their money where their mouth is" and personally invest in their endeavors. As he states, "If I were going to invest in a company, I would want to make sure that the entrepreneur had a whole lot invested in that company's success on a personal level. So at the time, I put up every penny that I had, all the money I had, into the deal."

Despite the fact that they were operating in an extremely competitive market, they were confident they could succeed. It was a strategic acquisition because they knew the business, the customer, and the prospects, and were committed to the process. As a result, Strategic Partners, Inc. now operates independently and has seen phenomenal growth since the LBO.

Buying a franchise

Looking for an apportunity with structure?

Although this entry strategy could be classified under many headings, it is listed here because the journey of franchising often requires a significant amount of funding. If you are an organizational entrepreneur but haven't found the right opportunity, or if you are a sales entrepreneur but haven't found a worthy concept, franchising may be for you.

Franchise should be proven success.

A franchise is (should be) a proven process, a national identity, and a structure on which to build. It is an opportunity to be exploited by those with passion. Currently, in excess of 60% of all retail meals are purchased through franchises. The coop-erative advertising of all franchisees creates a higher success rate for start up restaurants (and most categories of new ventures) as compared to Mom and Pop restaurants.

Do you want to do it their way?

However, serious challenges exist for entrepreneurs in franchises. There are rules and processes that are dictated and demanded by franchisers. You do it one way—their way. Why? Because consistency of product and of delivery are key. If you enter one outlet of a national franchise and receive a hamburger that is larger than expected, when you go into the same franchise in another town and the hamburger is smaller, you will feel cheated. If you walk into one franchise and find a dirty restroom, you may boycott that franchise altogether even though every other location's restroom may be spotless.

Consistency means conforming to a set of standards, which can be difficult for entrepreneurs.

"Subway knows sandwiches. It knows how to bake the bread, and how to build sandwhiches the way the customers want them, but with a prescribed formula that's the same coast to coast."
-Steve Ginsberg, Owner, Subway Franchise

Up Front & Personal: Subway

Steve Ginsberg got first hand knowledge of the food industry during high school and college when he worked in a family restaurant and at a hamburger stand. When it came time to open his own business, he wanted a national identity and knew that his model business dictated that he find a business with a structure, where many decisions are made for him.

Subway, the third largest franchising organization in the country, seemed a natural fit. It tells franchisees how to bake the bread and how to build sandwiches the way customers want them. It has a prescribed formula that is the same coast to coast.

Ginsberg believes in the concept, which he feels is a necessity for success. He feels he benefits from the fact that he doesn't "have to worry about menu design, décor, advertising, and what to purchase because they do all that for you. Those headaches, those arrangements that you would normally have as an owner, you don't have to worry about."

Working as a team and following the franchiser's guidelines is part of the deal, a process with which Ginsberg is quite comfortable.

Franchising can be a costly business from the outset as many franchisers require high up-front fees and royalties. Ginsberg did his research and was attracted to Subway because he felt "it afforded the least capital to get into business. A lot of businesses require hundreds of thousands of dollars up front, but Subway didn't." He recognized that he was building a business for the future and had to calculate what he could afford in the beginning while still being able to repay loans, make money, and grow the business.

Franchising as an entry strategy fit Ginsberg's model business. Does it fit yours?

Form a spin off

Look to what companies are outsourcing for opportunities.

As the world becomes more and more virtual, many corporations are reviewing their operational techniques and are analyzing what really contributes and adds value. What doesn't fit or doesn't add value is being outsourced or divested. For example, multiple new companies emerged in the late eighties when the Southern California aerospace industry experienced a cut back in defense spending. Employees who realized that their work and therefore their livelihood was being farmed out, acted on the opportunity. They quickly realized that they were the most qualified to perform the services being outsourced and therefore many negotiated and were then hired to do the outsourced work. Essentially, they used their employer as a customer in hand and embarked on their journey.

Others who ran mail rooms and copy centers realized the inefficiencies of a large corporation and successfully negotiated to do the same services, on contract, saving the firm money and creating their own venture. An opportunity recognized, an opportunity exploited. Forming a spin off is a proven entrepreneurial entry strategy.

Final thoughts on skill sets

Are no rules in entrepreneurship.

Keep in mind that there are always exceptions and, as we know, there are no rules in entrepreneurship. The number of individual successes born from market knowledge, not sales, from a product developed (without a first customer), or brought together by an organizational entrepreneur are unlimited. There are no absolutes—no formulas. Everybody will find their way from their own starting point. What is common is the need and ability to sell yourself and to attract associates.

Start when it's right for you.

The focus of this chapter has been on both the timing of starting your venture (entrepreneurial lifecycle) and the best entry strategies for certain skill sets. In the final analysis, the best time to start a venture is when you feel it is the right time and when your research confirms it.

Common for teams to start ventures.

Additionally, it is best to embrace the notion that rarely will one person possess all of the skill sets—sales, product, and money—which is why it is so common for teams to start ventures, that is, partners with skill sets that complement each other. The adage "no one is an island" is very true for the entrepreneur.

> *"Tony possessed some skills that I did not and I possessed some skills that he did not. And one of those skills when we first met was that he wasn't one of those people who could go up in front of people and talk to them. The combination of our talents, and there are a lot of our talents that overlap, but the combination just makes us that much more potent out there."*
> -Stefan Bean, Co-Founder, Avanteer

Chapter Summary

- Knowing how entrepreneurs start firms versus how managers start projects by understanding the four stages of an entrepreneurial company.
- Myriad of variables that lead entrepreneurs to action. Asking what triggered it for everyone you see is important.
- Products, industries and companies go through predictable lifecycles much like people.
- Transition points from product to market and market to management are areas of greatest opportunity.
- Entrepreneurs can act quickly and celebrate their smallness in order to meet demands of customers.
- There are three primary foci of a business and two complementary skills sets fall under each one.
- Knowing what you are good at will help to determine the best entry strategy for you.
- Variety of entry strategies fall under each skill set.

It's now time to "get physical fast" and enter the ambiguous world of generating new ideas. Go talk to a stranger.

> *"Today's business is so complex that and changing so rapidly that it's very difficult to do it all on your own and have all the tools and expertise to do it on your own. I think you're going to see more and more of these teams of entrepreneurs or organizational entrepreneurs working together because they do need a balance of strengths to be able to execute a business plan. I think investors will want to see that as well."*
>
> -Bill Sanderson, Founder, Popcorn Palace

Chapter Four Exercises/Discussion Questions

1. What is the meaning of an industry lifecycle?
2. Where do your strengths lie? List two entry methods that might be appropriate for someone with strength in marketing.
3. What entry strategies are used by QAD, Trick R/C, and Strategic Partners? Why did these strategies work for them?
4. Think of three businesses that have been started with a customer-in-hand. Have they been successful?
5. What are your hobbies? Can you turn any of them into a business?
6. Try to think of individuals or the qualities of an individual that might make a good partner for you.

Journey Four: QAD

While Pamela Lopker may not yet be a household name, Forbes magazine has distinguished her as the "richest self-made woman on the Forbes 400." Despite being ranked among tycoons like Bill Gates and six spots above Oprah, Lopker is described by friends and associates not as a success in business, but more importantly, as a success in life. She is living proof that success is not measured solely by what you accomplish in business, but by how you manage a balanced life.

The Company

Her company, QAD (NASDAQ: QADI), is one of the 30 largest public companies to be led by a female and completed its initial public offering in August 1997 after experiencing a four year annual growth rate of 46%. Founded in 1979, QAD (which stands for Quality Added Design) adds value within the business arena by providing integrated management solutions.

As a pioneering leader of the 'total solutions approach' to management operations, Lopker has more than 19 years of experience collaborating with companies to optimize employee productivity and efficiency. QAD's mission is "to increase our customer's competitiveness by improving the speed of their organization." QAD software technology enables manufacturers to speed up order fulfillment cycle times which, in turn, minimizes inventories and maximizes operating efficiencies.

The Customer

Described by a long-term colleague as "the Mary Tyler Moore of the software industry," Lopker has built a worldwide company focusing on her customers. In designing our installations, Lopker states the objective is the same: "We look like we come from that industry." Along with her life partner and CEO of her firm, Karl Lopker, she has created a culture at QAD: "Don't talk programs, talk the customer's business."

QAD boasts a clean record and has never been sued by a customer, an unheard of feat in the world of software manufacturing. Lopker attributes this to the fact that if a customer is unhappy, she always offers to refund his or her money. She will personally call a dissatisfied customer to find out the reason and figure out how the situation can be rectified. This approach immediately puts the customer at ease and in control as opposed to feeling like a caged animal. Since the company was founded in 1979, Lopker can recall only three times in which she has actually had to refund any money and two of the customers came back to QAD within the year.

QAD's customers include AT&T, Philips, Kraft, Pepsi-Cola, Colgate Palmolive, Johnson & Johnson, Ford Motor and Rockwell, to name a few.

The Products

The flexibility of QAD's products help manufacturers adapt to business challenges, including growth, organizational change, and business process reengineering. Specially designed for deployment at the plant or division level of global manufacturers, QAD's MFG/PRO software is targeted to manufacturing environments with extensive supply chain management issues. This includes the electronics/industrial, food & beverage, consumer-packaged goods, and medical and automotive industries. MFG/PRO is truly global in scale. It supports 24 languages and multi currency formats.

Lopker's Early Years

Born a military brat in Japan, Lopker is the middle of three children. She spent her childhood moving frequently and attended eight schools in 12 years. Her father, a Navy Engineer and gifted scientist, passed his love for math and the sciences onto Lopker. Despite her many attempts to broaden her horizons with heavy doses of philosophy, psychology and sociology, her comfort level took her back to the structured world of calculus at UCSB where she finished with a double major in Economics and Math.

QAD's Early Years

QAD started by building a software product around its first customer's needs. Opportunity recognition occurred for Lopker when a friend at the time, Karl, was looking for software for his sandal manufacturing company. After examining everything that was on the market, they concluded that there was nothing available that met the needs of a multinational manufacturing company.

Because he believed in her and her expertise in this area, the owner of the sandal company talked Lopker into starting a company to provide the essential software. He provided the office space, bought the original hardware, licensed the necessary software, and they cut capital needs to the bone. As Lopker recalls, "What we really needed was capital for salaries, and so I said o.k., I don't need a salary for two years and then if I sell something, I can use that money to pay someone else's salary."

With her future husband, Karl, as her customer in hand, QAD was born. By 1983 Karl sold his interest in the sandal company and the two began to build QAD.

Growing the Company

After joining the company full-time, Karl developed an aggressive business plan to grow the company from $1 million to $3 million to $6 million and then to $12 million over a few years. He planned everything out in stages and clearly outlined what they needed to accomplish in terms of selling, distribution, recruiting, and financing.

QAD was internally financed from its inception through 1997 and operated as a traditional bootstrap company, financing operations through internally generated revenue. The com-pany's first loan was for $300,000 from Santa Barbara Bank & Trust, the only bank that would lend QAD money solely on the merits of its business plan and without requiring outside collateral. For 15 years, the company grew steadily, with growth sustained by ongoing profits.

A Balanced Life

As their company grew, Karl and Pam began to fall into their separate roles – she the vision, research and product definition, he the sales and marketing. That sharing of duties continues in their home life. He, the morning person, is in the office early; Pam does breakfast and drops the kids at school. Karl leaves early and often prepares dinner.

Pam had originally planned to have children at age 30, four years after getting married, enough time, she figured, to get her business underway. When she turned 32, she realized that there was never going to be a convenient time, but that she needed to figure out how to fit it in. "You must spend time on that," she states, "make a decision and plan how you are going to do it."

Their home life is about their family—no trophies or trappings of their business success mark the walls. They remain in the house they bought in 1984, and there is no home office. Rather, it is the place where they preserve a normal family life despite the demands placed on them by their company. Even when important clients are in town, they are never both out at the same time. One is always at home with the kids. It is also a family rule that one of them will be home for dinner every night with the children, which means that they do not travel together or at the same time.

Initial Public Offering

Most companies go public to raise capital for growth alone. But at QAD there were additional pressures from employees and customers to do so. Employees with stock options wanted to reap the rewards of liquidation. As for QAD's potential and existing customers, they were becoming reluctant to buy software because of a concern that if QAD were squeezed out of a tightening market, they would be buying software for which upgrades would not be available. "When you're buying software," says Pam, "you're not buying what the company delivers you today. You're buying what they will be able to continuously deliver you over a long period of time. So it's important to have stability."

So, in 1997, to please its customers and employees and to maintain a credible balance sheet, QAD went public. Fortunately, the company was running smoothly and could afford to hire the appropriate legal and financial experts to help in the process. The Lopkers were also able to retain a significant stake, 67%, in the company after the offering.

Lessons Learned

Lopker has learned over the years to trust her intuitiveness and anticipate what people want. She recognizes the importance of market research, but when it comes right down to it, "you have to trust those feelings and go with them. If you are right, you are right; if you are wrong, you try again."

This was driven home for her when she was sent a survey from Ford Motor Company asking about her Windstar minivan. Because Ford was a good QAD customer, Pamela decided to fill it out. One of the questions asked whether or not she would like to have a fifth door on the minivan. After thinking about it, she decided to fill in "no." However, when Chrysler came out with a minivan with a fifth door, she saw it and changed her mind. So, she called Ford to tell them about her mistake and was told that it was too late. Ford had already dropped in rank for the minivan and it would take an additional 50 weeks to come out with a new design. At times, going with intuition is better than market research studies.

Lopker has also learned that people are an important asset and it is necessary, but also challenging, to properly motivate your employees. What she and her husband have done is to create as many profit centers as possible, giving complete responsibility, within certain guidelines, to each division head. This allows for rewards based on performance. As Pamela states, "If they feel the buck stops with them and they are in control, they are going to make it happen."

When asked how it feels to be successful, Lopker always responds, "I'm not successful yet, but I am going to be soon." She feels that we are at the beginning of a major change in technology, and the Internet is the backbone of that change. The next step will be the integration of what she calls the virtual supply chain, whereby the company is integrated with its suppliers, its customers, and its customer's customers. "I believe that in five years, 50 percent of the information you use to make decisions in your company is going to come directly from your customers and suppliers." Today, it comes from within the business.

If entrepreneurship is truly a journey, then the Lopker's have proven that it can be a full and balanced journey.

"Being an entrepreneur is not necessarily about being or becoming rich. It is about doing what you want to do the way you want to do it and thinking for yourself on a continuous basis. It's about being optimistic about the future and what you can do. Entrepreneurship has everything to do with thinking how you are going to make something out of nothing—or whatever you have. It has to do with continuing to move on your business plan."
-Pamela Lopker, President and Chariman, QAD, Inc.

Journey Four Case Questions

1. How did opportunity recognition occur for Lopker?
2. What type of entrepreneur is Pam Lopker? In what area are her greatest strengths?
3. What type of entrepreneur is Karl Lopker? In what area are his greatest strengths?
4. What were some of the difficult issues that Pam has had to face in growing her company?
5. What entry strategy worked for Lopker?
6. How do the Lopkers manage to maintain balance in their lives?

Chapter Five
Getting Past the Idea

Chapter Five Major Concepts

- From idea to concept
- Vital area and niche

Journey Five: Zanart Entertainment

Up Front & Personal: Chem Trans

Up Front & Personal: A-1 Turbo Industries

From Idea to Concept – The First Discipline

Ideas begin to flow.

When ideas begin to flow, you will know your journey has begun. Committing to an industry, studying the competition, and forming an inner circle of associates to foster creativity will bring ideas because you have positioned yourself to recognize opportunity.

Popcorn heads with ideas exploding.

Additionally, "getting physical fast" will generate more ideas than you can imagine; you must be careful not to become a popcorn head. As described in Chapter Two, popcorn heads are people with so many ideas that the ideas explode in their heads one after the other. At this point, you must concern yourself with discovering the merit of your many ideas, rather than with finding ideas. Are the ideas any good? How do you determine whether or not an idea is "good"?

Define the variables.

Enter the role of a concept. An idea is a random thought; a concept is the beginning of a structure. An idea can be a statement about anything (an entry strategy, a distribution point, or an invention); a concept is a demanding, exacting statement of the key elements of a potential business. A concept is the hypothesis of your new venture and a premise for success. In essemce, a concept is a clear, concise articulation of the critical components of a potential venture that propels it beyond the loose, random, and freely structured thoughts that create ideas and opportunities.

What do the customers need?

The types of questions asked while getting physical fast form the basis for concept development. When exploring and recognizing opportunity, the first question asked should be "who is the customer?" which, in effect, introduces a structure to your search. "What do they need?" "How do I reach them?" "How do I deliver the benefits my customer wants and needs?" Answering these questions is the challenge for every new business, but, once determined, provide the necessary components of a concept.

> A concept is the clear articulation of **who** your customer is, **how** you will reach that customer, and **what** the benefit is that your customer wants. The concept takes you from a generality (idea) to a premise from which to launch your business.

Sales & Distribution Channel

Benefit

Customer

Testing the concept.

Once a concept is formulated, a logical progression of steps can be taken. Having defined the components of a concept, it is then possible to test each of those components. For example, a customer can be tested to measure interest level and even to determine the possibility of becoming a first customer thereby creating a customer in hand entry strategy. However, you can't determine interest or reach that first customer without first knowing who he or she is!

How to reach the customer?

Once a customer is defined, can you reach that customer? What marketing tactics can you employee? At what cost? Do you need a retail store? Is direct mail the appropriate sales method? Once decided, how do your sales tactics match your model business and your skill set? Finally, can you build your customer's benefit? When? At what price? With what reliability?

Three critical elements comprise the concept.

The complexities of starting your firm can be defined and executed through this single thought—the concept. Within it, the three critical elements of customer, benefit, and sales channels are brought into clarity.

Ideas need direction.

It is no longer enough to profess your interest and passion for food because that is a statement of desire, at best. Saying "I like natural foods" is more precise, but still a desire and not yet even an idea. If you take note that society's patterns of change suggest better eating habits, then you are beginning to have a direction. On the other hand, declaring that you hate fast food because it's not nutritious or tasteful is a personal observation indicating your bias; it is not clearly demonstrated in the buying habits of the general public. The lesson is that while you may choose your preference in the model business, you do not have that luxury in developing your concept. Your preference is not a business fact and cannot launch your journey.

They die without structure.

Exploring the nutritious food desire further would take dedication, talking to strangers, researching the industry, and pursuit of a defined concept. But without the structure of a concept, the idea will die. You will then be labeled a "would be, talkative" entrepreneur who is the center of attention at a cocktail party but never seems to get past the "hot" idea of the week.

Don't be fooled. It will take a great deal of discipline to reach the concept stage. You must commit to talk to strangers, structure your search, keep a record of your actions and contacts, and live by the 11th commandment: don't lie to yourself in the data gathering process. Sounds simple, but it's not.

Defining a Concept

Concept of popcorn.

Let's explore a basic business opportunity: popcorn. Assume this is your area of interest and you want to start a venture based on popcorn. How do you begin?

Secondary research.

First and foremost, you need to know everything possible about popcorn. Your search cannot be limited to secondary research, i.e., research gleaned from reference sources, such as libraries, the Internet, or trade journals (classic research). This type of research will give you important information, such as what percentage of the adult population eats popcorn, when and where they eat it, and even why they choose which popcorn to eat.

Primary research is more critical.

Primary research, on the other hand, is gathered first-hand and is therefore of greater value. It is information extracted from customers, competitors, and other relevant strangers. Further, it is knowledge gained by getting physical fast and best done by dedicated entrepreneurs.

Asking questions helps to formulate the concept.

Returning to the popcorn idea, the first question you must ask yourself is "why am I interested in popcorn?" Are you in love with the product? Are you a solution looking for a problem?

As you seek to answer those questions, are talking to strangers (including those from whom you buy popcorn—outlets in the store, at the movies), and meeting with friends and associates, you are exchanging thoughts to create new ideas and to formulate your concept.

Now it is time for concept definition. So, Mr. Popcorn King – who is your customer?

Who is your customer?

If your answer is that it's the person who eats popcorn, then you haven't been paying close enough attention. Rather, you are falling into the trap of doing it the way the large food companies would and are going to end up with a plan that requires a huge Procter & Gamble-size budget and hurdle rate just to get started. Think like an entrepreneur: who is the customer?

Customer vs. consumer.

The person who eats popcorn is the consumer, who is *possibly* your customer, but not necessarily. If your concept is to sell popcorn in movie theatres, then the movie theatre is your customer and their customer is the consumer. If you envision your popcorn being sold at retail stores in a mall, then your customer may be the individual retail storeowner or it could be a company that sells to various retail mall stores throughout the country.

Customer writes your check.

For you, the entrepreneur, the customer is the one who writes the check, the one who pays you directly. That person or company is king. Part of your learning process is to discover how your product or service travels from its original source to the end consumer and to determine at what stage within that process you fit in. To whom do you sell directly? Who will write you the check?

You must keep an open mind as you explore, recognize opportunities, create ideas, and seek to answer this first question—**who is your customer?** Structure your search in broad categories and begin by developing a list of all possible customers. Start with the end consumer and work backwards. Your list will be longer than that listed below but would include:

List your potential customers.

- general consumer
- movie consumer
- at home consumer
- mall consumer
- retail mall outlets
- movie theatres
- specialty stores
- mail order companies
- internet sites
- internet malls
- *and the list would go on*

What do the customers want?

The next question is: "what do these customers want?" General consumers would be the most varied so slide past them for the moment. What do movie consumers want? Taste? Price? More than simple popcorn? Would they pay more for premium popcorn? For flavored popcorn? Remember they are captive customers in the theatre, which is an interesting question to explore. While mall consumers have more choices, such as alternative products and alternative outlets, the movie consumer does not have a lot of options. So, will mall consumers pay for higher quality and greater variety? How will you learn the answers? Only through primary research—by asking them. Ask both the consumers and the storeowners. Build a large mosaic on what exists in the market and on what people want. Your task is to generate ideas and structure them into concepts so that you will then be able to test their feasibility.

If consumers indicate that they want better quality, more flavors, and better prices, you need to keep asking because these answers are too general, you need more focus.

Be sensitive to both customers and consumers.

Being sensitive to both your customer and the end consumer is critical. Given the limited space available at a movie theatre concession counter, will your customer, the movie theatre owner, want to carry a variety of popcorn? What is the benefit to your customer? Popcorn and sodas are bought seconds before a movie begins and theatres need to get people in and out of line as quickly as possible. Will the theater want their counter staff spending time suggesting the new "popcorn of the month" flavor? Probably not. Their focus is on a high margin, high frequency product. Most theatres today even have the melted butter on a separate side table so you spend less time in line. Other tactics the movie theatres use are to limit the candy selections so you don't take too long to decide. They have also learned from the fast food "combo" model and offer a package of soda and popcorn to get you to buy more at a faster pace. Regardless of the consumer's desire, without meeting the benefit needs of your customer, the movie theatre, you will not succeed.

Different customers have different benefit needs.

The mall retailers are the opposite. They need repeat customers who pay higher prices. They need you to supply specialty popcorn that carries higher margins and offers new varieties, i.e., reasons for their customers to return. The benefit they seek is variety, consistent service, and a margin that supports their high cost of overhead; a benefit very different from that of the movie theatre.

This is all still relating to popcorn, and if you are following this free flow you should learn two primary lessons. First, this is how ideas flow and are initiated. Second, your immediate reaction when you hear the word customer should be: why? and what's the benefit? The benefit for the movie theatre verses the mall is very different.

Self serve candy at the theatre.

One bright entrepreneur came up with a unique theatre candy service as a result of this type of free flow analysis. The concept was to provide free standing, self-serve candy kiosks that offer candy, but not behind the counter. Theatergoers with the time and desire can serve themselves and then go to the counter to pay. This method benefits both the customer and the consumer. It doesn't take away from the high volume, quick turnover at the counter thereby appealing to the customer and it enables consumers to choose the amount and type of candy they desire. This is a clear example of understanding both customers and delivering both of their benefit needs.

Alternative customers?

To continue the free flow relating to customer definition, we must consider other alternative movie theatre consumers. If popcorn and movies go together so well, why not sell to homes as in video rental and popcorn combination?

New benefits defined every step of the way.

Is popcorn sold at Blockbuster, Inc.? Some Blockbusters do sell microwave popcorn, which is another means to fulfill the benefit. Consumers want popcorn but Blockbuster doesn't have the space for popcorn machines. It does have the space for a microwave popcorn point of sale display. One successful independent video rental company competed with the big guys and did well by giving away a small, and fairly inexpensive, bag of popcorn with each movie rental. It bought both mind share and repeat consumers.

Specialty popcorn connoisseurs.

With another potential customer being the connoisseur of specialty popcorn, are you limited to selling to mall outlets that specialize in popcorn? What about other specialty stores? Will people buy popcorn in unique places? What other sales channels do you need to explore to get to this segment either directly or through a channel. There is always direct mail with catalogs that specialize in popcorn or high-end catalogs that could carry your popcorn. These represent two different customers to further explore—the catalog company and the consumer. We'll discuss that when we explore marketing tactics. What about the Internet – does popcorn flow through the world of e-commerce. Who are the customers? How do you reach them? Can you afford to reach them?

What business are you in?

If you want to reach a high-end mall consumer, you can use existing channels that sell to mall outlets. If you want to do it yourself and be a mall outlet, you are no longer in the popcorn business, you are in the retail mall business and your benefit offering will need to expand. Before entering the mall business, you need to consider the cost of entry as you explore your ideas. What does it cost to open and maintain a mall store? A lot! What does it take to sell to a mall store? Less than a lot, a lot less. What business are you in—popcorn or retail mall specialty store? To answer these questions, you must first review the model business and decide what route to take. Then, you must define your idea and passion into a concept.

Thus, a "popcorn head" with ideas popping like popcorn is great, enjoyable, and provides neat party talk. But, if you are an entrepreneur and exploring the world of popcorn, then you must seek to define a concept that can be tested. You must focus on the opportunity to start your journey.

Develop your concept.

Getting physical fast will bring industry knowledge and allow opportunities to be recognized at which point the mindset of structure, discipline, and focus must come into play. This will enable concept development, which can direct your search to your business.

Up Front & Personal: ChemTrans

Reggie Latham, a veteran executive at Bethlehem Steel's shipbuilding division, decided to go into trucking because he thought his better business skills would give him an edge in the industry. "There are no MBAs in trucking," he notes.

After buying a toxic-liquid transport company in 1987, Latham soon discovered new areas to explore and develop into businesses. When he bought ChemTrans, Latham did not own any land nor did he own the washing facility needed to clean his chemical tank trucks after use. Rather than pay others to clean his trucks and in order to control costs associated with the cleaning, Latham decided to build his own washing facilities.

He estimated that they'd be doing about 10,000 washes a day, which did not happen. The tank was only at 30% capacity. Latham's wheels started turning and he came up with new concepts to test. With 70% idle time in his tanks, Latham went to the government and asked if he could treat other people's non-hazardous wastewater. He got permission to do so.

This led to the formation of three new businesses. His spin off companies include Avalon Premium Tank Cleaning, Avalon Environmental, which treats commercial and industrial waste water, and Avalon Intermodal, a depot for larger shipping containers.

As Latham now states, "The companies, I'm embarrassed to say, have dramatically exceeded our expectations. The environmental company is a good business, the container, intermodal service has grown nicely for us and it is also a business that feeds the truck company and feeds the wash rack. The tank cleaning we have found to be a good margin business. They are all doing well independently."

"If you have a dream, dream it. Believe in it and go do it, and don't let anyone tell you no. I had so many people tell me I couldn't do what I've done, so many people not return my phone calls. I used to have a ratio that if I got one phone call back for every ten calls I made, I was doing well."
-Sky Dayton, Founder, EarthLink Network

Entrepreneurial Exercise

For this exercise, you will need to choose a business that you feel is successful and then answer the following questions about that business. Discuss your findings with others.

Can you identify what the original business idea was?

_____

List possible customers for the business? What do you think was the process of elimination for this company in determining which customer(s) to go after?

_____

_____

_____

What is the business' concept?

_____

_____

_____

What customers does the business focus on? What distribution channels does it use?

_____

_____

_____

Has the business' concept changed from what it was originally? If so, what is that change? How has it redefined its concept?

_____

_____

_____

⇒   **Tear out and move to your entrepreneurial road map binder.**

Beyond the Concept – Vital Area

Entrepreneurs seek to identify two critical elements of their business: the vital area and the niche.

Success for one and failure for another. Why?

When examining and testing ideas to turn them into concepts, you will see many successes and learn of many failures. It's true of every business. How often have you driven a major thoroughfare and seen vacant restaurants with a For Lease sign? Frequently there will be three or four within a mile. You will then see one restaurant with a line of customers stretching out the door and people pushing to enter. Why? What does that one restaurant do that the others couldn't or didn't? What led to their success? Luck? Chance? No.

Could be any number of reasons.

Typically, luck and chance have little to do with success, except in the lottery. In fact, that restaurant did many things right and so did its competitors. But, that particular spot won for a reason. Somehow, they created a value that brought customers time and again. They did something that separated them from the rest; most likely it was an intangible. It could be the way they met their customers, their service, or the cleanliness of their facility. It could be high quality at sensible prices. We don't know. What we do know is that it was something or a combination of things. Perhaps it was location, environment, or motif?

Vital area.

In seeking opportunities, try to identify why the store you are in or the web page you are surfing has won. Ask owners, competitors, and customers why that business is successful. The answer is what entrepreneurs call the vital area.

> **Vital Area**—the critical component of a venture that is the underlying cause of success.

The vital area is how entrepreneurs create value. It is the essence of the business. It is the differentiating point that counts.

What is McDonald's vital area?

Let's return to the McDonald's example. What is its vital area? Some declare that it is critical mass, consistent product, or mass advertising. Certainly all are true, but a recent survey of McDonald's consumers revealed that clean rest-rooms and a safe environment is what brings them back to McDonalds instead of going to the competition. What do you think? Why do you choose one over another? Are you getting sensitive to your potential customer?

Niche

Segment of market in which you want to compete.

In turning ideas into concepts, the final area entrepreneurs seek to identify is a niche. In the most exacting definition, a niche is that portion of a larger market you wish to explore. It is the battleground on which you choose to fight for market share for your company. Certainly this is an acceptable definition.

To others a niche answers the question: "what business are you in?" This describes what you do and where you do it, i.e., your arena.

How do you add value?

For many entrepreneurs a niche has an additional connotation, which includes <u>why</u> you are able to compete in this area. In other words, the definition of a niche should also describe what you bring—what is the value or proprietary position that will enable you to effectively compete in this arena.

> **Niche** – that portion of a market in which you wish to compete because you bring value and/or a proprietary position, which you believe, will lead to your success.

What's your proprietary position?

A proprietary position is not to be confused with protection and is not limited to legal protection, such as a patent. The proprietary position you have may be industry or customer knowledge. It may be location. It may simply be you and your passion.

Up Front & Personal: A-1 Turbo Industries

Carving out a niche in a vital area is exactly what Tony Haywood did when he combined his teenage passion for turbo racing with his training as a bus mechanic. The county agency for whom Tony worked decided to outsource its bus maintenance, Haywood's livelihood. When the contractors came in, "it was more work and half the pay," Tony recalls.

He decided it was time to take the skills he had gained throughout his career and life and put them to work—for himself. He "figured it was now or never." But with a million repair shops in the market, Tony wanted to establish himself in a niche where the customers would have to come to him. He wanted to do something that most mechanics avoided and felt that the complexities of turbochargers provided the ideal market. While they have been around a long time, turbochargers are not a well-understood product.

Haywood was able to refine his expertise in this arena by "experimenting on my own, learning the dos and don'ts" and then he was able to "master the technique for my own self, and start a business." The result is A-1 Turbo Industries, an automotive repair business specializing in rebuilding turbo chargers. He further delved into this niche by discovering a widespread design defect in turbochargers and became known for his expertise in correcting it.

In the nine years since Tony started the company, sales have skyrocketed from $900 to more than $600,000 a year and he gets customers from all over the world. "I have customers in countries that I can't even pronounce, they call me on the phone, or they email me on the Internet or they mail me letters," he says.

Chapter Summary

- If you get physical fast, if you are constantly seeking to recognize opportunity, then ideas will come; slow at first and then with greater speed.
- As ideas flow you will need a structure to articulate them in a meaningful way.
- The articulation of customer, benefit, and sales and distribution channels is your concept.
- In defining your concept, you need to seek and answer why you will succeed—your vital area and the way that you will add value.
- Finally you need a place in the market to compete—a niche—but you need to know how you will build a proprietary position to fend off competition.

> *Our niche is probably the fact that we deal with the minority population more. That's what I choose to do, hispanic, black, african american, I choose to do that. Our nurses will go into areas that other nurses will not. They are familiar with the areas and I want to do that. That's our niche. In terms of another niche though, we also do pediatrics. And we take care of developmentally disabled children a lot."*
> -Carolyn Colby, Founder, Colby Home Health

Chapter Five Exercises/Discussion Questions

1. Articulate the A-1 Turbo concept. How did Haywood test his concept? Can you articulate your business idea into a concept? How will you test that concept?
2. Find a potential customer within the sphere of your model business and pick his or her brain for customer needs.
3. Identify ways that you can test your business idea.
4. Discuss the evolution of Reggie Latham's business concept. At what stage in the entrepreneurial lifecycle is ChemTrans?
5. What is A-1's niche? It's vital area? How did Haywood translate his idea into a concept?

Journey Five: Zanart Entertainment*

A cartoon revolution is about to happen. Bob and I expect a major change—from a market with no merchandise being available to Baby Boomers who want to buy something from their time period—to a market waiting for this demand to be filled. This expected phenomenon created a constant urgency and self-imposed pressure for us to drive this potential market. I know we are on the right track. But I have no control over the company I work for.

Copyright © 1981 Alan Aldridge

Tom Zotos summarized the conversation with Bob Stein in the deli that summer morning. Tom felt a great deal of pressure on himself at OSP over the Walt/Mickey proposal. Without the Disney deal, OSP would be hurting for sales volume; but even with this deal, his position was not secure and there was no upside for him.

Tom needed time to reflect. He went home to Massachusetts for a week and talked with his Father. The two philosophized, the senior Zotos advised his son. Dad shared that he might not have made the right moves in his life because of personal and family security reasons. Costa at age 80, was reflecting on his own earlier indecision and suggested that Tom go for it; because Tom had a clear vision on how to go forward.

Tom had the $20,000 saved for his daughter's college fund which he did not want to touch. He knew he could fall back on his credit cards. He avoided sharing the impending storm at OSP with his wife. He had to isolate her from stress as she was expecting their second child and was also ill at the time. It became a silent time. Tom knew that if he started a new company, and it failed, he would be buried financially, but he only focused on success. He felt the weight on his shoulders.

Bob was single; his pressure was not similar to Tom's. He would gladly give up his legal position. His Dad agreed to make a loan of $15,000 to help his son over the same time period. Bob never had any self-doubts.

Zany Art Was Born

So Zanart Entertainment (ZE) was launched. Tom Zotos and Bob Stein decided that they should pursue their common dreams together—publishing zany art. Why is the word "entertainment" in their name? It indicates what the two felt they were always involved in. ZE believes it produced entertainment that you hang on a wall: visual entertainment.

Bob had worked on "blind pools" that had been raising money with an eye toward investing in various companies. The pool was called Xuma and controlled about $50,000. Zanart ultimately merged with this pool and now had access to limited funds.

A friend of Bob's, Steven B. Adelman, the son of a Polish emigrant father, became the third original shareholder. His investment in ZE was to do legal work and share, for two and one-half years, his penthouse offices and office equipment in the Unisys building in Westwood Village.

The company initially consisted of four equal owners: the shell provided $50,000 in cash for 25%; Adelman got 25% for providing free rent, advice, and the use of equipment; and Zotos and Stein would get 25% each for the sweat equity to come.

Even though the offices made them look good, the active partners were so cash poor they had to park on residential streets in Westwood to avoid building parking fees. When and if any money came into the company—there was not a lot of it at the beginning—Bob felt he had a moral obligation that the majority of money would go to Tom. Bob knew that for ZE's survival, the first funds had to go to Tom to support his family. But Tom took no funds and lived on his credit cards.

The first effort the fledgling company undertook would take all of their available cash. They wanted to but the Looney Toons® and Batman® licenses from Warner Brothers for wall decoration art. Tom felt that Warner Brothers characters had not been exploited to the extent that the Disney characters had been, and thus was an opportunity for Zanart.

> Does anybody remember Mickey Mouse cartoons? No, except for ten seconds of the historical 'Steamboat Willie.' But people certainly remember almost every chase scene of Bugs, Elmer Fudd, and Roadrunner.

There was no marketing research. All of the players just "felt" that spending all of the company's money on the two licenses was right. They were trying something new. Older people feel adult art—cartoons on a wall—is a waste of money. Baby Boomers yearned for nostalgia.

> We felt like the one Warner brother who held out for sound added to movies. We felt like the people who introduced the paper towel: everybody used rags for chores, but Scott Paper pushed disposable towels on rolls. We felt like Las Vegas and the Nevada desert: "you're going to gamble where?" We were pioneers!

The two principals sat on their rent-free chairs at their rent-free desks in their rent-free office and contemplated how quickly they had changed their entire lives while waiting for the rent-free fax machine to run. The calendar read February 1990.

Reality

ZE had spent the majority of its initial funds for the two licenses. The owners had not yet agreed on where or how to sell the products. The license was for high-end art and artistic print derivatives of that art. The license covered one industry category: "wall decoration." Tom and Bob asked themselves, now that we have the two licenses, where can we sell our product—Warner Brothers characters—as wall decoration?

The sales plan was that the balance of the funds would be spent on two trade shows, the first, Art Expo in LA and the second, a major show in New York. An elaborate last minute, "smoke and mirror" booth was constructed. In addition to their Looney Tunes® and Batman® art, they negotiated a consignment license arrangement. This deal provided no up front payment, but paid a higher percentage for products sold from a portfolio of Marilyn Monroe photographs and the work of a little-known art deco artist, Tamara DeLempicka. With these two additions, ZE's product retail price line at the show would range from under ten to over a thousand dollars.

Interest and sales at both shows did not materialize. The gallery buyers would look at Marilyn and Bugs prints placed next to each other in the booth and come away quite confused. The pricing and positioning left some buyers puzzled. The costs of the shows were not even covered by their few sales. Everything was wrong. The good news was the Batman creator came by the booth and remarked at how fine the art was. Tom was devastated! Bob was more philosophical:

> I'm in tune with rejection from my music experience, being turned down wasn't really new to me. What would keep us going was basically a lot of things: owning popular art was a smart thing, but there was not yet a natural sales channel, for enough sales to sustain our business.

ZE explored other distribution channels. It thought that its line might be a new visionary product, an "executive gift." Would sales go through Sharper Image, Hammacher Schlemmer or American Express?

ZE felt it could do better than Scoreboard. It was producing a high quality collectible that was different from the products people already had seen. It was not like a thousand baseballs stamped with a signature. The issue became, can ZE go out and sell a higher-end collectible?

This experience really tested Tom and Bob. Bob trusted Tom's instincts. Tom instinctively knew that the market for popular art was coming. The two returned to LA with no cash, but with more determination. The calendar read April 1990.

Credibility

The first "significant" order came across the rent-free fax machine when an art print company distributor bought six $12.00 prints. "What is it? It's a PO!" They didn't know what to do with it but it sure felt good. During the next several months, more and more small orders dribbled in from the shows. The two spent all their time in sales. Bob was on the phone with every show attendee and a long list of art distributors. Tom spent his time constantly visiting the studios. Anything was important as long as it rang the cash register.

> We can't refuse any business. Even if it's only ten percent over our cost, we have to take the order. We need to build credibility. We need to let buyers know we are out there and can do a great job.

Tom received a call from the Spielberg organization. A major party was to be held the following weekend to introduce Tiny Toons, a new generation of baby Looney Tunes® characters. Spielberg wanted to give each guest a memento about the film. ZE was contacted about making 2,000 souvenir art prints. Tom quickly designed them and called back with a price of $10 each. "Too high," said the buyer and Tom went back to the drawing board. He came up with a new printing technique, which allowed an inexpensive print to be done on glossy stock. It took on the look of an expensive cel. "Pseudo-Cel" was the newly-coined product name and this new concept would later provide the major breakthrough for Zanart. ZE got the order and the bragging rights that came from making an innovative product for Spielberg's company. Tom used the proceeds to buy the license rights to classic movies such as Casablanca. These new products showed the world that the young company might have a good idea. Tom summarized their thinking:

We were skirting around limited editfon art, just to show the world something. We looked like an art company and we looked like a merchandise company. We were trying every avenue until we could find a breakthrough. I knew three propertfes were enough. Bob and Steve felt limited. We looked better than we were, top quality on all. Bob thinks we have changed the company. I think that the credo was the same.

The Warner Brothers Era

Zanart's positive reputation traveled around and opened doors in this select industry. Tom and Bob received a call from an account executive at Warner Brothers. WB had recently decided to begin to market their library of characters in direct competition with Disney and others. Prior contacts, mutual friends, and knowledge of the industry created a type of situation where the account executive at WB was supportive and wanted to work with ZE. WB wanted to use ZE because they were capable of delivering. There were no surprises; WB liked the products that Tom had done for Disney in the past. The real value recognized by WB was the creativity seen in Tom's Disney experience and the fine art work they published with Tamara DeLempicka.

It was a combination of all the things that gave us credibility. They knew we were in a penthouse, though they never visited us there. WB had seen the 70 color piece we had done with Tamara and they loved our creativity in the Disney and Lennon posters. They wanted to do business with Zanart Entertainment!

Bob and Tom knew the WB people needed help in finding a direction for its lines. They worked long hours at no charge—free consulting. The first Warner Brothers offering would be a catalog of its line. Steve Adelman had a contact at the new division and opened the door wider. The question was what pieces would be included? Certainly the existing licensed products. But WB wanted something special. So did ZE!

When Mel Blanc passed away in 1989, Variety ran a commemorative tribute page that showed a spotlight on a lone microphone with the WB cartoon characters standing silently by with their heads bowed down. Tom wanted to work with this piece and make it ZE's flagship. He experimented at length with the printing process he used on the Tiny Toons® Pseudo-Cel. Trying different combinations of glossy papers, filtered inks and application techniques, he created a product that was even richer and still could be produced at affordable costs. It looked like a real cel even though it was much larger. When matted and framed, the image jumped off the wall. It was the right look and gave the impression of being a one-of-a-kind- custom work-of-art—truly a collector's item.

"Speechless" was the first item produced by ZE for the WB catalog. It carried a $150 retail price. It was new and daring. Most of the catalog items were lower priced. Items in the catalog began to sell. "Speechless" began to sell. ZE felt it had turned the corner.

WB and ZE debated about "Speechless" as a retail item. WB felt that it would be construed as an old product. Bob sang "Unforgettable" to the retail group of WB executives to demonstrate that "Speechless" would not go away in a few months. It was a standard—timeless. The "Speechless" original was scheduled to be a limited edition but ZE persisted and WB made it an open edition. It would have been limited to 1000 pieces; but has sold many, many more. ZE knew that the piece had a great deal of emotional grabbing power. WB & ZE had synchronicity about this Mel Blanc concept. But ZE was still just a vendor—each day it had to prove itself all over again.

Bob and Tom were willing to put in the time and be persistent enough to wait and earn the right to meet very busy people. ZE provided value-added by providing an idea source. This was key to getting into WB, the biggest entertainment company in the world.

> We knew that getting further involved with Warner Brothers was very important. We had no idea what would keep selling our products. We knew what was right but we didn't know how big. This was a point where we began to generate money. The niceness of "Speechless" impressed other buyers and what we could do for them. It was an exciting time!

The first Warner Brothers Studio Store was close to opening. Warner Brothers wanted to make a big splash. Casablanca was a Warner Brothers film and Tom knew the Hollywood Wax Museum manager. He was able to "borrow" the Bogart wax figure for the store opening. Warner people thought the ZE people were real team players. They did more than just favors; they made the buyers look good!

Outside retailers saw the success of ZE at WB. The WB store carried litho prints and lobby card portfolios made by ZE. Suncoast/Musicland saw these and contracted ZE to make similar items for their stores. Sales materialized and ZE used the funds and added more licenses.

> We were like Cannon Films who would sign hot stars to their studio without money, but gave the talent a bigger piece of the deal. We may not have been that smart to think of this so we copied their idea and began to give higher royalty percentages than what others would offer for licenses, but we paid less up front.

In the early years of movies, 11x14-inch promotional placards were displayed in theatre lobbies. This was the only way movies were promoted from the early 1900's through the 1960's. The placards became a new collectible. "Do you have a program?" buyers would ask (which meant a line of products). "We don't sell programs, we sell lobby cards." Bob thought the buyer meant the type of program ushers handed out in theatres.

As ZE continued to get closer to WB, it began to get better market feedback and the learning curve got shorter. The "sell through" issue is very important to retail, especially with impulse items. ZE got close enough to WB stores that it tracked what shipped last Friday through when it went on the shelves giving them quick measurement of sales—or not. This channel flow of products was in real time so ZE and WB could react quickly; they could add more similar products if they moved, or change lines if they did not.

When did Tom and Bob think "it" would really happen? Tom remembered exactly, it was September 4, 1991, a Saturday afternoon at the Beverly Center when 5000 people were fighting to get into WB store. Tom sat and watched from the floor above the Warner store:

All my life I had waited for this moment. This was the fulfillment of my vision. The revolution was happening and I was not only watching—I was a part of it.

Bob reflected:

We got a first down and stayed in the game. We went into this black tunnel, an unknown area, without any money flowing through. We were taking out small draws now. We tried to start repaying my Dad, but he kept sending the checks back to us. Unless you have a backer (or are independently wealthy) you will have to use the money from your family and friends in order to take it to the next level. And you do not have to be ashamed of this.

An Investor

ZE had grown to the point where it had employed a part time accountant to do its books. The management realized the company needed financing to grow. Growth could not be financed in a trickle down manner any more. There was a payroll to be met! Bob's family was aware of a gentleman who had just successfully sold a large company and who liked to do private investments. A meeting was arranged with the investor who was the chairman and majority shareholder of a major public corporation. Previously, he had successfully built another company and sold it for stock.

I recall going down there with a copy of every art piece we had ever done and laying them out in the conference room. We wanted to dazzle him. It was an impressive array of products.

The investor enjoyed the principals of Zanart and the chemistry was good. He was more impressed with the perseverance and conviction of Tom and Bob than he was with the product. He was amazed that they had gone almost two years without a salary and that every dollar had gone back into buying more licenses. Tom was certain that something would come of the meeting, and when the investor asked why they didn't put characters on other products, like paper plates, the duo explained the intricacies of the licensing business and the capital required to expand to other product categories.

The investor was so taken by the focus, conviction, and the strong reaction of the team that he agreed to make a $500,000 bridge loan on the spot. He concluded:

If you two guys could do this much without any money, imagine what you could do with money.

With funds now in place, the tempo of the game increased. Bob and Tom were able to enjoy their first real payday. Additional personnel were hired and additional licenses purchased. During this time, Zanart hosted a University of Southern California Management Internship Program project. Based on the MBA's recommendations, prices were raised, with a positive result and very little impact on customers. Dr. Ben Enis of the Marketing Department was the professor. Both Zanart principals felt that the experience was very enjoyable and profitable.

With time, money, and people now working for them, ZE made plans for the next stage of growth. They produced a catalog of their new offerings, organized their sales efforts, and built a distribution system. The two and one-half years of free rent was coming to an end and new offices were needed. But the most important thing that the bridge funding did was to give Tom and Bob the time to build their company.

The next 18 months saw growth in revenues with sales in the $2 million range. The com-pany's reputation and product line grew. Companies now came to ZE looking for it to do things for them. As Tom's efforts moved more into product development and sales, Bob took on the additional challenge of exploring the feasibility of taking the company public.

When asked when he first thought about going public, Bob replied without hesitation:

> Day One. We knew we were not property capitalized. We never questioned that we couldn't go public. But we knew we needed enough substance to get there. We had to!

Using his legal contacts, Bob quickly found the difference between someone saying they were interested and someone actually willing to seriously take on the challenge of taking a marginally profitable company, with untested management, public. He felt the challenges would never end. A new challenge seemed to arrive just as the last one was answered.

*This case was researched and written by Professors William H. Crookston and Thomas J. O'Malia. This case is intended to be an ontroduction to the Enterprise Formation process. Some details have been changed to protect the confidence of actual individuals and companies involved. Copyright © 1995.

Journey Five Case Questions

1. What is your analysis of Zotos and Stein and their concept/company development?
2. What are the chances of continued success? What are the limiting factors?
3. Will they be able to raise significant public funding?
4. What are the next steps for the company? How should the principals spend their time? What would you do if it were your company?

Chapter Six
Feasibility - Part One

Chapter Six Major Concepts

- Feasibility funnel
- Industry knowledge
- Concept filter
- Market risk filter
- Sales/Distribution filter
- Benefit filter

Journey Six: Vessel Assist Association

Up Front & Personal: Autopsy/Post Services

Feasibility - Part One

Has your attitude changed?

In the early stages of our journey we have focused heavily on you, the traveler. How do you think—inside or outside the box? If it is still inside the box, what are you doing to change your attitude? We have looked at many entrepreneurial characteristics including passion, integrity, and perseverance. We have also examined the many myths associated with entrepreneurs, such as risk takers vs. risk managers and born vs. made. Entrepreneurship is first about *who you are* and if you have not yet made that determination, it is time for you to do so.

Journey recap.

Much of our initial journey has also been focused on opportunity recognition. How do you position yourself such that opportunities present themselves? What role does creativity play in discovering new ideas? Concluding the first leg of our journey was spent not just on seeing new ideas but also on structuring them. We learned of concepts, vital areas, and niches.

Who is your mentor?

We have also changed our approach to life by getting physical fast. Meeting strangers, going to trade shows, talking to industry leaders, and interviewing entrepreneurs should now all be part of your daily routine. Hopefully, you've even started a mentor relationship with one or more of the entrepreneurs you've met. If you have broadened your horizons, moved beyond your normal comfort area, and gotten physical fast, then you are well on your way and have taken responsibility for your actions. Congratulations.

Tool sets.

It's now time to learn *how* entrepreneurs become successful. We need to learn more than just *who* they are. We need to study their actions and explore their tool sets to become successful.

As we learned in Chapter Five, entrepreneurship is not about ideas or perfect new products, it's about turning ideas into concepts and testing ideas to determine their viability. Entrepreneurship is about the mindset that asks not whether an idea/concept is good or bad—a personal judgement—but asks whether the *customer* considers it good or bad.

Feasibility is essence of entrepreneurship.

Entrepreneurs test their ideas through a series of tasks known as Feasibility, which is the essence of entrepreneurship. It is how entrepreneurs think and a process whereby entrepreneurs filter information and tweak concepts based on feedback from strangers, experts, potential customers, and competitors whom they meet and converse with. It is how entrepreneurs test the ideas and concepts that have been boomeranging around in their heads. Feasibility is the point at which entrepreneurs decide whether their concept is a "go" or "no go." Feasibility answers the critical question: under what conditions are you willing to go forward?

Ask critical questions.

To answer these questions, entrepreneurs must look to the outside. The comments and suggestions collected from getting physical fast now need to become more focused and be taken more seriously. As you begin to understand feasibility, you must clearly define the answers you seek. Ask the critical questions of successful entrepreneurs: where did you find your opportunity? What were you doing at the time? How did you test your concept to know that you could go forward as a risk manager? Learning from those who have traveled the journey before you is the key to your success.

The Feasibility Funnel

Feasibility helps to funnel out the good and bad.

Feasibility is best viewed as a filter in the form of a funnel. The top of the funnel is where ideas enter and where thoughts abound. The end of the funnel is where your journey will begin as is demonstrated below.

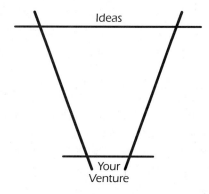

Funnel begins with ideas and ends with starting.

Series of tasks on your concept.

Which ideas will become new ventures? The filters in the funnel help make that determination. You will perform a series of tasks on your concept at each filtering point thereby testing the feasibility at that filter stage. Those concepts that pass the tests move through the filter and continue down the funnel; those that don't are eliminated.

> *It's a little bit scary when you actually take something to market, whether or not it's going to work. So that's a trial right there. When it does work, when you take something to market, you find that out from the acceptance of the customer. If the customer calls and says, yea, this is a great idea, it creates a great feeling in here. And, that's what happened to me."*
> -David LaMontagne, Founder, Vessel Assist Association

Industry Knowledge Filter

Industry knowledge is critical for success.

Industry knowledge is a critical component of starting your venture. As we have learned, a very high percentage of successful entrepreneurs, some estimate as high as 89%, experienced opportunity recognition in an industry that they already knew. They didn't jump into a strange, foreign environment and start a business. Rather, working in an industry, becoming intimately familiar with its processes, and learning its ins and outs created opportunities, which generated ideas and concepts that could then be tested.

Look beyond the obvious.

For this reason, the first filter in the feasibility funnel is to determine how an idea fits into a particular industry as is demonstrated in the diagram on the next page. In so doing, it is very possible for you to learn that your idea is more appropriate for an entirely different industry, and you must be open to that shift.

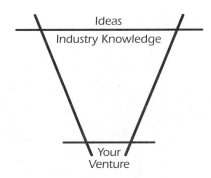

Industry knowledge is first filter your concept must pass.

What is your approach for gathering information?

How do you learn about your industry? Three primary activities should be undertaken—interviewing, doing secondary research to learn industry status, and recognizing patterns of change. You can develop an elaborate, formal approach or a simpler, more casual effort. Each entrepreneur has a different tact for soliciting information. But solicit you must because industry knowledge can only be gained if you are meeting the leaders and learning of successes in your sector, i.e., if you are getting physical fast.

Interviews

Interviewing should be your most common and most enjoyable task. At this point, it should be clear that asking a lot of people what is new, what they see coming in the near future, and what they would pursue if they were starting a new business today provides the backdrop for your journey.

At a bare minimum, you must talk to your potential customers and the ultimate consumers of your product or service. However, suppliers can also be an informative source as they are extremely knowledgeable about the inner workings and patterns of change in an industry. Furthermore, suppliers are always listening to their customers and constantly learning of changing needs and desires.

Talk to everybody you can.

Essentially, you should be interviewing anybody who knows anything about your industry to effectively increase your knowledge base. Complete and facilitate your interviews by attending trade shows and reading trade journals.

Industry Status

Secondary research is also necessary.

Interviews will give you a good understanding of your industry, but the basic statistics must also be learned. This includes knowing the size of your total industry, the size of your specific niche, and everything possible about those who are already in your niche—your competitors. Be sensitive to why certain firms succeed as you gather this information. What is their vital area?

> *"We went to the libraries, we went to search engines and looked up plus sized, full-figured. We found information that would be good for the business plan. Then we went out and developed a questionnaire that only had about 5-6 questions and we asked women of all ages, where do you want to shop, where do you shop. We got the same answers over and over again. They weren't truly satisfied with their options. So, everything kind of validated what we were finding in our primary and secondary research."*
> -Kim Camarella, Founder, Kiyonna Klothing

Patterns of change

What's happening in your industry?

Learn to recognize patterns of changes in your industry. What was your industry like 10 years ago? How and why has it changed? What will it look like in another 10 years?

There were 22,000 travel agents in the United States in 1980. Today there are less than 8,000. If your interest is in travel, you need to know why. What does this tell you about the future for travel agents? Will they come back? Will they disappear completely? Why?

Can you spot developing trends?

You'll realize that you are starting to understand your niche as you see trends developing. Being able to recognize changes before they occur will enable you to properly prepare and position yourself to capitalize on those trends when they do take place.

> *"I read through the Surgeon General's report and found that public understanding of the importance of exercise is on the rise. People know that exercise is important and now they are demanding it. So, the business traveler is expecting his hotel to have a gym. Corporate fitness also. There's evidence now that employees are more productive if they exercise."*
> -Michael Garvey, Owner, The Dumbell Man

What type of changes do you see?

Some patterns of change are global and some are location specific. You'll need to know and learn to judge both. For example, a well-known nationwide pattern of change is that baby boomers are aging, which has created and will continue to create tremendous demand for new services as this large sector of our population becomes more needy. As a result, the number of assisted living complexes has been on the rise in the recent past as has been a focus on alternative medicine to guard against aging. Can you think of any other businesses that could develop from this trend?

What does the pattern suggest?

We have also seen a dramatic increase in the number of single parents and dual income families in which both parents work. This pattern of change requires the creation of more services for children, such as day care, nursery care, and transportation assistance. What happens when both working parents need to be out of town at the same time? Is there a business there?

Who is affected?

Patterns recognized give a strong indication of where opportunities lie. More importantly, they provide foresight into whether your ideas and observations are flowing with the tide or going against the grain. In the 1950's families ate all but two meals a week at home. Today they eat an average of two meals a day away from home. What's the opportunity?

Global Patterns of Change

Global patterns of change can and do affect everyone and every business. While these patterns do not dictate a business structure, they are indicative of the world in which your business will operate. Thus, you need to be aware of these global changes and mindful of how they will effect your business venture.

The distribution channel is shrinking

Historically rigid distribution channels have existed with as many as five steps in the chain. For example, toys went from manufacturers to wholesalers to dealers/distributors to retail stores to consumers. Each step creates a value and adds a cost. With the advent of large national chains, such as Toys R US, the need, value, and cost of certain steps came into question. Was a wholesaler or distributor really needed or did the large retailers handle that function best? Today, buying direct from the manufacturer cuts the chain to two steps—manufacturers to consumers. Will toy companies sell directly to you in the future? That is the promise of ecommerce and the Internet. What will your future distribution look like?

The virtual corporation and the virtual employee are a reality

The world is no longer real in the sense of formal organizations or companies. Instead, there are loose confederations among different, often smaller companies that perform services for one another. Together, they combine to provide all the components of a classic company without ever truly being a real company.

This change diminishes the need for "in-house" full time employees. Instead of incurring a life long commitment to pay and care for employees, companies now contract with third parties for the services previously done by employees. A reliance on temp agencies or contract employees as opposed to a permanent labor force is more prevalent. Using "temps" during busy periods does not leave the company with idle capacity at slower times.

The same is true of the distribution channels. Historically all goods were purchased from physical locations—retail stores. We now buy from catalogs, which are essentially virtual stores. Increasingly, we are also taking advantage of electronic catalogs—the Internet. We shop in virtual stores.

Virtual employees and virtual distribution represent the pattern for the future. Will you have employees and buildings, or will you be virtual? Will your entry strategy include supplying products and services through virtual distribution channels?

Depersonalization of services

As distribution channels shorten and the world becomes more virtual, we have begun to rely on new forms of communication, which has led to less human contact. We now communicate by voice mail, e-mail, and the Web. We have also learned to deal with machines and buy airline and lottery tickets from them. How often do you enter a bank and actually speak with a teller? Depositing and withdrawing money through a machine is now the norm.

In some cases this depersonalization has improved service. Certainly an ATM is a vast improvement over standing in line at a bank to cash a check (especially when they have the bulletproof glass and we don't). An added convenience is banking on the Web, a service that most of us didn't enjoy in the days of face to face contact. Ordering airline tickets, or at least obtaining flight information, on the Internet is certainly much better than calling multiple airlines and listening to music while on hold. Some airlines even offer low cost and/or bonus miles for dealing directly with their computer instead of one of their agents.

On the flip side, some depersonalization has not improved service. For example, the random assignment of doctors and the question of quality services at Health Maintenance Organizations have received much press and even more complaints. However, these trends will continue. How will you make and keep contact with your customers? How will you automate your services to enhance the customer experience?

Customers are relational

Forming a bond with your customer is critical in today's world. The time and cost of obtaining a new customer can only be justified by keeping that customer for an extended period. Repeat customers are essential; you need to keep their business, keep them coming back.

In order to effectively do this, you must create a value that they want. Even through shortened distribution channels and virtual networks, you must provide a service that will bind your customers to you. Develop systems that can learn, track, and adjust to their changing needs. You must continually anticipate and exceed customers' expectations for new and different products and benefits. Dealing with customers is not done at an arm's length, it is done on the basis of an alliance that needs to be maintained and nurtured.

Ecommerce is a reality

Many continue to believe that brick and mortar will win out over the digital world. How one can feel this way is surprising. Just ten years ago, larger banking organizations with their hundreds of retail offices seemed secure. Today those offices are considered liabilities and consolidation of the giants has been forced.

But this is only the first step of the ecommerce revolution. Digitizing what exists in reality is the low hanging fruit, it is the first to be picked and harvested. The change in sales methodology from a posted retail price to an auction environment is also just a moderate change.

Big changes are those that create completely new ways of doing business. For example, one clothing manufacturer was about to shut down his organization because he could no longer compete with off shore manufacturing prices. In the past five years, he examined the problem and turned it to his advantage. His corporate headquarters is no longer a manufacturing center, it is a computer based communications center. As orders are received, they are consolidated and sent out to multiple suppliers around the world for bids on supplying the material. The most successful bidders are coming from Indo China. The cloth producer is instructed to ship materials to the successful bidder—often in India—for dying the fabric. The dyed goods are then shipped to the best bidder for contract sewing—in Mexico—who forwards finished products directly to the end customers in the lots prescribed.

Shortened distribution in a virtual environment with many depersonalized services and between multiple customer supplier relationships has emerged and will continue to exist. Such models may even take over; they are all facilitated by and transacted on the Internet.

Summary

Change is the only constant in our future, which is great for entrepreneurs because it creates opportunities. With their nimble and flexible organizations, entrepreneurs can react instantly and satisfy customers at all levels.

Concept Filter

Define your concept.

As ideas filter through industry knowledge, we begin to articulate our thoughts in the form of a concept. We can now define our customer, the means of reaching that customer and the benefit to be delivered. As we already learned, without this structure we are simply popcorn heads with an unending number of new ideas, and no follow through.

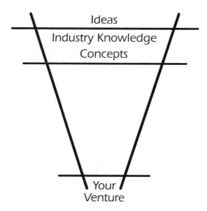

Ideas
Industry Knowledge
Concepts

The concept filter.

Your
Venture

To assist with the development of a concept, entrepreneurs use a tool known as a concept grid, an organizing structure that enables a concept to expand in a meaningful and controlled way. Below is the beginning of such a grid.

Begin to formulate a concept grid.

Customer	Sales/Distribution Channel	Benefit

A general statement of business interest forms the basis of your concept grid. Initially, it is very broad and expansive and is then refined into specifics when further developed. Let's return to popcorn. Your statement of interest could be as simple as *"I want a business that involves my passion for popcorn."*

Chapter Five explored concept definition and challenged you to focus your general interest. At that time, we briefly listed a number of popcorn positioning alternatives, which is reiterated on the next page.

You must keep an open mind as you explore, recognize opportunities, create ideas, and seek to answer this first question—*who is your customer?* Structure your search in broad categories and begin by developing a list of all possible customers. Start with the end consumer and work backwards. Your list will be longer than that listed below but should include:

List your customers.

- general consumer
- movie consumer
- at home consumer
- mall consumer
- retail mall outlets
- movie theatres
- specialty stores
- mail order companies
- Internet sites
- Internet malls
- *and the list would go on*

In our grid the list of potential customers would appear in a structure we can test. The grid would appear as follows:

Create a grid format for your concept.

Customer	Sales/Distribution Channel	Benefit
general consumer		
movie consumer		
at home consumer		
mall consumer		
retail mall outlets		
movie theatres		
specialty stores		
mail order companies		
Internet sites		
Internet malls		

"We knew at Decker's Corporation that we needed a package that could meet all our needs without spending alot of money and having it all pre-integrated. And, we looked around and we couldn't find anything to meet that need, so we figured if we couldn't find a package that would meet the need, there were lots of other people with the exact same problem. And, in fact, we were right."
-Karl Lopker, CEO, QAD

Mix and match customers.

Creating this simple grid enables you to mix and match customers to get a better sense of what business you are really in. For example, depending on your concept, a potential customer could become a distribution channel for another customer. In our example, many of our potential customers could be considered distribution channels for our first customer, the general consumer, as is outlined below.

Customers can also be distribution channels.

Customer	Sales/Distribution Channel	Benefit
general consumer	retail mall outlets specialty stores mail order companies internet sites internet malls	
movie consumer		
at home consumer		
mall consumer		
retail mall outlets		
movie theatres		
specialty stores		
mail order companies		
Internet sites		
Internet malls		

Explore different options.

With this structure in place, it is easier for you to explore options, move items around, and eliminate some that may not be feasible. With popcorn, reaching a movie theatre consumer may be difficult because the movie theatre itself owns and controls the distribution channel. As a result of this understanding, the concept grid shifts and the movie theatre becomes a distribution channel in addition to being a potential customer.

Distribution channels can become customers.

Customer	Sales/Distribution Channel	Benefit
general consumer	retail mall outlets specialty stores mail order companies internet sites internet malls	
movie consumer	movie theaters	
movie theaters		

Concept grid is evolutionary.

By listing customers and channels in this fashion your concept has both changed and grown, giving you a new alternative to consider. With that new alternative comes the need to talk to more strangers because you now need to know how theatres buy popcorn. What do they buy? Ingredients or popped popcorn? What is their benefit need? Good popcorn? A good supplier who delivers daily (they probably can't store a lot of popcorn)? Price?

All of these things need to be considered and entered into your early concept grid.

What are the benefits?

Customer	Sales/Dist. Channel	Benefit	Questions to explore
movie theaters		great taste consistent delivery price	who makes the decision ingredients or popped popcorn who now supplies what who is competition

To complete this overly simplistic example, we also need to examine how your company will sell to movie theatres. Do you call on theatres directly? In the early stages of a venture you, the entrepreneur, will wear all hats, including a selling hat. Expansion will occur later and you will need to recruit a sales team for this effort, but you must first define the process for these beginning stages.

Keep talking to strangers.

Talking to strangers, asking questions and getting physical fast will enable you to properly develop your idea into a working concept worthy of moving down the feasibility funnel.

Does each theatre buy individually? Probably not, but that is just a guess. Who is the decision-maker and what prompts them to action? Is popcorn bought from one source and candy from another, or is a "one-source solution" needed to minimize paper work and delivery challenges?

Questions need to be explored also.

The strangers you will meet hold the answers to all your questions and it is helpful to list your questions alongside of your concept grid as you can see below.

Customer	Sales/Dist. Channel	Benefit	Questions to explore
movie theaters	direct by entrepreneur using regional sales firms	great taste consistent delivery price one source solution	who makes the decision ingredients or popped popcorn who now supplies what who is competition

Concept grid can begin with any component.

Although customers are the best source for defining your concept, you can start filling in your grid from any vantage point. Michael Dell started his grid with a distribution channel for the sale of personal computers. Prior to Dell Computer Corporation, almost all personal computers were sold either through VARs (value added resellers) or retail outlets. In its infancy, this channel made sense for the industry because personal computers required technical assistance. The consumer needed to be educated about software and hardware configuration in order for the systems to be operable and of value to the purchaser.

Dell started with distribution.

Patterns of change occurred thereby creating opportunity. The industry grew and early adapters were no longer the only consumers. Dell targeted the same customer and provided the same basic benefits as a retail outlet, but did it in a virtual environment, which lowered its costs. To overcome resistance to change, Dell added

Define new benefits.

new benefits, including warranty work done in your home, which gave the user/purchaser peace of mind when buying a computer from a catalog. The obvious benefit to consumers was not having to pack up their computer and haul it to the retail store when they experienced problems.

Internet is new distribution channel.

This starting point, with a distribution channel, is the driving force behind the Internet. By its very nature, starting an Internet-based business dictates that you are competing for existing customers through a new channel. As such, a key part of your journey will be to explore existing businesses that may make sense as an Internet-based distribution company. Clearly there is a limitless pool of opportunity.

Or, start with a benefit.

Starting your grid with a benefit is also possible, but heed the product-driven warning once again. Returning to the popcorn example, if you have a vastly superior brand, you could take advantage of the market segmentation available on the web and open a specialty popcorn ecommerce site.

Define your customer though.

A great idea but testing it would first require you to define a customer. Who will buy your popcorn? How do you attract them to your site? Your research may direct you to a web mall in which case your concept changes. The web mall becomes your customer. You must then ask if it is a broker, an auctioneer, or a reseller? How does it decide who is in its mall? How does it decide if it will resell your popcorn? Who does it attract? What does it take to get into a web mall? What kinds of specialty products sell there? As is obvious, even with a benefit driven business, you must return to a customer focus to get started.

Focus your thoughts.

You will always be in the hunt for a new venture. A concept grid, otherwise known as a customer grid, is the best structure for focusing your thoughts as you mentally and physically struggle with defining your customer, your distribution channel, and your benefit.

Concept Statements

eToys.com

eToys.com, an Internet-based toy store, sells toys and other children's goods to parents who seek a simple, convenient means of purchasing toys for their children. eToys.com maintains its own warehouse, which houses its many products, and orders are shipped directly to the customer thereby ensuring timely delivery.

QAD

Pamela Lopker founded QAD, a company that designs, develops, and sells software technology directly and through VARs (Value Added Resellers) to manufacturers enabling manufacturers to speed up order fulfillment cycle times which, in turn, minimizes inventories and maximizes operating efficiencies.

Up Front & Personal: Autopsy/Post Services

Vidal Herrera had 24 years of experience in the death-care industry and had been an investigator in the Los Angeles County coroner's office for 14 years where his primary duty was to investigate the circumstances surrounding a death. But in 1984, Herrera hurt his back lifting a heavy corpse and was out of work for over four years.

Herrera had never given any thought to being out of work or having to find a new job. He even stated, "prior to that (the accident), I never took my education seriously. I felt my life was set, then one day, I had an accident and my life stopped." When he did try to return to work the only job he could get was working as an autopsy assistant at a Veteran's Administration hospital, which paid so poorly that he would have been better off remaining on disability.

After declining this offer, the hospital offered to hire him as an independent contractor operating on a per body basis. He calculated the financials of this offer and discovered that it was a substantially higher income level.

At the same time, Herrera noticed that a broader trend in health care was occurring. The consolidation of hospitals and downsizing of HMOs meant that there was a greater need for independent autopsies. Herrera noted, "the hospitals and HMOs took the position that they no longer need to pay for autopsy services because they are in the business of saving lives. When a patient has died, they just basically forget about them. But the families don't. The families have questions and they want answers."

As he was driving the freeways of Los Angeles, Herrera noticed the vast number of mobile businesses such as dog groomers, plumbers, and others that exist and he figured why can't autopsies be movable as well.

But, he had trouble getting a loan because there was no comparative business. "I was not a funeral director, not a doctor, not an investigator. I was just somebody who had an idea. But, we didn't have enough equity in our home, so therefore, we could never get a loan. To this day, I have never borrowed money."

With a $100 loan from his father-in-law, Herrera bought a beat up old Honda at a garage sale and borrowed surgical instruments from the hospital. After three autopsies, he was able to buy his own equipment and the business took off. "It just exploded," he says. His wife helps him run the business and they've built a Web site to help promote 1-800-AUTOPSY.

"What I do is not new, I just systemize it. I developed a customer service base and of course, quality assurance. Business is so busy that it just never stops. People die every day, every second, every week. We're basically on call seven days a week, 24 hours a day. I'm no different than anyone else, I'm in business to make money, but it's not about money, it's about service. I look at it from an introspective point of view. The money I make is a reward for the services we provide." As a result of his efforts, Herrera's business is profitable and growing.

Market Risk Filter

Filter down to market risks.

With a clearly defined working concept, you are ready to continue down the funnel and test your market risks. Ideally, your working concept outlines many possible businesses and you will spend a great deal of time refining some and eliminating others as you progress through this stage. Testing your concept will take a lot of energy. Are you ready for this challenge?

Feasibility funnel grows.

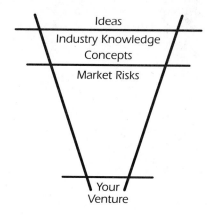

Are you sure it passed the industry test?

First, you must be certain not to marry yourself to one particular facet of your concept until you are certain that it passes the initial industry test. Does it fit in your industry? You will only learn the answer by discussing it with the industry associates and creativity circle friends that you have met. A concept developed in harmony with the patterns of change in your industry is critical to success.

Four aspects to market risk assessment.

There are four primary aspects involved in testing your market risks. The goal in this phase of the feasibility funnel is to hone in on the size and elements of your specific market, become intimately familiar with your competition, clearly define who your customers are, and determine how many customers exist for your product or service.

Market analysis

Primary research.

As with industry knowledge, market risks are best assessed through primary research, which is what you learn from personal contacts and by wearing out the bottom of your shoes.

You will also need secondary research, which comes from non-personal sources and is found in libraries, on the Internet, and in journals. As we mentioned in Chapter Five, this data is almost always statistical in nature and it may be difficult to find meaningful information about your specific niche. Be careful not to get caught up in secondary research because while it is the easiest to find, it is also the type that can lead to a "fatal flaw," or a condition under which you are not willing to go forward.

Small, customer, and niche driven.

Remember that you are not a giant and not market driven, but are small and customer and niche driven. It is unlikely that you will be able to attract resources sufficient to compete with the well-established players. As such, when you do your

What is your slice of the pie?

secondary research, learn about your slice of the pie—not the whole bakery. Knowing how many Americans eat pizza, how often, and where they eat it is critical to Pizza Hut. But primary research in your neighborhood (including standing outside pizza shops and counting the number of clients entering) tells you how many pizza shops exist in your area and how many customers they have. Primary research is the research you need.

Dave Thomas knew his market.

Dave Thomas certainly knew his market when he opened Wendy's back in the late 1960's. He did his research and discovered that customers wanted more choice and a fresher hamburger than they received at McDonald's. Thus, he provided customers with about 250 possible combinations of condiments, something they could not get at any other fast food restaurant. People also told him that he would waste a great deal of meat as a result of using fresh hamburger because he didn't buy premade burgers. However, he seized this opportunity to make chili instead of being left with extra hamburger meat.

Remember, execution counts.

As you get closer to your niche, you also need to learn the intricate details of execution. How did that box of popcorn get on the shelf or in the theatre? How did the popcorn get in the mall specialty shop or the microwave popcorn get on the grocery shelf or in the video rental store? You don't understand your business until you can answer all of these questions.

Competition grid

What's the competition?

Concepts need to be tested and the key variable is almost always the customer. But, knowing why each competitor is successful or why they appear to be failing is equally important. Although you most likely took a cursory glance at your competition when framing your concept, it is now time to do it with a much greater level of scrutiny.

Become a shopper yourself.

Many consider competition to be the window into your opportunity. Knowing what works and what doesn't establishes boundaries for your journey. A Japanese phrase typically credited to Mr. Honda states "if you want to catch a mouse, make a sound like a cheese." This literal translation may lose something, but not the message. The best way to know about your industry and initially validate your concept is to become a shopper. Try to buy what you perceive as your product or service. Be the cheese that draws the mouse.

"I did have a target store that I wanted to go into. It was essentially a store that I shopped at because I was basically a consumer creating a product that I wanted within a group of other consumers that would want the same. It was just very logical, common sense."
-Dineh Mohajer, Founder, Hard Candy

Estimate costs.

Acting like a buyer will teach you almost everything you need to know about your competitor. One potential exception is that competitor's cost and profit margin, but, if you are studying the competition in great detail, then you will be able to estimate that as well.

Create a competition grid.

How should you structure your competitive findings? You should do so by creating a competition grid, which is a format similar to a concept grid because it defines multiple elements of a single competitor. An example would be as follows:

What's important to know about the competition?

Competitor	Principal Customers	Principal Consumers	Price Points	How Customer Reached	Cost to Sell

Why are they successful?

What should you know about your competitor? You should know why they are successful. Too often entrepreneurs see only the weaknesses in their competition. They examine as if they were a general or a quarterback and seek vulnerabilities, where to attack. While this is an important vantage, you must also realize that your competitors have learned to live with those weaknesses and other competitors have most likely already attempted to drill holes in those weak spots. You will too.

What is (are) their vital area(s)?

More important is too discover why they succeed. You want to know how they satisfy customer needs. Is their pizza better tasting or better priced? Is their service superior or their location more convenient? What is their vital area? In the long run, companies remain in existence as long as they provide value for their customers. Always seek to provide value.

What's the indirect competition?

When exploring competition, you must also look past your direct competition, which is easy to find. Examine what is not in the industry, but perhaps could and should be. What alternative products or services exist? Be midfield of the patterns of change and anticipate what is coming. Will the current format of Internet-based selling disappear? What will replace it? How will you compete in the future? What will be the value you add in the future, your vital area?

Analyzing your competition also provides the added benefit of giving you further insight into your customer.

Customer definition

Who is the actual customer?

There are two common attributes of failed startups. The first is confusion over who is the actual customer. Countless stories abound of entrepreneurs with great passion and skills that have pursued the wrong customer. One illustrative example is an interactive computer training company that developed an alternative method of teaching car mechanics about new products and procedures in new models they serviced. The education system included videos illustrating new products, computer generated text about new products and services, and a procedures checklist.

Did they properly define their customer?

In the early stage of exploration, the new firm felt the primary benefit was that mechanics would not have to travel to a regional center for training. They could do it in their shop, which meant less time away from their job and saved the company from the costs of training. They met with their perceived customer—the local mechanic—and demonstrated their prototype. At the conclusion of their presentation, they asked if the system would work and received a positive response.

Why didn't they get a call-back?

Armed with data from their contacts and with the help of other contacts gained through a mentor, they arranged a meeting with the head of training and education for a Big 3 car company. In pre-meeting telephone conversations they discussed the system, their efforts to date, and the feedback received from the market place. A meeting was scheduled, a detailed presentation was given, and follow-up was promised. But it never came.

What was the benefit to the buyer?

Phone calls, letters, and even sitting in the lobby did not result in a single follow up contact with their perceived customer. Why? They offered no benefit to that buyer. Instead, they presented a potential threat to the perceived customer's place in that organization and to the power base of the entrenched organization. The new firm's effort was flawed from the beginning. In the interviews with the customer, the correct question to ask was "what would a system like this have to do to be of value to you," not "will a system like this work."

Critical to ask what is of benefit to the customer?

Asking what is of value defines the benefit need, not the product needs. While change may be a constant for entrepreneurs, it is not for the general mechanic. The mechanics are used to and enjoy playing by the rules and following a routine. In fact, they like going to regional training sessions; it gets them away from work. They learn about new products and services with their buddies and have some free social time. They like everything just the way it is—thank you.

We'll visit this oft-repeated scenario again when learning about entrepreneurial marketing in a later chapter. Good salesmanship would have identified the head of training as an obstacle to be avoided by entering at a much higher level. Perhaps the chief financial officer or director of quality assurance would have been a more appropriate target because that type of person is in a better position to recognize the timesaving and reduced cost benefits.

This new firm never made it past the prototype stage because they lacked proper customer definition. They tested the wrong potential buyer.

Don't confuse a compliment with a contract.

The second most common attribute of failed companies is confusing "a compliment" with "a contract," which is especially deadly. It is a self-inflicted wound that derives from the way entrepreneurs conduct themselves when contacting potential customers.

The entrepreneurial journey can be lonely and ambiguous. It starts with the premise that you must explore a hundred ideas to find one worthy of your time and can be discouraging to those not prepared or who lack the passion and perseverance for the effort. Tired entrepreneurs are vulnerable and can be ill advised by positive reinforcement.

Why wouldn't they say they like it?

Entrepreneurs presenting their products or services are likely to seek feedback and ask what others think; most respondents will say they like it. Why wouldn't they? We are social beings and are prone to being friendly. One customer focus group expert once indicated that asking "do you like it" is similar to showing someone a picture of your kids or your family. Nobody's going to tell you your kids are ugly. They'll give you a cursory compliment and get on their way.

What's the difference between a compliment and a contract?

So it is with an ill-conceived test of your customer. If asked in such a hurried and casual manner, you'll get the compliment, but never the contract. What is the real *difference* between a compliment and a contract? A compliment is just that, someone telling you they like it. A contract is a promise to buy. Whether it is in writing or in some other form, it is a formal commitment to purchase whatever you have said you will provide. Unfortunately, confusion of the two has often led to bankruptcy. Many an entrepreneur has walked to the poor house mumbling "but everybody said they loved it." Amen.

Customer test

Time to complete primary research on your customer.

You should now be aware of the logical flow of the feasibility funnel. You know what you like and have a vision of what industry you enjoy and feel you can compete in. From your concept grid, the various permutations of your vision have been brought into clarity. Similarly, your competition grid provides insight into the competitive landscape. Just like a hawk, you have circled your target; you now need to explore the bull's eye. It's time to complete the primary research on your customer.

When is enough, enough?

How do you know if you have gained enough information about your customer to launch the business? This is the hardest question in entrepreneurship and it is your challenge. When do you feel comfortable enough to launch? Because you are your risk manager, you are the only one who can decide. But what is the basis for that decision?

Is it time to jump?

Look to the outside. Ask yourself what an independent third party would say was adequate. What objective primary and secondary data do you have to support your going forward? When do you have enough to start? When is it time to dive in?

Herein lies the goal of the customer test portion of the market filter. What explicit actions are you going to take to confirm the existence of customers? The answers are obviously individual and unique to the business model you are forming. Is it a survey of potential users? Is it an order from a customer? Is it a formal written contact? Only you can decide when enough is enough and when you are ready to start.

Only you know when it is time.

For some, the business cannot begin until enough resources are amassed to get to the first customer. But obtaining those resources is dependent on your research and proof that a customer does exist that not only wants your services or products, but is also attainable.

How will you know you can support a business?

Entrepreneurial Exercise

For this exercise, you are going to analyze Dave Thomas, founder of Wendy's fast food chain, and try to recreate his concept definition and competitive analysis.

1. Whom should he have spoken with in doing his primary research?

   _____

   _____

   _____

2. What should his secondary research have discovered?

   _____

   _____

   _____

3. How should he have tested his customer?

   _____

   _____

   _____

4. Who else could have been defined as his customer beyond the obvious?

   _____

   _____

   _____

5. Which companies should have been included in his competition grid? What is the benefit they offer their customers?

   _____

   _____

   _____

⇒   **Tear out and move to your entrepreneurial road map binder.**

Sales Channels and Distribution Risk Filter

Once your concept has passed the market tests, it can then be filtered down to the sales and distribution filter.

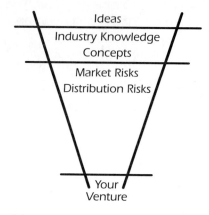

The filter grows.

Distribution filter deserves more attention.

Often this component of the concept receives the least amount of attention. However, it deserves more, especially today when rapid changes in sales and distribution have resulted from the Internet and the related movement to business to business commerce. This paradigm shift, coupled with the global pattern of change that distribution channels are shrinking, should signal opportunity for the entrepreneur because it marks a period of chaos, confusion, and ambiguity—the entrepreneur's dream.

Ecommerce may affect every business transaction.

Many believe ecommerce will leave no stone unturned and will, in some form or another, touch everything. In other words, this new business model has the potential to affect all normal business transactions. Physical assets including land and buildings that were the domain of industry leaders just a decade ago are now considered liabilities. What will tomorrow's winners look like? How will they create value for themselves and their customers?

Entrenched channels— opportunity?

In our analysis of sales and distribution channels, it is interesting to note that many later entrants in what appeared to be entrenched channels of semi-controlled industries were actually able to create value. Hindsight tells us that much of the value-add actually derived from overly simplistic alterations to an existing concept.

Domino's and Wendy's added new distribution to old concept.

Among the best known is Domino's, which combined the average pizza customer and the average pizza product with a new distribution channel—home delivery. In effect, this added a new, more important benefit—convenience. The doubters said home delivery wasn't affordable, consumers wouldn't pay for it. They were wrong. This change in distribution is now imitated by many pizza shops today. Similarly Wendy's provided the benefit of convenience to the average hamburger consumer when it added drive-thru windows and effectively changed the delivery point. Same customer, same product—new distribution point, new benefit. *So why isn't there home delivery for upscale hamburgers?*

The same is true in more sophisticated industries. Two of the five largest personal computer companies achieved market success through innovation in distribution.

Computer industry provides good example.

First was Michael Dell with direct sales to the consumer via catalogs. Same customer and same product, but with the additional benefits of direct delivery and a promise of home repair, which enabled consumers to allay their fears of buying a complex product from a catalog instead of in a store. Gateway followed suit providing additional benefits of a new channel—the Internet—that also supported another new benefit—a custom made computer.

Working through the various combinations of your original concept will enable you to find the channel that best reaches your customer and best delivers your benefit.

Concept evolution is dynamic.

As you saw earlier in the chapter, this sales/distribution channel component needs to be part of your evolving concept grid. As you continue to meet strangers, you also need to be asking yourself: if this were my customer, how would I get to him or her? How would I deliver my benefit? Concept evolution is not a static event, it is dynamic in nature and you must always try and test new permutations.

Keep a macro view.

You must also remember that while it is important to focus on the first stage of the journey, you must also be mindful of how you will progress into later stages. For example, your initial concept grid may reflect a direct sales method by you, which is certainly a common entrepreneurial tactic. But how do you get to multiple customers in multiple locations? Is direct selling going to prove fruitful in later stages? You must consider that the cost of direct sales is high. For example, in the pharmaceutical industry the salary, benefits, overhead, and travel costs of an average direct sales person exceed $250,000. Can you be priced competitively using this channel?

Is the Internet for you?

The Internet is a channel perceived to be "low cost" to enter and to maintain. It is, but you are fishing. Is that your model business? You are baiting your hook and waiting for customers to come to you instead of biting on your competitors line (their web site). Is this your optimum sales channel? Keep in mind that attracting people to your site is NOT a minor undertaking.

What does consumer awareness cost?

Industry reports indicate that "household" names—eBay, Amazon, Yahoo—have invested an average of $200,000,000 each to reach their level of consumer awareness. Are you prepared to launch a resource war? Again, refer to your model business to help determine the answer.

How will you know when you've discovered the "right" sales and distribution channel for your venture? What are the critical ingredients of testing your potential channels? Typically, three primary efforts are needed:

Three primary efforts to testing sales channels.

- examine your competitor's current sales and distribution channels,
- expand your competitive grid to include alternate channels, and
- explore both of these with an eye for cost.

Entrepreneurial Exercise

Refer to the just cited example of providing new benefits via changes in distribution channels. Dell Computer and Gateway were cited as examples. Think about these two companies and the industry in which they exist and answer the following questions. Share your answers with another and discuss.

1. At what stage of the lifecycle was this industry when these innovations were introduced?

   _____

   _____

   _____

   _____

2. Would their innovations in distribution have succeeded earlier in the cycle?

   _____

   _____

   _____

   _____

3. Would they have succeeded later in the cycle?

   _____

   _____

   _____

   _____

⇒ **Tear out and move to your entrepreneurial road map binder.**

Competitor's channels

What's average selling price?

As a risk manager you want to be prepared, and thus need to know everything you possibly can before starting your venture. Among other things, you should know the average selling price of your competitor's products. If your first reaction is that your competitor sells multiple products and you couldn't possibly track each one, you have reached a flawed conclusion.

Talk to suppliers.

Competitors with limited product offerings are easy to track. When multiple offerings exist, you need to learn the company's targeted gross margin percentage for each of its product categories. If something sells for $1.00, what is the company's cost? What is its gross profit margin? Only your tenacity will enable you to learn these numbers. Talking to suppliers about margin percentages at certain volume levels should be part of your efforts. Would you invest in someone who didn't know the sales price and costs of his or her competitors?

List alternative channels

What other channels are there?

This exercise is best done as part of a creativity lab. Bring your inner circle together and present them with the task. List your potential customer and the product or service you hope to provide and challenge them to come up with new sales and distribution channels. Remember the rules of the creativity lab? One dollar in the can for every negative comment or any use of the word *problem*. This can be a fun exercise that could expose a new value-add or may even turn up your fatal flaw.

Look outside your industry.

In addition, be constantly aware and observe channels in other industries to determine if they could also work for your concept. For example, bundling is a common practice in many industries whereby two products are sold together. You buy a computer that comes with software programs already loaded. The distribution channel for the software company is the seller of the computer. Can you bundle your product with another company's so that it becomes your customer thereby enabling you to use its sales and distribution channel?

What are costs?

Observe and explore what may work elsewhere and then apply it to your concept. In so doing, you must also be cognizant of cost. What does each sales channel cost to implement. How many direct sales people will you need or what are the fees associated with distributing your product through wholesalers? All of these variables will need to be considered in a complete feasibility analysis.

Prepare a price/cost schedule

What is the price?

The process of feasibility is often described as building a mosaic which, when finished, will give your start up direction. In a later chapter, when assessing financial feasibility, we will explore the many costs of implementing your business. At this stage, we will explore one of the key premises on which that financial model will be built.

Combine what you have learned.

In our market analysis, we began to define market and niche size. Examining the competition taught us actual pricing or the margins of our competitors. As we explored our channels, we became sensitive to cost. When these observations are all taken together, the following schedule begins to emerge:

Create schedule of price/cost.

	Product Description	Competitor	Us
Avg. Sales Price		xxx	aaa
Cost of sales and delivery		yyy	bbb
Price minus sales		zzz	ccc
Sales cost as % of price		26%	31%
Distribution cost as a % of sales		4%	3%

Gives you framework.

This simple chart is just the beginning and by no means answers your challenge of whether or not this is a viable venture. However, it gives you a framework on which to build and will be further explored in a later chapter on financial feasibility. Generating this initial price sheet and being sensitive to your sales and delivery cost per delivered customer is just one critical part of your journey.

Benefit Risk Filter

Upon filtering through the sales and distribution assessment, your concept is ready for the benefit risk filter.

Filter expands further.

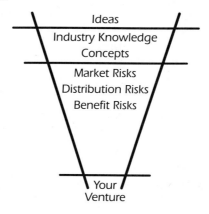

Ideas
Industry Knowledge
Concepts
Market Risks
Distribution Risks
Benefit Risks
Your Venture

What is a benefit?

Benefit assessment must begin with a clear understanding of the definition of a benefit. As with the definition of an entrepreneur, the answer begins by examining what it is not. It is not your product or service. It is not the functionality and uniqueness of your product or service. It is not the color or horsepower of a car. All of these are features and sometimes used to differentiate a car, but are not benefits. The speed of your computer, its disk size, or sound system are not benefits, they too are features. Benefits are not the bells and whistles or the uniqueness of the offering, which are the focuses of product-based companies.

It is not a feature.

Rather, a benefit is what your offering does *for* your customer—not what it *does*. Clearly customers need to know *what you do*; there is no argument about this. But it is more important that they know *what you do for them*.

Get customers to assist in benefit development.

You've been talking to customers, so you should know their needs. It is now time to focus on those needs and on what your customers want to accomplish. Then you must determine how you will help them accomplish whatever it is they want to accomplish. Have them assist you in creating the benefit they seek rather than building something with many features that are not important to them.

Don't just follow industry standards.

One company used its experience to develop a software program to meet a perceived need. Proper guidelines were followed and industry standards as defined by the major hardware and software companies of the time were met. However, despite having a prototype available for demonstration and the industry knowledge and experience to back their ability to deliver, customers were nowhere to be found. Not one potential customer indicated a desire to buy when told that such a system would be available.

Ask under what conditions would you buy?

The entrepreneurs persevered and when the question changed to "under what conditions would you buy?" they learned the customers' true benefit need. The early adapters shared that they had little concern over the software produced by the start up company. The potential clients also shared that as they shopped other vendors, they noticed a lack of a total solution. If the hardware, networks, or software didn't work, who was at fault? Who could they call? The hardware, software, or network company? The clients also wondered about implementation of such a system that would touch so many employees in their factory. Who would install it and how? Who would train everyone? These unknowns halted the purchase of any system., including this particular start up company's system.

Respond to benefit needs.

Ultimately, the solution was simple, but the execution was not. The young company returned and rephrased the question—"if we offered you a complete solution, a single source of all components, are you prepared to buy?" The potential customer assessed the start up's ability to deliver, satisfied itself, and said yes.

The customer designed the benefit and the entrepreneurs delivered it thereby birthing a new niche-driven company that successfully competed against giants like IBM and others. It offered a benefit that gave it a proprietary position in the market.

Build a brochure

Define benefits in a brochure.

How do you keep benefits and features separate? A proven exercise is to build a brochure. It can either be in a simple format using word processing techniques such as clip art software, or it can be created quite eloquently with state-of-the-art graphics. The primary goal of this exercise is to clearly state your benefits. The artistic value can be garnered at a future time with outside, perhaps professional, assistance and should not be of great importance at this stage.

Prominently display your benefits.

To help guide you through this process, first make a list of every feature of your product or service that comes to mind. Next to the feature, list the associated benefit it provides and if there is no associated benefit, then it is not a feature worth listing. You may include a section in your brochure for the features, but only a minor one. Listing the benefits in a prominent location is what will sell your product or service.

Brochure is a tool.

This written piece gives you a tool with which you can present yourself in a credible way. It provides both a checklist for review of your benefits in sales meetings and a tangible item that you can leave with your potential clients providing them with your road map and call to action (how they will contact you).

Brochure becomes multi-functional.

These early brochures will prepare you as you reach the second stage in the entrepreneurial lifecycle—seeking multiple customers. The brochure will eventually become multi-functional and serve as a customer qualification tool as well as a statement of benefits. Since you are most likely operating in a niche, not all customers will be interested in your offerings. As such, a brochure will help to weed out individuals who may have a misconception of what you can do for them. This can save you countless hours in sales presentations.

Other important assessments of the benefit filter section include the following.

Proprietary position risk assessment

Can/should your idea be protected?

You are openly talking to potential customers and they (and their friends) are learning about your vision, which brings up the two difficult questions asked earlier—can and should your vision be protected? Should confidentiality agreements be signed, and copyrights or utility patents be filed?

Investors will want to know.

"What is your proprietary position?" is a question that you will ask yourself and certainly your investors will ask of you. Proprietary position is a difficult phrase to define, but at the heart of it is why you will succeed against either existing or future competition. Are you just paving the raw path for the next competitor? What will stop some large firm from leveraging what you have done, adding its limitless resources, such as a large sales force and numerous programmers and technicians, and catapulting to the top? Why aren't you just the pioneer who will get the arrow in the back from competitors as opposed to being the first mover that builds a beachhead and grows it to dominance?

Only you know.

This is a challenge that can only be answered by you, the entrepreneur. Becoming intimately knowledgeable about your industry, your market, your competitors, your customers, and the benefits you provide will help to answer these questions.

Make a delivery timeline

Can you deliver?

As you have been busy listening to your customer's needs, the early adapters you first spoke with will want to know when they can count on delivery. As such, you need to know and be able to set mutual expectations for delivery time and sequence.

When will you deliver?

Can you deliver? How long will it take? Without knowing these answers, you risk responding in a less than supportable manner, which will cause you to loose both your credibility and your customer at the same time. You must outline your plans for delivery.

Timeline is an internal tool.

The timeline is an internal tool (and will be used for future investors) that needs to cover all of your activities—sales, legal structures, product development times, pricing, and every other action you envision taking place from that day forward until your expected initial success.

Involve team in development.

Involve your entire team of associates in the creation of your timeline and, depending on your relationship with your target customers, you may wish to have them tell you their expectations of time from initial order to completion. If clearly and precisely laid out in a timeline, you mitigate the risk of over, and under, promising.

Plan for future evolution and growth of your benefits

Find balance between being a "yes man" and delivering benefits.

As you close your initial customer, you will learn more and more of needed enhancements, which will create a mixed challenge. Saying yes to all customer requests will trap you into never-ending product design thereby inhibiting the actual progression of your company. Saying no means you risk losing a contract because of your admitted limited functionality. Your benefit development plan should therefore highlight how the potential client's needs and your enhancements co-exist. By the same token, be careful not to limit your initial offerings because you will then be surpassed by your competition.

Devise a structure to control initial design and future evolution and remember that your customer seeks and will buy benefits. Offering a system that supports future benefits and features will help close your early customers.

Feasibility continues.

This chapter has focused on the beginning filters of the feasibility funnel. Financial feasibility and people risks will be further explored in a later chapter.

"We tested some of the merchandise programs in the Krono markets, in the demographically correct Krono markets like the one in West L.A. And then when the first Trader Joe's opened, and it worked, especially the wine program, the photo finishing programs and some of the other things, we converted the demographically suitable Krono markets to Trader Joe's. And along the way we were learning, always learning."
-Joe Coulombe, Founder, Trader Joe's

Chapter Summary

- Feasibility is the essence of entrepreneurship. It is how entrepreneurs think and the process used to tweak and evolve concepts.
- The feasibility funnel serves as a tool that aids entrepreneurs in filtering aspects of their concepts into workable business ventures.
- Industry knowledge is the first filter that is best gained through primary research and learning of the patterns of change in your industry.
- A working concept grid helps entrepreneurs to clearly identify and work through various permutations of their concepts.
- The market risk filter includes gaining detailed knowledge about your potential customers as well as about your competitors.
- Sales and distribution methods are critically important to your venture and often provide opportunity in the least likely areas.
- Benefit development is critical to your success and should often be done in collaboration with your customers.

> *"Every morning to me is a challenge. Whether I make money or don't make money, it's a challenge because it's something new, something that's going to happen and I feel that if you have good spirits and you have a good head on your shoulders and you really want to succeed in your own business, then that's the way to go."*
> -Tony Haywood, Founder, A-1 Turbo Industries.

Chapter Six Exercises/Discussion Questions

1. Write down three facts about your industry that will help your business.
2. What are the features of a laptop computer? What are the benefits of a laptop? How do these differ? How do the benefits determine value? What benefits have evolved over time that were not originally offered on a laptop?
3. Consider an outdoor tent manufacturing company. Take this idea through the feasibility funnel and identify what would have to be done in order to properly address all aspects of the feasibility risks.
4. How did David LaMontagne, featured in Journey Six, test his idea before launching his business? How did his opportunity recognition occur?
5. Identify five people who will assist you on your entrepreneurial journey. Family, friends, associates?
6. If you would like to launch a restaurant, what would your customer survey look like?

Project Two: Value Chain Analysis

Your goal in this project is to better understand the distribution process and the value added at the different stages of the process for a product or service that is relevant to your interests. By the end of the exercise, you should be able to analyze the steps of a product's distribution, starting with its manufacturer and ending with its final sale, evaluating the value added and the revenue potential of each stage.

The product or service you choose to analyze should ideally be offered by the entrepreneur you interviewed for Project One, so that you are able to build on that relationship.

Begin by tracing this product or service from its current position in the market (from point of sale at the retail or wholesale level) back to its manufacturer and to its original form. For each step, analyze the value added and cost and pricing possibilities.

Since most products can follow more than one distribution channel, compare and contrast at least two channels for the product or service you've chosen. Cost, price and percentage of total value change should be identified as the product moves through the various distribution channels. Identify the cost associated with each distribution point, as well as the transfer price, which will allow you to determine the profitability of different channels.

Use graphics to depict the relationships of channel members and value exchanged. Use narrative writing to discuss what you found and what you learned from this experience. Be sure to compare and contrast these two channels you've chosen. Please limit this assignment to four pages of text, double-spaced, not including your graphics.

Again, you must also prepare a presentation of your results, which should include two illustrative slides for this presentation. As with the interview project, the slides should not reiterate your paper. Rather, they should highlight your findings in a captivating manner.

Journey Six: Vessel Assist Association

Early Environment

David LaMontagne grew up on the water and developed a love for boating at a very early age. He started sailing when he was six years old and was commodore of the yacht club while still a youngster. As he states, "I'm a bit of a product of my environment frankly. I love boating, I was raised boating and it's just always been in my life."

In 1984, LaMontagne was about to graduate from the University of Southern California's entrepreneur program and was watching all of his friends accept job offers with large firms for large salaries. He didn't think that route would qualify as his model business. "To me, at the time I graduated from college, business had a very stale perspective to it, and I was very concerned about entering the business world and just becoming a number, a statistic. To me, that wasn't who I was. I started looking at who I was, at myself, and tried to determine what's going to make me tick, what's going to motivate me."

Patterns of Change

At the same time that LaMontagne was trying to determine his model business, a Reagan Administration commission was studying which government services could best be privatized. It concluded that non-emergency boat services such as towing, jump starts, and refueling, until then performed by the Coast Guard, could be turned over to the private sector.

While this commission study provided opportunity recognition, LaMontagne's idea for his company, Vessel Assist (VA), actually came when he was 16 years old working on the docks. One of his tasks as an employee was working the ferry where he had to push cars that broke down off onto the land where the automobile club would come and tow them away. He thought to himself, "car breaks down, auto club helps. Boat breaks down, who helps? There's nobody there who helps. Why isn't there a boat auto club that helps?"

Having been exposed to the industry since he was a child, coupled with the opportunity presented by the government's commission study, gave LaMontagne the confidence to pursue his idea. He felt small boaters had a need for such services as towing when their motors broke down, jump starts when their batteries died, and refueling when they ran out of gas. But, he needed to further test his idea to determine if there were actually customers who wanted this service.

Testing the Concept

He began with market research by poring over statistics and talking with people from the US Coast Guard, local municipalities, lifeguard crews, and other groups that were familiar with recreational boating issues. He determined that a large enough percentage of cases would classify as "non-emergency" to support a business and decided to take the risk and launch Vessel Assist, which was not an easy decision. "What I did was I gave myself a year. At that point, all my buddies had graduated from college and were getting jobs from the recruiting firms. Some decent money. It was an uncertain time for me quite frankly. But I thought, gee, if it does work, I will be better off than my friends a year from now. So I'll go ahead and give it a year and if it looks like in one year, I'll break even or that it's going to work, then I'll stick with it. If not, I won't."

An uncle was kind enough to loan him $10,000 and he was able to negotiate a 100% loan on a boat as if it were a piece of machinery, capital equipment. This enabled him to launch; he had a boat and he had working capital to pay the bills.

As is often the case with entrepreneurs, his main resource was himself and he made every effort to cut costs to the bone. He operated the boats, he did the marketing, and he went to the boat trade shows to gain exposure.

Concept Development

LaMontagne soon had to modify his business concept because a number of others entered the towing side of the business. He decided that it was not in his best interest to spend his capital on more tow boats and compete with these smaller operations in the various harbors. He met with the tow boat operators and "so, what we did was we said, o.k., you guys run the towing side of it and we'll run the marketing side of it."

Through this effort and by joining with other towers, LaMontagne was able to hurdle the obstacle of his limited size and expand his one-man band into a service company that spanned the country. The tow boat owners became independent contractors working for VA, which calls them out whenever a distressed boater radios into VA for help. The towers sign up with VA and receive exclusive rights to tow within a specific geographical area.

Another modification to his business model came soon thereafter. When he started out, boat owners were paying him a straight hourly rate—up to $150 per hour—for a VA boat to come to the rescue. People were upset by having to pay this high fare, which was understandable. So, he added the American Automobile Association concept whereby VA became a membership group with annual dues and free service whenever needed. As LaMontagne says, "pay us now or pay us later, either way, we come and get you."

David feels fortunate that he did not have to provide a great deal of education regarding this model as it already exists on land in the form of AAA, which has various chapters around the nation. Using the AAA as its model, VA seeks to provide a host of benefits. As one dispatcher comments, "we're basically the AAA of the water. What we do in this office is we take calls and find out what the problems are and then dispatch people. We do it 365 days a year, 24 hours a day, and anywhere in the country."

Challenges

David's journey has been fraught with many challenges, the greatest of which has been fending off the reversal of the commission study's policy on non-emergency services. At one point, the government was very close to bringing non-emergency services back under its own roof. David did a great deal of lobbying at that time and testified in front of Congress and the Department of Transportation at two of 13 public hearings being held around the country. It was a troublesome period. "We invested a lot of time, a lot of money, and my whole future was wrapped up in it. Knowing that they could, with a stroke of a pen, take it all away, was really tough."

In the end, the policy remains, the private sector is in control of non-emergency services, and Vessel Assist Association is thriving. From its small start, it has grown to 30,000 members assisting in about 10,000 rescues per year with $3 million in annual sales.

Furthermore, VA benefits from lots of free public relations. "When you get mom, dad, and two kids out there stranded and we come to the rescue after they've been out there for an entire day, and they're just scared and terrified, we become their best friends. We get letters in the mail, we get articles in the press, they talk us up all along the docks, that's the best PR we could ever have."

"What really became nice was that after doing this for a number of years, I was actually making a living and at the same time I was actually doing something that had satisfaction and felt right. At that realization, I thought, wow, it's working. Wow, it's great. This is the way it's supposed to be. That was really satisfying to me."
-David LaMontagne, Founder, Vessel Assist Association

Journey Six Case Questions

1. How did LaMontagne come up with the idea for his business?
2. What types of research did he do to test his concept?
3. Did he recognize any patterns of change that pushed him to move forward?
4. Why did he make changes to his original business concept?
5. What benefits did he originally offer that turned into new benefits?
6. What have been his keys to success, his vital area?

Chapter Seven
Entrepreneurial Marketing

Chapter Seven Major Concepts

- Celebrating entrepreneurial advantages
- Entrepreneurial marketing
- Guerrilla marketing tactics
- Writing the entrepreneurial marketing plan

Journey Seven: Cardinal Laboratories

Introduction to Tool Kits

Status check.

You should now be getting a sense for how entrepreneurs become successful. Chapter Six introduced you to feasibility and the process of testing ideas to determine their viability in the marketplace. Feasibility asks the question: "under what conditions am I willing to go forward?" It works your concept, reworks it, and reworks it again until you can convincingly say that you have found such conditions.

Feasibility introduced you to how entrepreneurs become successful. To continue learning about the how, we will now focus on entrepreneurial tool kits. But before delving deeply into tool kits, we will explore entrepreneurial advantages and must keep two primary lessons in mind.

Lessons learned.

1. There is no "one type" of entrepreneur; each is unique and every journey is different. Entrepreneurial characteristics vary, but most successful entrepreneurs describe passion, perseverance, and integrity as the basis for who they are.
2. Entrepreneurs are not the same as business managers. Doing things in stages as opposed to focusing on a full project is the primary difference. The approach to the amount and type of resources available in the beginning stage is another differentiating factor.

Wannabe entrepreneurs.

Beware—danger ahead. This is the point where most "wannabe entrepreneurs" fail. They internalize and think "yeah, I'm a person with passion, I have perseverance, I have integrity." "Sure," they continue, "I don't want to be a bureaucrat. I don't want to measure success by the size of my office or by whether or not that office has a window, I want to control my destiny—do it my way!"

Failure looms.

But, they then start by trying to raise a million dollars because they have "an idea." Or, they want to hire a team to come up with an idea. However, these resource driven actions are against the most common entrepreneurial model as well as the entrepreneurial mindset.

Loneliness and self-doubt.

So what happens to many of these "wannabes?" What do they physically do? They start by competing for potential customer attention. After having gotten physical fast, attending trade shows, meeting strangers, and even formulating a concept, the wannabes must now begin to execute that concept and all of a sudden they feel like they are in a battlefield all alone. With that loneliness comes self-doubt. They think, "who wants to talk to me? How can I compete against all the others? How do I compete against those with serious budgets and existing organizations?"

Employ entrepreneurial tactics.

If you want to be an entrepreneur and are not a "wannabe," then you must employ entrepreneurial tactics and not get scared or feel alone. And, being shy or sheepish is going to leave you in the wannabe category. You must be aggressive and move forward with clear goals in mind.

How do you compete?

You should already be thinking outside the box. So, if you are a small, fledgling startup with little or no money, how do you compete with the bigger companies? Outside the box thinking says you do it by celebrating your advantage—your smallness. While others may view this as your fatal flaw, you know that it is your strength and can use it as such.

Celebrating Your Entrepreneurial Advantages

Don't apologize for a weakness.

There are many advantages of being the little guy. What the big guys may perceive as your disadvantages, you must make your strengths and use to your advantage. Success has never been achieved by apologizing for a weakness.

Your clients have access to the president

That's not our policy!

Have you ever had a bad experience dealing with a company? When a problem arose, were you given the run-around? Were you told that there was nothing that could be done to help you? Or, sorry that's not our policy, we have to follow procedures!

You are the company.

Those are the responses you receive from larger organizations. Comparatively, think about what you have to offer your potential clients. You are the company. You are the decision-maker. The buck does stop here. You can guarantee your client that you are there to listen, to react, and to service their needs.

> *"My persona around the organization is to talk about the customers first. Everybody knows around the organization that if he wants to get through to me, he can get through to me."*
> -David LaMontagne, Founder, Vessel Assist Association

Alliances become critical.

Our virtual world that is a reality means that smaller companies, downsizing, and focusing on niches are the wave of the future. These trends dictate a continuing need for outsourcing thereby leading to the formation of strong strategic alliances between the larger firms that formerly handled all outsourcable functions internally and you, the entrepreneurial startup. An alliance of this nature must function with the same fluidity that two internal departments would. It must appear as one organization, when in actuality, it is two.

Can you deliver?

As today's larger companies become dependent on outside firms, they know that the entire operation can come to a complete stop if they can't get an immediate answer or resolution to a problem. When competing for that alliance (customer), you need to understand that getting that contract could, in large part, be dependent on your ability to get the job done quickly. To be the ally and to get the contract, you, personally, have to be available to your customers.

Clients deal with you, not a switchboard.

Your position as an entrepreneur gives you that power. Your clients can deal with bureaucrats twelve levels deep or they can deal directly with the woman or man at the top. What do you prefer? What do you think they prefer?

Celebrate this advantage, it should be part of your mindset.

Quick response time

Speed to delivery.

Being able to access you, the president, is a communication advantage. For that to be beneficial to your customers is often dependent on the speed at which you do things.

Can you supply the need?

Consider the following scenario. You are part of an alliance and dependent on a strategic partner to supply a part. Further assume that your customer is about to order but they need the part in red, the standard is green. You call your supplier to say, "we need to change our Friday delivery to red, not green."

Bureaucrats can't.

If that supplier is a bureaucratic organization, it may respond with any one of the following answers—a.) We don't make red and if you want a custom order, you need to file a request with new product development and they'll call you in 90 days. b.) We don't make anything but green. Period. c.) If we could make red it will require a minimum order of xxxx units (three times what you need). d.) You have reached Mr. xx, I am unavailable to take your call, but leave a message and I will get back to you as soon as possible (likely to be in three weeks).

Build it into your culture.

Which of these answers is acceptable? None. But because of your size, because you are small, quick, and nimble, you can move fast and respond to the request quickly. You can call another supplier. You can paint the part yourself! You can do whatever it takes to make your first customer happy. And, if you remain entrepreneurial as you grow, you'll build a culture that responds in the same fashion.

Celebrate this advantage—be quick to respond.

> *"If I get three or four phone calls about a problem that anyone's having building, I know that I've done something wrong in the instruction book and I can correct it. And I get that feedback immediately, because I'm available, my phone number is on every piece of literature I give to the customer and my email address. I get emails daily, phone calls daily."*
> -Jerry Teisan, Founder, Trick R/C

Knowledge of key players

Learn the players.

You should still be meeting new strangers everyday. Networking, attending trade shows, giving presentations at trade events, and getting to know the important key players in your niche are critical to your success.

Build lasting relationships.

But you should not be only meeting them, you should also be building relationships with them. Get to know them personally. Meet their spouses and learn the names and activities of their children, which will enable you to know them—not about them.

Be at the forefront of suppliers minds.

The day will then come when one decision-maker needs a new vendor. You have properly positioned yourself so that he or she knows your strengths (and weaknesses) and that you are the company, therefore, you can respond immediately to his or her needs. The choice is ultimately in the hands of that decision-maker, but you can convincingly argue that you will be there for the duration—that your company is and will be there for the long haul to service his or her needs. Other, larger companies will most likely change sales people and primary contacts many times, but you will not.

Stranger or you?

This decision-maker can choose to deal with a stranger, who, if good, will likely get promoted and, if not good, will be fired. Either way, that stranger won't be there for an extended period of time. As a result, a new relationship will have to be built each time a new sales rep or new primary contact is hired and/or fired. So, the decision-maker must choose: deal with a stranger and hope for assistance in times of need, or, deal with you whom he knows and can trust. What would you choose?

Celebrate this advantage—build relationships in your industry.

> *"Great Changes was our first customer. They saw us at the BAT show, which is when we first launched our line. That stands for big and tall, a trade show we go to twice a year. It was a great order, we were very excited. They actually knew our name because we did send out some promos to a lot of stores announcing who we were."*
> -Yvonne Buonauro, Founder, Kiyonna Klothing

Fewer customers means more personnel attention

Niche vs. entire market-what's the advantage?

You are resource constrained. You are focusing on a niche. Your larger competitors are not resource constrained and are attempting to service an entire market. They have more people but do they have the right people on each account? No! That's your advantage.

As an entrepreneur, you are focused. You know you can't be all things to all people and so you choose your customers carefully. A wrong customer or too many customers before you are ready and able to service their needs will shut down your organization. Don't over-promise.

All resources or appointed personnel?

For your targeted customer, you can devote all of your resources. You can bring all 2, 3, 5, or 10 of your associates to bear. You can bring the entire company. A large company usually designates one sales person or one sales person and one technical person to handle your account. It is likely that your team outnumbers that company's designees for the account. You will win in a direct competition.

Committed for the long haul.

In addition, your team is there for the duration. Sell your potential customers by asking if six months from now he or she wants his or her company dependent on a support person who will see the account once. You can offer an assurance that your team will be there, will have first hand knowledge of the account at all times, and will deliver.

Celebrate your advantage—concentrate on the select few instead of trying to service the many.

Summary

Entrepreneurship is not for the weak of heart.

You will not succeed if you are weak of heart. If you attempt to enter a relationship with a customer while fearing your larger-sized competitor, you will not get that customer.

Allow your entrepreneurial mindset to recognize that you can't do it like your larger-sized competitor because you don't have the resources, nor do you want them. Adjust and play your strengths. You will win if you celebrate your entrepreneurial advantages.

Your clients will choose you because

Celebrate your advantages.

- they have access to the boss,
- when they need you to, you can quickly adapt,
- you have built an ongoing relationship that will stand the test of time, and
- you can deliver an entire team that can service their needs.

Celebrate your advantage—celebrate your smallness.

The Great Mousetrap Fallacy

If a man can make a better mousetrap than his neighbor,
though he builds his house in the woods
the world will make a beaten path to his door.

Ralph Waldo Emerson

If a person can efficiently satisfy a customer's need,
regardless of where they build their benefit
the world will make a beaten path to their door.

Entrepreneur

Marketing & Sales - How Do I Get To My Customer?

Marketing versus selling.

Positioning and closing a sale with your first customers are two distinct processes, which are effectively the difference between marketing and selling, your first entrepreneurial toolkits. In this chapter, we will focus on marketing.

Marketing is positioning.

In its classic sense, marketing is the positioning of your product or service in such a way as to attract and educate a customer. Advertising, promotions, and public relations are the primary tools used to create an image and inform the public of the your company's advantages.

Selling is systematic.

In contrast, selling is a systematic approach of educating both yourself and your potential customer of each other's needs. You learn client requirements while they become aware of your benefit. A mutual understanding will result in an order.

Pull through approach.

Both marketing and sales have varying levels of intensity and personalization. A commodity product, soap for example, is positioned primarily through a great deal of advertising and price point marketing. Such a commodity relies heavily on this non-personal means of completing a sale and is commonly referred to as "pull through." As the phrase denotes, the goal of this medium is to get you to buy. You are "pulled through" by the television or newspaper ad or the coupon mailer to purchase the product.

Push through approach.

The opposite of pull through is people intensive and is referred to as "push through" whereby the education and sales propositions are made by a sales person directly. In this case, marketing plays a minor role and is not usually aimed at getting you to buy, but merely at learning of your interest to buy and at understanding your needs. A classic example is selling cars where the marketing role is to get you to the dealership and an actual sale is dependent on the salesperson in the lot.

Entrepreneurs push through.

Historically, entrepreneurs start businesses in the latter format and are dependent on their people and direct sales. Being resource constrained, they do not have the budget to launch significant campaigns and "pull through" customers. They are not a Procter & Gamble or a PepsiCo and cannot spend $20,000,000 to launch a new product, nor can they saturate television and newspapers with ads.

Niche focus is your advantage.

By the same token, large companies find it very difficult to support the cost of a field professional. It is expensive to have a fully paid, fully supported person trained, experienced, and on the road selling. Therein lies the advantage of the entrepreneur. You are trained and experienced and credible in your niche as opposed to a large market. Your target customer is just that and not a target market and so that is where your energies are expended; therefore, you will win the majority of head to head combats, despite your size.

Is yours a marketing or sales oriented business?

In the model business, you evaluated what type of business is right for you. In assessing your skill sets, you again determined the entry strategy that matches your strengths. This part of the journey explores the same type of question from the business viewpoint. Is this a marketing or sales dependent business? Does the answer fit with your model business profile and your skill sets?

Entrepreneurial Marketing

Know your limitations.

To identify the best marketing (positioning) strategy, you must first know your needs and limitations. As an entrepreneurial venture, you cannot compete on the same level as a company with vast resources. If you wish to enter the cola industry, you will face companies such as Coca-Cola and PepsiCo that are well known for their huge advertising and marketing budgets. This is a battle of dollars and one that you are not likely to win.

How do you want to compete?

So, should this be your business strategy—competing on strength of resources? Is expenditure of funds your initial priority? If you have or can get funding, do you want to spend it in this way?

Entrepreneurship is not about resources. Entrepreneurs know and accept the difference between themselves and their competition, which bring vast resources. Startups are created—they are not purchased. Give birth before you push growth.

What's your budget?

Expensive and very involved are the starting points of a large company's classic marketing campaign. Market focus and target profiles are developed. At a minimum, focus groups, market surveys, and a framework for market reaction are developed and conducted by outside experts on a contract basis. Typically, anywhere from $250,000 to several million dollars is budgeted for the "information gathering stage." Do you have $250,000 to test a market? If you did, would you spend it to test the market?

How are you perceived?

If entrepreneurs identify market research as their initial use of funds, investors become wary. Lacking the drive or being unable to create value is what investors will perceive. Often, investors will then dismiss those entrepreneurs as people who want to be President, but not the driving force—the entrepreneur. They merely want the investor to buy the company so that they can be president.

Low cost market research exists.

Getting to know your customers, doing your own counts of traffic at a competitive store or restaurant, and/or setting up a booth at a trade show are low cost alternatives to market research that serve the same, if not a better, purpose and represent the creation of value, not the management of resources.

> *Marketing for an entrepreneur, or entrepreneurial marketing in the same vein, is to take a clipboard and a pencil and stand in a mall and ask people questions about why they are buying your competitors product. Or, to stand outside a restaurant and notice the flow of people through the restaurant. Or, going down to the county and getting the traffic reports for the boulevard that you're thinking of putting your new facility on."*
> -William H. Crookston, WHC Associates

Apply the same tools differently

Marketing tools don't change.

The basic tools used by classic marketers are no different from those used by entrepreneurs and entrepreneurs still need to learn about their market and how to attract prospects. However, the distinction is in how and when the tools are used as well as in the level of intensity of tool usage.

Identify low cost alternatives.

Prime examples are advertising and promotions. You need to make people aware of your product or service and to gather prospects. Classic marketers would launch a huge direct mail and advertising campaign. You can use the same tools in a different manner. Place a simple ad in the classifieds or elsewhere that costs no more than $50 or $100 and will launch your business. Or, instead of a fancy brochure, your mailer can be a letter to the president of a firm with which you wish to do business. A simple phone call, not a large telemarketing effort, can also be effective.

Focus, sensitivity to timing, and the level of intensity are the keywords in preparing your entrepreneurial marketing strategy.

> *"Back in '89, we got a local newspaper, put an ad in there, and advertised for turbo rebuilding. Two days later to my amazement, I had a customer. I turned a $100 ad into a $900 profit. Just rebuilding the customer's turbo and he was happy."*
>
> -Tony Haywood, Founder, A-1 Turbo

Focus on first customer, not target profile

You don't need vast resources.

Even though large companies invest significant dollars in learning about initial customers, the process does not have to be resource dependent. That's your difference and your advantage. Think in terms of first customer—not percent of market share you can obtain.

Clearly defining target profile is theoretical.

Your needs are then focused. The cost to identify and prove a target market profile is much more intense, and frankly, theoretical at best. Large firms spend significant dollars to get a conceptual framework that identifies their target market. Entrepreneurs spend few dollars—and a lot of legwork—to secure a listing of their first ten sales prospects. This is the classic difference between the entrepreneurial and large company approach.

Kiyonna Klothing

Kiyonna Klothing sought its first customers by attending a trade show in its industry. With a series of professional, but inexpensive pre-show announcements, the company invited key prospects to stop by its booth and learn about its company and its offerings. Kiyonna's first customer, a Hollywood, CA retailer named Great Changes, had received one of the announcements and were intrigued by the new line. Great Changes stopped by Kiyonna's booth at the show and placed an order.

Result? First customer. *Cost?* Minimal. *Excitement and fun level?* Very high.

Timing is everything

Know the status of your industry.

Be sure to choose an industry that offers entry opportunities. A well-established consolidated industry with only two or three primary players will have a very high entry price. Competing with Coca-Cola and PepsiCo will be expensive. Battling with existing car manufacturers requires a nine-figure bankroll. Both are obtainable, but at the far end of the probability spectrum for a fledgling start up.

Where are you more likely to succeed?

Choosing a niche in which competition is not yet embedded is not resource dependent. Nor is one that is undergoing change because it creates new customers. Finding early adapters and innovators in segments too expensive for larger companies to explore has a higher probability of success.

> *"Personal care, personal touch, entrepreneurs go the distance. For example, if someone calls us at 5:00 and they have a case for us, we'll take it, we'll take care of it, other companies won't. If someone calls us and they need someone for two hours instead of four, we'll still do the two hours, most companies will only do four."*
> -Carolyn Colby, Founder, Colby Care Home Health

Classic Marketing – The Four P's

4 P's well known in marketing.

Almost every traditional marketing class will begin with the four P's of marketing—product, price, placement, and promotion—which represent the time tested, true-blue approach. As part of our philosophy of using the same tools, but differently, we will first review the traditional P's and then redefine them to match the entrepreneurial way. As an added entrepreneurial edge, we have added a fifth P, People, not found in textbooks.

Classic vs. entrepreneurial approach.

Classic	Entrepreneurial
Product	Customer
Price	Value Added
Promotion	Guerrilla Tactics
Place – Position	Alternative Channels
Paid People	Passionate People

Product versus customer

Products are core competency.

Large firms are driven by their core competencies—what they perceive they do best—which is often their ability to produce and distribute products. To them, value added is created in their products and efficiencies and thus, products are their major focus.

Customers should be core competency.

Entrepreneurs do not have the advantages, or limitations, of core competencies. What they seek to do is to attract customers and determine the best means by which to do that. Through practice and experience, they are able to develop a core competency of reaching customers.

Production is often outsourced.

As such, value added is in attracting and keeping customers. Entrepreneurs start with customers and end with benefits. Production and distribution are not the critical components and are often outsourced to firms that are better equipped to meet those requirements.

Therefore, entrepreneurial marketing places customer ahead of product.

> *"When I took a look at the business and my partner took a look at the business, we spent some time to really look and see what's happening in the industry. We felt that everybody can produce, but nobody was really servicing the merchant. Unlike most everybody else in the industry, who believe that they have to produce, produce, produce, production's really the the most important thing. We believe that production is a by product of service. So, I think that's what really sets us apart from everybody else."*
>
> -Joe Kaplan, Founder, Superior Bankcard Service

Price versus value added

Price is competitive advantage.

Efficiency is a core competency of a company built for high output and capacity; therefore, the most effective way for them to compete is based on price. Their facilities, equipment, and contracts already exist and large output quantities are needed to survive.

Sunk costs are high.

Having evolved over time, costs in the books for these companies are low. To build similar factories from scratch would be very, very expensive for a new start up. By competing on product price point, these companies have the advantage and can keep new entrants out of the market. Controlling price to make entry for others difficult is a key part of their strategy.

How do you add value?

Entrepreneurs are careful to avoid competition where price is the leading determinate. Competing on price eliminates your ability to celebrate your advantages, particularly of size. You provide better, faster service and you can win by finding niches in which these advantages are paramount. That is your point of differentiation.

Pick a niche in which the competition is based on value you add, not on the efficiency of output or low price.

Promotion versus guerrilla tactics

Big guys have huge advertising budgets.

Classic marketing is based on the premise that a firm needs to spend inordinate amounts of money to build and maintain brand awareness, which is how resource driven firms operate. A $20,000,000 annual advertising budget to maintain awareness for a consumer product is considered minimal.

Be a guerrilla.

Finding creative, eye-catching ways to attract attention is the entrepreneurial alternative. Such tactics are often compared to the heroic acts of soldiers who find unique ways of penetrating the enemy's headquarters to capture territory without having the resources of a massive army to support them. Guerrilla tactics are not based on over powering nor are they resource driven. They are creative, back-door, alternative routes for which entrepreneurs are known.

Place - Position versus alternative channels

Classic mindset is to follow fixed procedures.

In classic marketing, place is how you position your product—your sales and distribution strategies. Placement focuses on how and where sales occur. The size of classic consumer product marketing companies dictates the need for fixed procedures that manage the flow of goods, which leaves little room for and few alternatives to existing methods of selling.

Entrepreneurs find new routes.

As we have discussed throughout our journey, the channels of distribution are changing and new ventures are cropping up exponentially. There is little doubt that the Internet and ecommerce industry will create new opportunities for generations to come. You are innovative, flexible, and do not need (or have) the bricks and mortar of your competitors. As a result, you are free to find alternative channels to get your product to market.

Paid people versus passionate people

Marketers don't think in terms of people.

The final P is not found in classic marketing textbooks. But when building a marketing plan, you, the entrepreneur, are the critical component. You are the driving force and your plan is dependent on you and the inner circle of associates you have gathered.

Why do you get up in the morning?

It's always about people. Some work primarily for a salary and they are the paid people, constantly managing their careers. Others have different motivations. Historically, large companies offer higher salaries, both in base compensation and in bonus. Entrepreneurs are doing what they love to do and what they would do if they could work for free. While they do want the potential for upside, more importantly, they want a great and fulfilling journey.

Build and celebrate entrepreneurial spirit.

An entrepreneurial phrase simply states, "people that come for money, leave for more money. People that come with passion, stay." There is no doubt that you will need a full team to be successful. Choose that team based on passion and skill sets and find associates who want to share in the ownership of the company.

A final thought on the P's

Marketing is often viewed as a department on a company's organization chart and exists to perform the duties of advertising, promotions, and customer feedback.

Foster a marketing culture.

To be effective, marketing needs to be more than a just an integrated department within an organization that coordinates with other company functions. Instead, marketing needs to be a culture and in the mindset of every person in every department. Marketing needs to be the company.

Share emphasis on customer.

Entrepreneurs think of marketing plans as both internal and integrated. The internal encompasses the fact that it is part of your culture and is known and understood by everyone. All parties associated with your company should know your emphasis is on customers and delivering their benefit desires.

Make everyone accoountable.

By being integrated, the entrepreneurial marketing plan identifies that all personnel should be judged and rewarded by the extent to which customer benefits are met. The sales department is not solely responsible for generating sales revenues, retention of customers is everyone's duty, and all must recognize that risks and rewards are shared equally. Your culture dictates that opportunities exist for all employees and that nothing is guaranteed for anyone. The customers pay the bills, including employee paychecks, and everything is measured against customer satisfaction.

> *"I think a customer is king and its something that's almost innate for a company and starts with the founding of the company. To me, it the most important thing, if you don't have happy customers, you don't have a company. I think some people start companies with the idea of looking to make money, what can I do to quickly make a bunch of money? And they're almost like, I don't care if a customer is happy as long as I get the money."*
> -Pam Lopker, Founder, QAD

Entrepreneurial Exercise

For this exercise, you will need a partner. Together, come up with a company that offers a product or service with which you are both familiar. Separately, determine whether you feel their marketing efforts follow the classic or entrepreneurial model. Then identify each of the 4 P's in the marketing mix if it is a classic company and indicate how that company could follow the entrepreneurial model in the rest of the table. If your company is entrepreneurial, do the opposite. Don't forget the fifth, entrepreneurial P, for both models.

Classic

Product: _____

_____

Price: _____

_____

Promotion: _____

_____

_____

Place - Position: _____

_____

_____

Paid People: _____

_____

_____

Entrepreneurial

Customer: _____

_____

Value Added: _____

_____

Guerrilla Tactics: _____

_____

_____

Alternative Chls: _____

_____

_____

Passionate People: _____

_____

_____

When finished, compare tables with your partner. Discuss your findings.

⇒ **Tear out and move to your entrepreneurial road map binder.**

Comparing the Classic and Entrepreneurial Marketing Plan: A Scenario

A developer bought land next to a popular ski resort on which he wanted to build and sell homes. He hired a marketing organization to develop a marketing plan. The firm started with the product and designed a brochure describing the homes. They then did market research, conducted focus groups, and developed a profile of the projected target customer.

That customer was a professional individual with a family living within 100 miles of the resort. After purchasing a mailing list, they sent out a mass mailing to those names that matched their profile. Including the mailing, the developer had spent $500,000 in fees for focus-group research, materials, and brochures. Three months later, the developer had yet to make a sale. The end of the ski season was fast approaching and he was facing bankruptcy.

This classic approach to marketing used by the outside experts was both expensive and flawed. Flawed because it sought a target profile for a one-time purchase and used a "shotgun" approach to get customers where an aimed "rifle" would have been more appropriate.

The marketing firm's product driven, expensive approach did not even address two critical questions: Are you a skier and, if so, do you like to ski this mountain? As it turned out, a very small percentage of those mailed to were skiers and an even smaller percentage liked that mountain. The third critical question was whether or not they would be interested in buying a home, which could not be asked until the first two questions were answered.

With bankruptcy looming, the developer regrouped and brought in his entrepreneurial network. They held a creativity session and focused on finding the customers—not on pushing the product. Where should they look for people who like to ski, who liked to ski on that mountain, and who might be interested in such a home? The answer was obvious. They needed to look on the mountain at the people who were skiing.

So, the developer put a sign at the top of the slope offering free hot chocolate to skiers interested in touring his model homes. The people reading the sign were already qualified. They were skiers on that mountain. The third critical question could then be asked: under what conditions would you be interested in buying one of these homes?

The sign attracted visitors. Proximity to the mountain, ease of skiing in and out of the house, a promise of skiing into the your home in bad weather or for a quick lunch thereby avoiding the long lines and crowd at the mountain cafeteria were the benefits the customers sought and the homes delivered.

After the first weekend promotion and a cost of $300 for the sign and hot chocolate, the entire first phase of the development was sold out.

Guerrilla Marketing Tactics

Entrepreneurs are creative.

As we have learned, entrepreneurs and administrators differ in many ways, the most significant of which is in how they start businesses. Administrators are resource dependent and measured by the efficiency with which they utilize those resources. Entrepreneurs seek opportunities without regard to resources, which leads to creativity.

Finding inexpensive ways to attract and secure customers is perhaps the most exciting part of entrepreneurship. It is where creativity and ingenuity flourish.

Creativity in starting a restaurant.

How do you start a restaurant? Two primary challenges face those who wish to do so. The first is managing the logistics of a new kitchen. Orders typically get lost, the time needed to prepare meals will be longer than anticipated, and the quality of the food and expectations will grow as customers and employees become familiar with the menu and physical layout of the kitchen.

Noone enters an empty restaurant.

The second challenge is that customers don't come to an empty restaurant, it will detract them. An individual walking by a new restaurant does not know whether it has been open for a week or a year and empty tables lessens the probability of that person entering and ordering. A crowded restaurant is associated with good food and entices people to walk in. In almost every business, the primary cash flow challenge is how long will it take from start up to break-even—getting enough customers and cash coming in the door to meet operating expenses.

Many restaurateurs begin with a large surplus of resources knowing that it will take time to iron out the logistics and build a clientele, which is very expensive.

What's the vital area?

Is there an alternative? The entrepreneur using guerilla tactics says yes. One entrepreneur with a strong background in catering to the restaurant business knew the vital area, that friendly, quick service and quality food were critical for success. He wanted to open a specialty, healthy, fast food restaurant in Southern California and his price point would be almost double that of a McDonalds. With adequate, but limited resources, he had to be good and he had to work through the kitchen logistics in a hurry.

How was he to address the two challenges? How could he quickly and effectively train a new kitchen staff and fill his restaurant with customers upon opening?

Solution: a guerrilla tactic

Give it away.

The young entrepreneur decided to invite individuals and groups that would create excitement and draw attention to his new restaurant. He began four days prior to opening and first invited the tenants that shared the shopping center in which he was located to come in for a free lunch. Who was going to pass up a free lunch? The price was right and so he received nothing but praises. In return, he asked that they place a small sign near their cash register announcing his grand opening. They graciously agreed. As a result, every shopper in the center would be aware of his restaurant. His primary benefit was that training had begun in the kitchen using real customers.

Create a scene.

Three days before opening, he invited the local fire departments to come any time from 11:00am to 7:00pm for a free meal. His only requirement was that they come in their fire trucks. Many fire trucks pulling up in front of his restaurant clearly grabbed people's attention—the new restaurant was gaining recognition. At the same time, the kitchen logistics were improving and internal problems were being resolved. Faster order time and better food and service were the result.

Invite locals.

On the second day prior to his official opening, the entrepreneur invited the regional police department to his restaurant. As long as they came in a police car, any individual on duty could receive a free lunch or dinner any time that day. Again, the kinks in the process were being ironed out.

The day before he opened, he was confident that the food was improving and customer awareness was increasing. His final "free lunch" visitors were the local ambulance companies. Once again, he built awareness and logistics were now perfected.

Close to breakeven in one day.

Opening day came with receipts that reached ninety percent of his breakeven sales point. His first day volume equaled what he had projected for six months later. What could have taken many months and thousands of dollars in operating losses, occurred within four days. His total cost for the four days was less than $10,000 for the food and labor.

Find ways to hunt in the beginning.

The message is simple, even in the resource-intense restaurant business and an area in which you are dependent upon your customer's actions to make a sale (fishing), guerrilla tactics can be employed to hunt for your first customers.

So, what are the most common ways that guerrilla tactics are employed by entrepreneurial startups? The number is unlimited and is as many as your imagination can create. Some of the most common are described below.

Offer free seminars

You are an expert, share your knowledge.

Changes in the marketplace occur on a regular basis and success for all parties is dependent on keeping current with what is happening. Assuming that you are "an expert" in your field, then information is available to you and it is likely that others, including potential customers, want that information. Giving something of value away (for free) will create awareness for your product or service. As a result, your potential customer will notice you and you will be closer to that customer.

An entrepreneur launched a consulting business in the area of environmental care and compliance. Her firm's specialty is to assist companies in their understanding of both the legislative mandates placed on them as well as their required actions to maintain compliance.

Cold calls were being stopped.

During the startup phase, her initial tactic was to cold call and direct mail to several regional firms, but she met with great resistance and little success. "Gatekeepers" stopped her calls and mailings were not answered.

Free seminar offer.

She decided to employ a different tactic and offered a three-hour seminar, free of charge, on changes in legislation affecting environmental standards for manufacturing companies. A simple, professional announcement was mailed to 100 firms in the area and twenty-two sent representatives.

Make potential customers aware.

As a result, all twenty-two firms are now aware of her consulting firm. Six of the attendees were sufficiently pleased with the benefits being offered by her start up that they turned into potential customers and two firms signed consulting contracts for work to be done. Her total cost including the mailing, the handout materials, the guest speaker, rental of the room, and coffee and donuts was under $2,000. A very creative solution to what could have otherwise been a significant advertising and awareness campaign.

Write articles for trade journals

Cost is your time.

Every industry has a trade journal as well as editors looking for insights into their industry by individuals and firms that have the ability and desire to share such content. The cost of writing an industry article is your time and the reward is free exposure and instant credibility.

Article doubles as marketing tool.

Your article becomes your marketing tool. Send reprints to target customers, which educates prospects of your expertise, credibility, and benefits. They then have the information needed to justify choosing you over a competitive firm.

The alternative to an article and direct mailing is mass advertising, which is very expensive. Such advertising is typically sent to many individuals not in your target profile or geographic area. Writing a trade journal article and sending it to prospective buyers is a time tested guerilla tactic.

Create excitement and enthusiasm

Spread your enthusiasm.

You are part of an exciting journey—the start up of a new company. You are in control of your destiny and passion and excitement for your work abound. It is contagious; everyone around you can feel it.

The majority of individuals with whom we communicate every day are without excitement or enthusiasm. On the phone or at a check out counter, we are greeted with a large dose of ho hum! People often appear bored and can even be rude.

Every word counts.

Because you are different and sincerely wish to service customers, meeting the public is pure joy for you. Even the way you say good morning will have an effect and attract potential customers. Smiling is a simple, cost free tactic that markets you and your company.

Build personal service

Personalization at every level.

Informing customers that they will deal with real people, not an impersonal company or a voice mail, will set you apart from the competition. Respond to a phone call by saying: "it's nice to hear from you." End a conversation with "it's a pleasure to do business with you" and it could be the difference between success and failure.

Establish personal relationships with customers.

As you have already learned, keep a diary and record your conversations. Learning something personal about those with whom you speak will be appreciated. Knowing when to ask about their vacation, their golf game, or how their child's soccer game went will endear them to you. Personalization is equated with trust. Customers will know that they can count on you and that you are not a cold, bureaucratic machine that shuts off at five o'clock when they need you most.

Sending a card or calling to say Happy Birthday will distinguish you from the pack.

> *"Some of the old-fashioned service techniques that we have instilled along with some new technology have really set us apart as a service company. One of the things you'll get when you call Superior Bankcard Service that you won't get when you call one of our competitors is you'll get a live person."*
>
> -Tim Jochner, EVP, Superior Bankcard Service

Establish integrity and build credibility

They can count on you!

Buyers are concerned about who will be there to assist them when something goes wrong. Inevitably, companies run into problems and knowing how someone will react in the worst possible situation is an important part of the buyer's decision. If you build trust, they will know they can count on you.

Be honest at all levels.

Achieving a comfort level is critical to your success. Building a sense of integrity and delivering what you promise will separate you from the pack. Simply returning a phone call when you said you would is important. When a customer asks how quickly you can deliver, be honest. If you cannot deliver within their time frame, tell them, even if it means foregoing that particular order. You want to make them aware that when you promise a delivery date, it will be met.

Not only should you develop a sense of comfort so that they know they can call if anything goes wrong, but you also want to exceed their expectations. Be one step better than you promised and have an attitude worthy of all entrepreneurs.

Maintain mind share

Consistently cross their desk.

As an entrepreneur one of your greatest challenges is maintaining awareness. If customers have a problem, your name must come to mind as having a solution. You do this through entrepreneurial guerrilla marketing.

It's important to cross their desk on a regular basis, which can be done in a variety of ways. We have already mentioned two—sending copies of ads or trade journal articles. Another alternative is to send quarterly newsletters filled with informative occurrences in their industry.

Get visible. Celebrate your successes with present and future customers by announcing your accomplishments, which can be anything from a significant new alliance formed, customer established, or a product milestone crossed. Sharing such events enhances your credibility and visibility as a leader in the industry.

Doesn't matter what you send. Competitors often send gifts, tickets to a ballgame, or some bright colored, attention-getter to customers, which are not bad either. Regardless of what you send, consistent personal contact with customers will reap the largest dividends. Don't just send something once and expect results.

Make personal calls. In your diary, you should track when contact has been made and when next contact should be made. If it has been ninety days since last contact, call the individual, but don't turn every call into a business call, make it a personal call. If they attempt to talk about business, try to change the subject and let them know you are calling to find out how they and their families are doing. If the conversation ends in business, fine. But if it doesn't, it may be even better because that individual will be pleased that you called to be personal.

Get referrals

Ask for the referral, don't expect it. The most expensive part of a start up is the cost of attracting and solidifying relationships with customers. Once you successfully meet the needs of an existing customer who thanks you for your efforts, you should first say "thank you." Your second immediate reaction should be to ask for a referral. If they are satisfied or their expectations were exceeded, they will have no problem making an introduction to another that needs your services. A credible introduction to a potential customer is more likely to close a sale than any amount of advertising or marketing. The best part is that it's free.

> *"To establish a solid relationship with my customer, it took some time. It took a lot of personal meetings, to show them that we were not working just for the profit and that we want to build a long term relationship with them."*
> -Miguel DeLeon, President, DeLeon Enterprises

A Favorite Guerrilla Tactic

How do you reach the president of a mid-sized or large company? How do you get to the decision-makers to inform them that your fledgling start up is alive, is capable of meeting their needs, and wants to do business? How do you get past the gatekeepers at the reception desk or the administrative assistant that runs blocker?

One successful entrepreneur found a way. He determined that six minutes was all he needed with the president of a firm to share why his startup could service that president's needs. He knew that six minutes would not close any deal; so, his goal was to get either a return phone call or for a phone call he made to be answered.

His approach was unique. Intrigued by the technology of miniature VCR players, he figured most people would also find them interesting and bought several. After recording a professional, six-minute message addressed to the president, the small player was loaded and put into a box with a very simple, hand written card that said, I really believe this is worth six minutes of your time, please press play. An administrator couldn't ignore or throw this away and the president almost always received the tape and pushed play.

The entrepreneur had gotten through, his message was being heard. A very high percentage of presidents either placed or received a phone call. An even higher than normal percentage either agreed to a face to face meeting or arranged for a meeting with the appropriate person inside of the company. The total cost of breaking through barriers and getting to the president was a $622.00 VCR.

The back of the instruction card had a return address and a request that after the message was heard, the VCR be returned. The entrepreneur's accountants argued that this was a silly and expensive tactic, reasoning that individuals would keep the VCR and sales would not result. The entrepreneur on the other hand was thinking outside the box and knew that if the VCR wasn't returned, it would still be cheaper than the cost of a plane ticket for a salesman to visit.

Every VCR sent was returned. A guerrilla tactic par excellence.

Writing The Entrepreneurial Marketing Plan

Focus thoughts and vision in plan.

Being an entrepreneur does not give you the right to be a loose canon. On the contrary, entrepreneurs are extremely focused and have a keen sense of priorities. Writing a marketing plan helps to structure thoughts, provides a framework for action, and expands communication within the company.

Ask everybody for opinions.

The largest benefit that derives from writing a plan is the exercise itself. Before actually putting pen to paper, you must solicit input and insights from associates, which can be done anytime, even during a simple one-hour coffee break prior to work some morning. Involving the entire company in the planning process not only enables you to communicate your goals for the upcoming year or years, but also to incorporate ideas you may not have considered into the plan. Investing the time into asking for opinions and communicating goals will cement the culture that you have been building. Having the chance to provide input means that your associates are committing to delivery of the output.

Don't write a promo plan.

As detailed in classic texts, most marketing plans quickly boil down to promotional plans and identify the level of, efficiency of, and return on the expenditure of advertising, public relations, and in many cases new product development dollars. These are plans based on the 4 P's, and not an entrepreneurial approach. So, what specifically should your plan include? Only a select number of topics should get your attention.

Components of the marketing plan

Who is your customer?

Plan is a roadmap.

The entrepreneurial marketing plan is essentially a roadmap that leads you from your current position in the market to your targeted point of accomplishment. On that map must be a clear definition of your customer because there is not a goal in business that can be achieved without a customer. It is only through customers that accomplishments are made.

It's not a sales forecast.

Be careful not to confuse the marketing plan with a sales forecast. A sales forecast is part of the overall marketing and financial strategy, but it is not the explicit goal of either.

Customer is king.

In the marketing plan, review both existing customers and the potential customer base and then define how to expand your niche to gain additional customers. Identify your accomplishments to date, highlighting the characteristics of your current customers, including why they purchase from you. Then, identify the entire customer base, with a focus on those customers giving business to your competitors as well as changes that might be occurring in the marketplace that could affect purchase habits.

How will you make your customers aware of you?

Use guerrilla tactics.

Everyone can shine in this section because it is the essence of entrepreneurship— how do I reach and close customers? Critical to this discussion, particularly in the early start up stage, will be the inclusion of as many guerrilla tactics previously

Establish your brand.

discussed as possible. Solidify your commitment and that of your associates to personal relationship building, enthusiasm in dealing with customers, and allegiance to the motto that the customer is king. A unified thrust to how your company's name will be shared with the marketplace is the final challenge. You are sowing the seeds for branding.

How will you reach your customer?

Don't get stuck in a rut.

Society is constantly changing and daily demands often prohibit us from making necessary internal changes. Reasonable success with a direct mail campaign or a telemarketing campaign leaves you reluctant to stop that effort. But you must experiment and maintain the culture of your start up in which trial and error is embraced. Try something different or try the same things in a different way. Perhaps this is the year that you hire sales agents and representatives from other parts of the country to sell your products or services. Or, maybe it is time to seriously consider ecommerce or Internet opportunities for your company.

Full and current knowledge of all potential channels available, detailed information about the sales channels used by competitors, and being aware of successful new channels being introduced are an important part of your written marketing plan and your ultimate marketing strategy.

What benefits will you offer?

Why you?

Why do customers buy from you? What is your vital area? What does your product or service offer that will make or has made it successful? Equally important is to consider why potential customers may choose the competition instead of you. Are there valid reasons that you can address? Or, is it simply price or geographic location differentials against which you elect not to compete?

How do the customers in your marketplace buy?

Why not a competitor?

To many entrepreneurs this is the ultimate definition of industry knowledge. To every successful salesman, it is perhaps the most important question. What is the basis by which a potential client chooses between your company and another company? How do your customers rank their priorities? Is price really first and all else doesn't matter? Is there value placed on experience, service, industry reputation, and market share? Who has to approve what and at what price? Who can agree to hire the best supplier, not the lowest priced supplier?

Embrace failure.

Part of your annual marketing plan must explore each of these questions in depth. Without feedback from customers that don't buy, you lack a clear picture of how your company is viewed in the market. Learning from a short-term failure can often be more important than celebrating success.

Get an objective view.

A good tactic that lends credibility to your plan is to get a third party (with a good reputation) to review and perhaps make direct contact with potential customers that did not materialize. An unbiased opinion regarding what you are, are not, and should be doing can be very valuable.

Is this a worthy opponent, a worthy business?

Does this fit your model business?

On an annual basis, you should reevaluate the questions asked at the start of your business. What is your market niche? What is its size? What does the primary research (contact with clients and potential clients) tell you? What does the secondary research (libraries, the Internet, etc.) tell you? Has your penetration improved, but the target shifted?

Highlight changes in your niche.

Only by answering these questions can you decide whether or not you are still playing on the right part of the battlefield. Has the niche you sought really moved? Have you moved with it? Have you really determined where the market is headed or are you catching up to where it was and finding entrenched competition? The makeup and size of your niche are critical components that need to be clearly identified in your marketing plan.

> *A corny definition between sales and marketing is that marketing does what selling can't do and vice versa. Or marketing makes the sales person's job easier. Or marketing is the planning function and the support function behind personal selling and you can't do one without the other. An entrepreneur who goes out and makes personal sales calls is doing something vital to that particular enterprise, but if he or she does this without a marketing plan, it's just making sales calls."*
> -William H. Crookston, WHC Associates

Entrepreneurial Exercise

For this exercise, you are going to start to think about your own entrepreneurial marketing plan. In hte spaces below, answer each of the questions in the greatest detail possible.

1. Who is your customer?

   _____

   _____

   _____

2. How will you make your customers aware of you?

   _____

   _____

   _____

3. How will you reach your customer?

   _____

   _____

   _____

4. What benefits will you offer?

   _____

   _____

   _____

5. How do the customers in your marketplace buy?

   _____

   _____

   _____

⇒ **Tear out and move to your entrepreneurial road map binder.**

Chapter Summary

Entrepreneurial marketing differs from classic marketing in a variety of ways that we have explored. As you seek to define your entrepreneurial marketing plan, be sure to keep your advantages in mind. Do not be shy and celebrate your smallness.

Comparing and contrasting the classic marketers view of the 4 P's with the entrepreneurial approach provides evidence for the effectiveness of an entrepreneur's approach.

As you cogitate the components of your marketing plan, keep the following questions in mind:

- Who is your customer?
- How will you make your customers aware of you?
- How will you reach your customers?
- What benefits will you offer?
- How do the customers in your marketplace buy?
- Is this a worthy opponent, a worthy business?

Include as many guerilla tactics in your plan as possible and always be thinking of unique and innovative ways to make potential customers aware of your product or service.

Chapter Seven Exercises/Discussion Questions

1. Discuss the difference between the ways traditional companies and entrepreneurs view marketing.
2. Think of creative ways other entrepreneurial ventures marketed their products or services.
3. Consider some guerrilla tactics you could use in your business. Discuss.
4. Start a diary of information on your potential customers. Learn how and why they buy.
5. Discuss the benefits of being new and small and think of some real world examples of the advantages.

Journey Seven: Cardinal Laboratories

Cardinal Laboratories is a chemical manufacturing facility that produces a specialty line of animal care products, including shampoos, conditioners, skin care, and eye care. When the company had difficulty getting retailers to recognize its products, Tony de Vos, president, told his marketing staff that in order to survive, sales revenues needed to increase by millions of dollars. His marching orders were "to create something different."

Finding Innovation

Whether she was fully aware of it or not, Barbara Denzer, Vice President of Marketing, was given this challenge of employing entrepreneurial tactics. Rather than look to resources for new product development, she had to innovate. "He (de Vos) was pretty open to what the product was or what the innovation was, but we had very strict parameters in terms of what we could manufacture in this plant, what our budget was, and where our market was."

In addition to the normal challenges of increasing sales, Cardinal also faced fierce competition in a pet-care market already saturated with suppliers.

Denzer began her quest for innovation by gathering market information. As she states, "it's mostly knowing the competition, knowing what's out there, understanding all the products that are on the market now, and finding a niche that nobody has addressed."

Denzer went out into the market and began observing. She paced the aisles in retail stores, examined the products, analyzed what was available, and assessed what was missing. She noticed that most products had pictures of live animals and seemed to be quite serious in nature, not a characteristic she associated with pets. "My point of view is, no matter how bad my life is going, when I come home and my Rufus comes running toward me wagging his tail because he's so glad to see me, it's a good part of my life. It seems to me that this is the good part of everybody's life and something that we should be celebrating."

Crazy Pet

She then had to translate this instinct into something that could be put on the shelf. She felt the new products needed to have a character, a mascot of sorts. So, she discussed her thoughts and observations with the graphic designer, brought samples of designs she liked, and stressed the importance of certain colors. As they went through the design process, everyone involved seemed enamored with "this one crazy little dog." After gravitating toward this dog over and over again, Denzer finally realized that this was her character—crazy dog.

de Vos was skeptical at first stating that "my gosh, my grandchild could draw this character." Fortunately, he allowed the creativity to flourish and the initial crazy pet shampoos and other grooming items were received quite well by the retailers. As de Vos recalls, this led to the next challenge, "we said, gee, this is an unlimited opportunity, but how do we get there? We wanted to build a brand. But, when you have no resources, that can be a very difficult task."

Innovation in Expansion

So, Barbara had to figure out how to expand her product line, still with limited resources. She knew she wanted her brand name on other products, but needed a way to make that happen. The only thing she could think of was to pool resources and "somehow convince them to put my label on their products." The increasing competition from the larger, chain stores led Barbara to believe that working together would appeal to the smaller companies in the same position as Cardinal.

Her first challenge was to convince her boss of this idea. She recalls, "hands down, across the board, everyone thought I was crazy." However, persistence and determination paid off and Denzer was able to convince de Vos of the potential of her innovative marketing concept.

Approval in-hand, Barbara called a meeting of several smaller companies and explained her concept. Knowing that they were all being hurt by the big chains who preferred to work with the larger manufacturers, Denzer figured that if they were six smaller companies working together, they could effectively compete with the big guys.

Crazy Pet LLC

The plan was a success. The limited number of items that Cardinal was getting onto the shelves turned into more than 50 new products distributed under the crazy pet brand name. Cardinal would approve the other companies' products, which would then sell the products and pay a royalty fee to what became a new company—the Crazy Pet Limited Liability Corporation.

The new cooperative branding effort was not only a sales success, it was also a public relations coup for Denzer and Cardinal Laboratories. "We had the thrill of being chosen as Inc. Magazine's marketer of the year in 1997, which was really a thrill," remembers Denzer.

Barbara Denzer's concept, Crazy Pet, was a perfect solution for a small manufacturing company that faced increased competition in the pet supply industry.

Journey Seven Case Questions

1. How did Denzer utilize entrepreneurial tactics in her marketing scheme?
2. How was her approach different from how a large company might operate in a similar situation?
3. What was her growth strategy?
4. Did Denzer exhibit entrepreneurial characteristics? If so, which ones?

Chapter Eight
How Do I Sell?

Chapter Eight Major Concepts

- The classic 5 step distribution channel
- Changing channels
- How will you sell?
- How do you approach sales?

Journey Eight: Hard Candy

Up Front & Personal: Trick R/C

Distribution and Sales Channels

Distribution and sales tool kits.

As an entrepreneur your tool kit is growing. You have a clear definition of a concept and know that entrepreneurship is not about the idea but about testing a concept, which is a clear articulation of a customer, the channels by which to reach that customer, and the benefit provided to that customer.

In this chapter we will explore distribution and sales channels, which are the ways that entrepreneurs first reach and then transfer goods and services to their clients.

Distribution can mean opportunity.

The center of the concept grid, the sales and distribution channel, is the area of greatest opportunity to folks in the entrepreneurial world because it is an arena of creativity. In many industries customers are already clearly defined and the competition is doing whatever it can to reach and hold on to its customer base. Benefit needs of these customers are also well defined. This is especially true in maturing industries where innovation and minimal changes to a product's features are more the norm than is innovation.

Entire industries can be created.

The sales and distribution channel has also been defined by competitors, but this is where entrepreneurs can thrive. By changing the sales and distribution channel, entrepreneurs can change and create an entire new industry.

Pattern of change.

Of the most prevalent patterns of change today, shortening the distribution channel, or the distance between the customer and the desired benefit, is the most prolific. It has been the primary pattern of change that marked the 1990's and will continue to do so well into the 20th century.

More new companies have been created by changes in the distribution channel than are created by new products or services. Just look around you. Consider how things have changed over the past several years.

The changing world of flowers

Flower sales have even changed.

Until twenty years ago, 95% of all flower sales were on a relational basis. Your mother and grandmother had a favorite florist who knew them, what they liked, and what they wanted to spend. This represents the perfect profile of a relationship customer, one that has been built over time. But retail stores could not maintain that customer. As our world began to expand, our friends and families spread out and we had the need to deliver flowers all over the country. Beginning with FTD, the number of sales that occurred outside of the retail florist shop expanded.

Benefit remains the same.

Today if we were to build a simple working concept grid for flowers, the customer profile would likely be the same, that is, the end consumer. The nature of flowers or the features, such as additional arrangement options and the way flowers are packaged, have and will continue to change but the benefit of beautiful flowers remains a constant.

What has changed and what is exciting are the many ways that flowers are sold—changes in the sales and distribution channels. See the working concept grid on the next page as an example.

Working Concept Grid for Flower Sales

Customer	Sales/Distribution Channel	Benefit
general consumer	Internet	beautiful flowers
	Florist	
	Flower of the month club – mail	
	Flower of the month club – phone	
	Grocery store	
	Shopping mall kiosk	
	Airport kiosk	
	Street corner vendor	

Many distribution options.

Reviewing the selling of flowers reveals that flowers can be purchased in many, many places. They can be purchased on the Internet, from the "Flower of the Month Club" via mail or telephone, in a grocery store, at a kiosk in a shopping center or an airport, and they can be bought from a vendor on a busy street corner.

Home delivery of flowers!

One very bright entrepreneur found an entirely new industry through weekly home delivery of flowers. Every Thursday morning, he delivers fresh flowers to the homes on his route, which are those of upscale families. In the morning, as his customers retrieve their morning newspaper from the front stoop, they also receive the flowers that have been carefully left on their doorstep. His customer's home will be properly decorated for the upcoming weekend.

> *"There are over 22 million people in America who are involved in industrial or commercial selling, not retail. So, there are a whole bunch of people out there who are behind the lines, involved in one-to-one calling on customers, calling on buyers, making transactions happen. Hopefully, they are developing clients who will repeatedly buy thereby bringing the manufacturer's goods through the distribution channels to the next eventual user or in some cases all the way down to the consumer."*
> -William H. Crookston, WHC Associates

The coming change in distribution

Only constant is change.

Entrepreneurs are extremely excited when there is change in a marketplace. Chaos and confusion create opportunity. The core competencies of certain companies have now become their liabilities. In a world of change the only constant is change. How big are distribution changes? How big are changes in the sales channels? To understand this source of opportunity, we need to review the past and understand the value chain of how a product got to market just a generation ago.

To do so, we can again look at flower sales, but this same model also applies to many other items including refrigerators, most household goods, and other daily products.

Entrepreneurial Exercise

Think about the product or service you would like to offer in your new venture and answer the following questions to get you thinking in terms of the variety of distribution channels that may exist for your offering. Be creative!

Who is your target customer?

_____

What is your benefit offering?

_____

How many distribution channels can you identify?

1. _____

2. _____

3. _____

4. _____

5. _____

6. _____

7. _____

8. _____

9. _____

10. _____

$\Rightarrow$ **Tear out and move to your entrepreneurial road map binder.**

The Classic 5 Step Channel

Manufacturer ➔

Manufacturer starts the process.

The product you purchase starts with a manufacturer. You must also recognize that even the manufacturer is a consumer. A distribution channel also exists for manufacturers so that they can purchase the products and services needed to assemble their products.

However, the first step of the classic distribution channel is the manufacturer or producer. In the floral example, it is the grower. For a refrigerator, it is the company that builds the refrigerator. Historically, depending upon the nature of the industry, the manufactured product is sold either through an agent or a distributor.

Manufacturer ➔ Agent\Distributor ➔

Agents can add value.

Agents exist because they have contacts with the next step in the distribution channel. Their value add is the consolidation of their fragmented contact's requirements and coordination of purchases for the manufacturer they represent. In certain industries these agents have ultimate control. A mid-sized grower of flowers may not have the margins or level of expertise needed to build and maintain a sales force that could sell directly to their customers. As a result, agents hold them captive.

Agent supplies personal contact, which is needed.

In the manufacturing arena, this step in the channel is often known as a distributor and, depending on the nature of the particular industry, the distributor falls before or after the wholesaler. Initially, sales requires face-to-face contact and therefore the need for an agent\distributor. Accessibility, new communication tools, and the relative ease and prevalence of travel have diminished this need, which is why it has been one of the first channel points to be eliminated. However, it is still prevalent in certain industries.

Manufacturer ➔ Agent\Distributor ➔ Wholesaler ➔

Wholesalers provide credit.

The agent's customer is the wholesaler. The major value add of the wholesaler is that they are responsible for credit (they purchase goods from the manufacturer) and maintain inventory in key geographic locations throughout the United States or the world. It is the wholesaler who is then prepared to satisfy the retail store needs. Occasionally, this includes other value-added services, such as training the retailer's personnel in function or the coordination of regional sales events.

They manage inventory.

This value-add of credit and inventory responsibility by the wholesalers can be of significant value to a manufacturer. Without credit, manufacturers would have to carry huge amounts of debt as they finance the sale through the channel. Without regional inventory supplies, manufacturers are at a disadvantage because their customer—the retail outlet—would have a limited selection of inventory to offer. The wholesaler brings this significant value add to the table. By having a distribution point in the channel (regional inventory supply), the manufacturer is willing to forego some profit while the retail outlet pays more. A distribution point—either an agent or a wholesaler—could add up to 20% to the cost to the end consumer.

What was Magnavox's key to success?

Historically, some companies found that they could increase market share through these classic sales and distribution channels. In the mid-1970's, large consumer electronic stores had not yet become standard. Televisions, for example, were sold in regional stores throughout the country. Magnavox was among the leading suppliers of high-end televisions. Despite what was claimed as superior manufacturing, Magnavox's key to success was a distribution channel that avoided the cost of the agent or wholesaler. The company built a large in-house distribution channel and guaranteed its retail dealers that they could have any television set they wanted delivered in 72 hours directly from the factory. No middle man, no added cost. At the time, it was unheard of to avoid the classic distribution channel.

Lots of trucks.

As such, Magnavox had a complicated logistical problem to conquer. Its manufacturing and assembly came from Fort Wayne. Some clients were in California. How could the company promise a 72-hour delivery? By using 270 trucks that were constantly moving. Trucks to key geographic locations left every hour or two depending on distance, whether they were full or not. The dealers profited more on the Magnavox set because it cost less, but was still high-end. Magnavox didn't have to forgo profit to the middleman.

Savings passed onto consumer.

The cost of such an enterprise, the personnel and equipment, had to be staggering. In 1975, Magnavox's return on investment was one of the top ten of American corporations. They must have saved a great deal through this channel innovation.

Manufacturer ➡ Agent\Distributor ➡ Wholesaler ➡ **Retailer** ➡

Wholesaler controlled the channel.

The small size of retailers' orders and/or the limitations of space and credit to carry inventory left no alternative other than to use a wholesaler to purchase goods. As a result, the wholesaler was in the order fulfillment business for the retailer and thereby controlled the channel.

Super stores became the norm.

Wholesaler dominance of the channel began to change as the super retail stores came into existence. This movement was led by companies like Toys R Us and spread into all industries, especially sporting goods, electronics, and home repair and supplies, and the channel was eliminated. In return for reduced price, one-stop shopping, and vast product choice, consumers no longer benefited from relationship-based purchases with much hand holding and advice. Instead, they entered retail outlets that were impersonal and had a find-it-yourself, carry-home environment.

They held manufacturers hostage.

With such a large volume, these large super retail stores were able to hold manufacturers hostage. Representing such a large portion of the manufacturer's revenue, they could demand (and get) lower prices on goods purchased, advertising credits, stocking or shelving fees, and rebate programs.

Successful mass merchandisers became channel kings.

Manufacturer ➜ Agent\Distributor ➜ Wholesaler ➜ Retailer ➜ **Consumer**

Cost is added with each step.

Last but not least is you, the consumer. You are the person who walks into retail shops and purchase goods or services that you need. Historically, your flowers or your refrigerator arrived after travelling through five steps of distribution.

Each step takes time, money, and resources. A product that was manufactured for $1.00, transferred through an agent for a 20% to 30% commission for maintaining contacts, bearing a credit risk, and delivering the product to a wholesaler, could cost you $1.30.

Mark ups are significant.

The wholesaler needs a profit in the same magnitude, which means that the product arrived at the retailer 30% higher than at the wholesaler (for carrying the credit risk and maintaining inventory). As such, the retailer's direct cost of goods (varying with freight charges) was in the neighborhood of $1.75. Depending upon the nature of the retail shop, its overhead, and cost of doing business, the norm is for that price to double before being sold to you, the end consumer.

Cost of channel is majority of price.

In this simple illustration, that which was manufactured for a $1.00 (with material costs of probably 50 cents) will cost you, the retail consumer, $3.50. $2.50 of this $3.50 sales price (or nearly 70%) came from the cost of the channel.

How to reduce costs?

At a time when credit was not easily obtainable or when it was difficult to find information on your customers, then each step in the channel added value. Additionally, when there was inventory exposure and responsibility for logistics of shipping, delivering, and accepting bad products, then each of these steps provided a valuable and necessary benefit. However, the cost of doing all of this is prohibitive. Clearly such a structure is a point of opportunity for the entrepreneur.

The Changing Channels

Channels must change.

Changes in channels have had the most dramatic effect on the consumer. As a result of consumer sophistication and access to information, channels are being eliminated and manufacturers are seeking to serve consumers directly, both by their own volition and because they are being forced to do so by margin pressure.

Value added is lessened with industry maturity.

Consider the ramifications of buying a television just two decades ago versus buying one today. Under the successful Magnavox strategy, the consumer felt a need for education and assistance with choice, set-up, and delivery. The same was true of the computer in the mid-1980s and of satellite-based television in the 1990s. The common thread among these examples is that as an industry matures, the value-added from each channel becomes less. When that channel no longer contributes, it is eliminated.

Internet opportunity is endless.

The movement to reach a consumer without the cost of a channel is not new. Direct sales and catalogs have sold certain specialty items for some time. Currently, today's excitement is the Internet, the reality of this new marvelous communication medium is that its business application is endless. The essence of the value added of the Internet is that this channel takes us from supplier to customer in one step.

Can increase margins and decrease cost.

Look at the same manufacturer who would sell you a product today on the Internet. There is certainly additional cost by selling directly to the consumer. But that additional cost is not as much of a markup as what the consumer would experience if the product traveled through the five traditional channels. Today, many manufacturers have found ways to spend a portion of that margin thereby increasing their final margins and at the same time decreasing the cost of sales to you the consumer.

PC industry.

Think about the often-cited example of the personal computer being manufactured and transferred through the classic distribution channels to see how far we have come. Today it is possible to order directly from the manufacturer (Gateway or Dell) and have your computer shipped directly to you, the consumer. The difference is that a good deal of overhead is removed and the result is a more competitive computer manufacturer and a more satisfied consumer.

Determine your own strategy.

Why then should we study the classic distribution channels? The answer is simple. Every entrepreneur will be dependent upon a sales and distribution channel. Understanding the many possible steps will allow you to first establish what is the best way to reach your consumer and then to decide at which point you should sell. Should your customer be the wholesaler? Will you sell to a retailer or directly to the consumer? Who is your customer? Answering that question allows you to decide where to begin your penetration and where to grow as your volume increases.

How Will You Sell?

Every company's future depends upon its ability to attract customers. As you well know by now, you are not in business until you have a customer.

Lots of options.

What are alternative ways to reach customers? How can you educate, inform, qualify, and close sales with those customers? There are many options. A few of the most prominent follow.

Sales Channels You Control

Direct sales by you

People take a chance on you.

As we have shared throughout, one of the many ways entrepreneurs distinguish themselves from managers is by starting ventures in stages. The first stage entails going from an idea to a first customer and the most common way of reaching that first customer is by selling yourself. People are likelier to take a chance on you than on a product or service. People will believe you before they will believe in your product or service. The burden of selling yourself to get to those early customers will always be on the shoulders of you, the entrepreneur.

Burden is yours.

It is not acceptable to be the driving force in a start up venture and not be responsible for sales. If your company is technical in nature and you are not, this can be to your advantage because it means you can sell without the obstacle of delving into technical details. Your team will handle that aspect on your behalf, but you must control when, how, and by whom those technical questions are answered.

Continuously learning of needs.

An additional benefit of personal selling by you is that you will learn customers needs. You need to adapt, be resilient, and create policies as you proceed. It is only through listening to your potential customer's feedback that you can provide the vision for your start up. What is your position if someone tells you that your product didn't resell and he or she wants to return it? How does that fit into your future growth plans and your choice of a distribution channel? If your customer says your product was damaged or that it didn't function as promised, what is your policy? Will you return for credit? Will you return for cash? If your product is not selling through, what seems to be wrong with it? Is it being displayed in a way that makes sales difficult, if not impossible? Is it in the right type of shop, in the right location, and in the right town?

Identify the policy.

By nature, almost everything that entrepreneurs do is evolutionary and so is the sales process and technique. You need to be extremely close to it to guide its evolution.

> *"I like talking to my customers and I like knowing if my product is selling or not. Does it sell when it's warmer? I like knowing why it's selling or why it's not and I like talking to the customers. Especially, I like hearing that they love our line, etc., which is great. But I also like knowing if there is a problem and being able to call the customer and saying ok, I'll call you back and I'll have a solution for you."*
>
> -Kim Camarella, Founder, Kiyonna Klothing

Direct sales force

Growing pains.

As your company expands you, the entrepreneur will experience a severe growing pain. You will need to be positioned one step removed from your customer and a sales force comprised of highly trained professionals will need to take over. They are not you. They cannot sell like you and they cannot imitate you. You need to educate them about your vision and share your techniques, but you must also realize that in the long run you are not in control, they are. As such, you need to incentivize them both financially and emotionally and provide them with the best available selling tools. Becoming dependent upon someone other than yourself to sell means that your world is changing and this needs to be a positive change—leverage your accomplishments and your firm and take it to the next level.

Can you afford a sales force?

Often, a direct sales force is not the best solution or may not be a tactic you can afford. We have shared earlier that a cost of $75,000 to $150,000 per year is what it takes to keep a professional sales person on the road selling your products and services. This means that each sales person must sell between $750,000 and $1,500,000 to cover the portion of your sales price allotted for sales expense. That's a big quota and you need to be assured of success before hiring such individuals, which means you are expecting three-quarters to one and a half million in sales. Otherwise, if your sales team is not successful, then you won't be successful.

Tough transition point.

Transitioning from a single entrepreneur selling himself, his credibility, and his passion to creating a group of trained sales people is a major change and many entrepreneurial companies have failed at this transition point. Before proceeding in this fashion, consider some of the alternatives available to you.

Non-Individual Dependent Sales

Be innovative.

Entrepreneurial companies like to use various unique distribution channels because they provide tremendous cost benefits. If the most expensive part of a sales team is the team, then consider the alternative of sales without people or at a minimum, sales without people on the road. There are several very common methods used to sell without incurring the cost of a sales person or the cost of travelling.

Direct marketing

Professional approach.

The initial reaction is often "oh no, not more junk mail." But, not all direct marketing needs to be junk mail. First understand what you are seeking to accomplish, which is finding a cost efficient means of exposing yourself to potential customers. The goal may be to get a person-to-person phone call or to determine whether or not any low hanging fruit—an easy sale—exists.

Not junk mail.

Direct mail need not be junk mail. A well written, personalized letter with a hand written note at the bottom addressed to the appropriate target in a corporation is a guerrilla tactic that has allowed many sales persons to receive a phone call or an in-person meeting. Many companies today are spending inordinate amounts of money on brochures. While this may not be the launch point for an entrepreneurial venture, it certainly demonstrates that it is better to spend money in this fashion than it is to attempt to harvest customers through a direct sales force.

Telemarketing

Again, be professional.

The initial reaction is always "oh no, not another phone solicitation." Telemarketing during the dinner hour selling subscriptions or burial plots is not necessarily the only form of telemarketing. Many companies have chosen telemarketing as their primary sales channel and use a very professional sales staff. Prior qualification and forwarding of information, follow-up to advertisements inside of appropriate professional magazines, and targeted at particular and specialized niches is the way to telemarket professionally.

How to telemarket successfully?

Some of the more successful examples are seen with medical implant and surgical equipment companies whose customer base is limited to a select number of medical doctors. The sales person must have a great deal of industry and product background. The individuals that they call have limited time, are usually not available during normal hours, and need to be kept current about changes in their industry. A combination of a direct mailing piece highlighting such changes and a professional telemarketing plan offering to share information with that customer, at their convenience, have proven to be very efficient and very controllable sales channels when targeted at customers with known and determined benefits.

Does another channel make sense?

In order to expand the company both geographically and in volume, alternative distribution channels will be needed. Often a telemarketing program is a necessary part of your sales strategy and is required in order to attract potential customers. The fact that the entrepreneur has had initial success selling to a consumer does not mean that the product, pricing, or benefit will make sense in a different sales channel. Telemarketing calls to retailers who would carry your product and to distributors who would supply retailers are valid sales channels that should not be overlooked.

Be consistent in strategy.

It is important to build your support materials to match the way you are going to present your benefit. A campaign to reach a distributor or retailer might start with a direct mail piece showing pictures of the product and how it might be presented in a store. This might be coupled with a telemarketing campaign to explore the benefits, the price points, the margins, and the purchasing requirements. With adequate interest, the final step may be a promise to send a sample for display to establish customer and consumer interest. Combining direct mail and a tele-marketing campaign are effective means by which a non-people dependent sales channel can function.

Reworking your concept grid

Keep working your concept grid.

What we are describing here boils down to the fact that entrepreneurs continue to change and expand their working concept grid, which is a listing of all potential customers and all potential means of reaching those customers. With a better understanding of distribution, we know that customers are not only the consumers of products and services, but they can also serve as any and all points in the distribution channel. Customers can be sales reps, marketing organizations, retailers, wholesalers, distributors, or manufacturers of the product. Entrepreneurs understand that each point in this value chain represents a new opportunity with a different challenge, price point, and selling need.

Target selling with different channels.

Further, it is not abnormal to use multiple channels segmented for each customer. For example, you could be selling directly to large retailers of your product while also using distributors to get to the smaller, more geographically diverse retailers that you could not otherwise reach. At the same time you may be using mass merchandisers who employ their own direct mail or catalogs to sell your products along with others.

Entrepreneurs must take advantage of each and every opportunity presented by the large variety of sales and distribution channels.

Trade shows

Large audience.

Educating and qualifying customers without a direct sales force can also be accomplished at trade shows where it is possible to share your benefits with a large number of potential customers. Since they are attending the trade show, you already know of their interest in your industry. You are both at that trade show for a reason.

Benefits of trade show.

Sitting behind your booth provides multiple opportunities. First, your presence both on the floor and in the program informs attendees of your offering. Although it's a crowded environment and mind share is difficult, your presence is known. Furthermore, in the future, you can mention your booth when calling on prospects. Indicating that you met at a trade show or suggesting a meeting at an upcoming show are effective and efficient means of gaining credibility.

Augment other channels.

Trade shows can also reinforce other sales channels if you are already reaching attendees through direct mail or telemarketing campaigns. Inexpensively, you can inform customers of your attendance and indicate your desire to arrange a meeting to help make their lives easier. This enables you to build personal relationships through face-to-face contact without incurring the cost of a direct sales force. How you use this tactic is, of course, dependent upon the nature of the product or service that you provide.

Customers approach you.

Secondly, being behind the booth allows interested attendees to approach you. They may have received your flier or seen your name in an industry article and don't quite understand your product or service. This provides you with the opportunity to educate them about your firm. A transaction will only occur if they know what you can provide and how they can benefit from your offering. Trade shows are an efficient format in which to do that.

Offer special viewing.

Additionally, pre-mailing notices of your attendance at a trade show gives you one more reason to cross the desk of a potential vendor. Finally, inviting certain prospects to a special, private showing of a new product or service is a great selling tactic used at trade shows.

Infomercials

Can be effective.

There was a time when infomercials represented a small if not immeasurable portion of available sales channels. However, they have gained recognition and can be effectively used to introduce new products. In some segments of the market, infomercials are even beginning to challenge catalogs for selling everything from shampoo to exercise equipment. Success is evident by the number of infomercials in the marketplace, but keep in mind that just as with every sales channel, they don't work for all products and are only useful for certain products at certain price and cost points.

Internal use as well.

It is also common today to see entrepreneurial startups spend a modest amount of money building a 5, 7, or 12 minute infomercial for their own use. Such a video piece will cost under $5,000 and can be used as a direct mailer to a targeted customer. An infomercial seen on a national network or used to educate and qualify potential customers is an important tool as a sales channel.

Sales Channels You Don't Control

Control can be an issue.

Thus far, we have focused on classic distribution channels and the modern changes occurring within them and in every example the entrepreneur was either directly or indirectly in control of the channel. When selling yourself, through a sales force, direct mail, telemarketing, or any combination thereof, you have control. Even with trade shows and infomercials as part of your sales tool kit, you are still in control of sales.

But as your company grows, the time will come when you must explore other sales channels that you will not control. There are several alternative avenues available that allow you to reach segments of your market without having direct control.

Among the new and exciting ways that people are selling include the following:

Value Added Reseller (VAR)

Is education or assistance needed?

If the nature of your product or service requires customer education as to individual needs and as to the functionality of your system, then a value-added reseller (VARs) may be the appropriate sales channel for your firm. VARs are independent firms that represent you; they know your products as well as those of other, similar companies and are able to combine such like products into a complete package/solution for the consumer.

Certain industries more attracted to VARs.

The nature of VARs differs. In certain industries, the VAR is a packager, educator, and implementer. In the sophisticated computer systems business, many companies have determined that a direct sales force cannot reach certain segments of their market for two reasons. First, the cost to identify and close a distant sale is prohibitive and second, if customers are smaller and do not have a complete staff or personnel capable of executing a complex system, then they will not buy. This is where a VAR is of value to you.

They build the relationship.

Both the potential customers (your consumers) and the supplier (you) may be best served by a relationship with VAR. That VAR, as the name implies, adds value to the resale by combining your product with hardware, with financing, with training, and with implementation assistance. They are often regionally located and have a working relationship with your potential customers. At times, especially at trade shows, you may team up with VARs to keep their understanding of your products and services current and to refer prospects to whom you could not afford to sell directly.

It is a difficult but exciting moment in the life of an entrepreneurial company when it recognizes that it cannot be all things to all customers and must find and implement new distributions channels. A VAR is one such example.

Corporate alliances

Create synergies.

By definition, a corporate alliance is when two companies bind together for synergistic value. Perhaps the most common example is in the travel industry. Every time you call a major airline to make a plane reservation, at the end of the booking, the

Can I transfer you?

operator invariably asks if you would like assistance with a car or hotel reservation. That airline is acting as the distribution channel for the car and hotel companies. At the same time, the car and hotel companies are serving as a distribution channel for the airline by offering airline miles for choosing that car or hotel.

Works for packaged goods too.

Corporate alliances also exist in packaged goods. Companies often enhance their standard offerings with other companies' products. A prime example is when computer software is bundled with the purchase of your computer hardware. This is also done in the swimming pool industry when supplies are included with the purchase of a stand-up pool bought at the local mass merchandiser. Having another company sell your product both as a means by which to introduce your product into the market as well as to build volume is an important entrepreneurial tool.

Relationship selling

A relationship sale is a sale that is based on positive past experience with the same supplier of a product or service. The basis of this relationship selling is customer satisfaction.

> *"For example, a household word for many, many families is Nordstrom's because its customer satisfaction level is so high that your good experiences there means that you will talk it up among your friends. Word of mouth is paramount and Nordstrom's grows just by internal growth."*
> -William H. Crookston, WHC Associates

Your culture.

Repeat customers should not be just a goal. They should be part of your philosophy, strategy, and culture. Chance will not bring customers back; you, your service to your customers, and the tools you have designed to keep customer mind share will.

Build an annuity.

Perhaps the greatest example of relationship selling, and thereby guaranteeing repeat business, is seen in Microsoft Corporation. It has built a product for which most of us have paid and on a fairly regular, if not annual basis Microsoft upgrades that product. For a price that is a fraction of the original price, we get an upgrade of its product that provides additional features and functionality. Microsoft has built an annuity into their product and we, the consumers, accept this to avoid obsolescence. For this we pay a fee, which means that Microsoft has guaranteed that every year or two, they are guaranteed a repeat customer.

Strategies like this are not happenstance; they are built into the original design.

> *"At ShopTrac we planned on adding three major and several minor features to our software each year. By doing that we kept 80% of our customers on annual maintenance for which they bought an upgrade for 12% of the original price. They usually bought one or two additional modules at full price. We built a guaranteed renewal of our sales each year through this tactic."*
> -Mark MacWhirter, ShopTrac

Customer incentives

Rewarded for buying.

Customers are often given incentives to take certain action so that nothing is left to chance. You are rewarded for returning to the same store, which can be in the form of special status at a retail outlet that allows free gift-wrapping or in collecting points to receive a free something. Certainly every time you take a trip, your decision to fly a certain airline is influenced by which company's miles you are accruing. Other examples are the frequent buyer cards that we all carry and are stamped every time we buy a cup of coffee, or a bagel, or rent a movie. Once enough stamps are collected, we receive a free coffee, bagel, or movie. While this is modest, the incentive maintains mind share for the supplier. We become accustom to thinking of that company or that store when it is time to purchase a specific product or service.

> *"If you sign up for EarthLink and you like the service, you will probably tell your friends. We recognize that early on and we want to reward you for telling your friends. So, when your friend signs up and gives us your name, we give you a free month of service. So, 20-25% of all new EarthLink customers that sign up every week are referred."*
>
> -Sky Dayton, Founder, EarthLink Network, Inc.

Multilevel marketing (MLM)

MLM can be effective.

As with some of the other sales channels discussed, multilevel marketing creates distaste for certain individuals. Despite its new name of network marketing, a certain stigma remains associated with this form of selling. However, there are certain niches that do find success with this format.

Network created.

Recall the classic distribution channel. Instead of transfer through the five classic steps of distribution—manufacturer to distributor to wholesaler to retailer to consumer—we go from manufacturer through friends and others that use the particular product directly to the consumer. This distribution channel is comprised of individuals who sell to their friends and associates, which creates a network through which sales occur.

Tupperware.

Historically, sales of this nature have been for select specialty products. Among the most common are vitamins, nutrition and beauty products, and household supplies such as those offered by Amway Corporation. This sales channel began with the sale of Tupperware products and Moms selling the plastic containers to their friends. Today, there are many new products that have achieved great success via MLM.

Stigma can be removed.

Some of the newer entrants include everyday products, even some that are considered commodities, such as long distance phone services and credit cards. The stigma of having to convince friends of their need for a certain vitamin or beauty product is removed if a measurable product is introduced, like phone rates or interest rates for credit cards. The ill will associated with convincing a friend of a need seems to disappear when selling products that are used on a regular basis, regardless of the sales channel.

You tell two friends and they tell two friends and so on and so on.

Further, MLM offers an enticing incentive program because it works in a succession. When you sell a product, not only do you receive a commission on that sale, but you also receive a commission when the person that you sold to makes a sale, when the person that he or she sells to makes a sale, and so on. The theory is that the initial seller will penetrate and build a chain of multiple sellers provided you are given both a reward and an incentive. The reward is the commission and the incentive is the commission on someone else's commission.

Significant dollars can be earned and many products distributed with a successful and ethical MLM strategy.

New Tools In The Sales Kit

Reverse email

Direct email.

A new sales channel has emerged that stems from the growth of the Internet, but it is not the Internet. It is the use of electronic mail, which is done in two ways.

In its worse scenario, it is junk mail received in your inbox that is neither solicited nor desired.

Use it effectively.

However, just as with a direct mail campaign, one that is professional, well done, provides education as well as a solicitation has a place in the sales tool kit. It is not the instrument that should be judged, but how you use the instrument.

At your discretion.

The second form of electronic mail is still in its infancy. Companies are now asking whether or not you wish to receive information in the form of email about their products or services. Do you have an interest in model trains and would you like to know when a new product is available? In reality, this is reverse email, or a catalog on demand. You receive what you want when it's available. If you don't want it, you just tell the company and you no longer receive the email updates.

Airline offerings.

Reverse email is a very targeted sales tool and its potential is unlimited. For example, you can sign up and receive discount airline fare reports. Major airlines and airline services are now publishing discounted fares for travel during an upcoming week-end. Late in the week, the airline will determine the number of excess seats available in a market and offer the seats at a discount for travel the upcoming weekend.

New customer base identified.

Some are even extending the offering for other than the upcoming weekend. What would have been a $2,000 coast to coast fare if bought on the Wednesday night for weekend travel can be yours for a few hundred dollars. Through this offering the airlines have developed a customer base of individuals who are willing and able to travel at a moment's notice, which is a tremendous sales tool. This same tool can be applied to advertising or liquidation sales.

Some are even predicting that reverse email as an information source, normally supplied by catalogs and direct mail, will dwarf all other forms of distribution within the next decade.

Internet

New, powerful tool.

You cannot end a review of sales channels without a discussion of the incredible impact of the Internet. There are literally hundreds of stories of small life style companies that have found a bigger, larger pool of customers because of this modern distribution channel. Only the future holds the answer to the widespread adoption of this new and powerful tool.

Are you a fisher?

From the perspective of the model business, the Internet is clearly a retail model whereby you are fishing. You cannot hunt down your customers; they must visit your site. This suggests that success will come to those who are capable of creating a brand name. Certainly Amazon.com and eBay have proven this to be true. But is this the realm of the entrepreneur or the creative manager? The cost of branding an Internet site similar to that of Amazon is estimated at $200,000,000. Clearly the Internet has become a resource dependent startup.

Future is uncertain.

How can the entrepreneur compete against such budgets? Initial success suggests that using the Internet to augment other sales penetration tools is one effective way. Simple steps such as placing a small ad for your site in a special trade magazine or in a classified section can help. Additionally, cross-pollinating your site with multiple key words will help to direct a broader audience to your site.

Only time will tell how large an impact the Internet will have. Certainly, it is a force to be reckoned with and not one that the entrepreneur can ignore.

> *"We advertise on the Internet through a company and it's really nice because we are able to reach people that we would never be able to reach in different countries. So, that works well for us and people seem to be comfortable with it."*
> -Tony Haywood, Founder, A-1 Turbo

Up Front & Personal: Trick R/C

Jerry Teisan started his model airplane business in his backyard. Through many different sales and distribution channels, he is now able to reach a wide variety of customers. In the beginning, he built the planes by hand and personally sold them directly to consumers. But when production levels increased, he had to determine how to mass-produce and mass sell.

While flying his own plane at a race, he learned of a new material that was "basically indestructible, it bounces, it bends, you just can't hurt it" and able to be mass-produced. This material enabled Jerry to grow the business beyond his original hopes and desires.

In the beginning, his sales and marketing efforts were what he termed "infection marketing." He would travel around and fly his planes on local hills with some friends. Inevitably, the hobbyists in that particular area would ask about Jerry's planes and want to fly them. So, Jerry would give them the transmitter and let them try it. Immediately hooked on the new planes, the locals would want to know where they could purchase one. As Jerry states, "once you get one or two on a hill to buy, the whole hill will buy. Everyone has to have one."

Jerry enlisted his brother, Joe, to expand the marketing efforts of Trick R/C. Joe was delighted to be a part of the business and knew just how to attract the customers. "The people who fly gliders, non powered, is a sub of a sub of a sub market. So, it was really a well-contained market, which made it easy to reach." He felt Trick R/C had an advantage because its first advertisement was placed in a magazine that is well known in the "slope soaring" industry. He expanded the distribution channel by selling to retailers in addition to the direct sales by his brother, Jerry.

As the business grew, the brothers asked their mother for assistance, which gives her great pleasure. "I'd rather be here now than anyplace else actually. Just working and seeing the business grow. It's amazing," she states.

The Internet has provided a unique opportunity for Trick R/C. It has enabled the company to save tremendous dollars on marketing because it can showcase its products in color without the expense of printing. Not only did Jerry have to learn about the Internet and how to use it effectively, he also had to learn how to use the computer because he wasn't even computer literate when he started the business. Through this knowledge and the use of technology, this small family business, Trick R/C, has been able to create a global distribution network at almost no cost.

As the marketer of the business, Joe is amazed at the speed and efficiency of the Internet. Referring to a Trick R/C customer in Sweden who recently bought a glider, Joe recalls, "that's 12,000 miles in 5 days. Being paid for, received, built, and flown, that's nice. Three years ago, two years ago, that would be inconceivable."

Entrepreneurial Exercise

Think about the many distribution and sales channels that have been discussed. Did you have an example of each in your last exercise? If not, could you have? For this exercise, you are going to address some of the common stigmas associated with certain channels. For each question below, try to come up with an example of a company's effective use of that particular channel.

1. What relationship selling tactic works on you?

_____

_____

_____

2. Identify a piece of direct mail that enticed you to respond.

_____

_____

_____

3. Think of a telemarketing campaing that actually got you to listen to the pitch.

_____

_____

_____

4. What multilevel marketing product or service might interest you? Why?

_____

_____

_____

Now, think about how you might use each of these tactics in your own business.

⇒   **Tear out and move to your entrepreneurial road map binder.**

How Do You Approach Sales?

In addition to the many channels available to you, it is necessary to also approach sales in the proper manner and understand the entire process. In its most basic sense, sales is the art of qualifying a potential buyer and then providing the necessary assistance to help that customer buy.

Sales people are often good entrepreneurs.

Strong observational evidence suggests that sales people do very well as entrepreneurs. Why? Some believe it is the outgoing personality that is typically associated with sales people. Others feel it is because they have people skills, which means they are both good at and enjoy working with people. Still others indicate that it is because they are customer-driven and have a need and desire to satisfy customer's needs. Finally, others suggest it is the first hand knowledge of markets and competition that allows them to recognize and exploit opportunities.

Selling is of primary importance to start up.

While all of these reasons may be accurate, the known reality is that entrepreneurs are dependent upon customers to exist and therefore must take on the sales responsibility as one of their major priorities. Doling out sales responsibility to an associate, a sales department, or even your partner would be shirking your number one responsibility. Selling is your business. Without it, you have no business.

Approach is cause for success.

Not everyone is a successful salesman. Why? While there is no one style or personality that dominates sales, there does appear to be a common underlying causality for selling success, which is in the approach. Just like entrepreneurship, sales is equally as dependent on what you do as it is on your attitude about who you are.

Qualify and assist.

The two challenges of qualification and assistance must be met in a sales approach. Qualification entails discovering whether or not the person wishing to buy has the power to buy. Marketing served to position the product or service in front of the potential buyer. Remember the ski slope example where the marketing tactic (placing a sign) led individuals to the model homes. Once inside the home, the developer then had to sell the home using sales tactics.

Products don't sell themselves.

You'll recall that the opposite of being sales and customer driven is to be product driven. Product-driven individuals believe that their product sells itself. They convince themselves that everyone needs one of what they have and that everyone else will love it because they do. An axiom of entrepreneurship is "don't fall in love with your product" because you will be blinded and loose all objectivity. Many bankrupt companies have resulted from products that did not sell themselves. Your company sells its products.

Know benefits and obstacles.

Assistance in buying is equally as important as qualification. Knowing someone can buy doesn't mean that they will buy. Assistance centers on knowing their benefit needs as well as the obstacles in their path and will enable you to define the former and remove the latter.

Learn all you can.

Many classes and seminars are offered that teach good salesmanship and signing up for one can be beneficial. Learn everything possible about sales approaches and techniques, of which there are many. There is a structure and process associated with selling, which can be learned and used to develop your own approach. Sales success results when sales people have their own process and don't just "wing it." Whether yours is the 3, 5, 7, 9 or 11-step approach, there are certain guidelines common to all. A brief review of a multi-step approach to reaching, qualifying, and closing your customer is given below.

Step 1 - initial approach

First impressions count.

How do you look when you approach your initial customers? Are you making a professional statement when you call on them? As you know, in the early stage of a start up, almost all sales are "people sales," which means that the sales process starts with you selling your credibility and capability. The first question is what is the initial impression you portray? What do you look like at your first meeting?

Don't be late!

Try to view yourself from the vantage of the other person. First, let's explore what would not be viewed as professional. Arriving ten minutes late for a meeting is a sign that you are not credible. Entering a meeting without having anticipated normal topics of discussion is a sign that you are not professional. Lack of a formal, or informal, agenda or prepared schedule is another sign. First impressions are crucial. Some indicate that they make a decision as to whether or not to do business with someone based on the first five minutes of their initial meeting. You need to be sensitive to how you are perceived.

Set up sales meeting.

Professional people are those who value time meaning that their time is important to them and know that yours is to you. As such, prior to a meeting they have called, spoken with the appropriate person in the company, and outlined a preliminary agenda (in-person cold calls aren't efficient, aren't professional, and are almost never successful). The phone meeting also enables them to gather preliminary information relating to that company's need. After the phone call and before the actual meeting, they send background materials (brochures) so that everyone planning to attend can be educated as to their benefits. Pre-meeting preparation for professional people is completed with some basic research on the company so changes and trends occurring within that organization are known.

Confirm.

Confirmation of the meeting is typically done in order to reaffirm the necessity of the meeting. You should ensure that this person wants to see you, understands the reason for the meeting, and is in a position to be the initial messenger between you and his or her company.

Aim high.

There is an old adage that you can never start too high in an organization. In other words, you are better served when starting with the president and being delegated down, than you are when starting with a purchasing agent and trying to move up through the political matrix of the organization. On an initial try, you may not reach the president, but that shouldn't stop you from trying.

Don't be rushed!

As for the personal aspects of entering a meeting, be cognizant of your presence. What do you look like when you walk in the door? Are you rushed, are you professionally dressed? Is your demeanor one of confidence? Do you have a presence that you are trying to understand their problem, their need? Or, are you there to present what you do? An inexperienced sales person is easily identified because he or she feels the number one priority is to present the company's offerings. The most important part of your sales call is to learn what your potential client needs. One old mentor always said: "God gave me two ears and one mouth for purpose." That purpose is to learn twice as much as is shared.

> "When you are meeting with a venture capitalist or an investment banker, you are making a sales pitch. So, you're a salesman, you have got to be wearing your sales hat, you have got to be selling all the time, you have got to have the conviction about what you're doing and that enthusiasm has to come through. Because if I don't see you being a true believer, I don't see that high energy level, I don't see that spark, that entrepreneurial spark and that enthusiasm, then I know that when the going gets tough, you're going to bail, you're just not going to be there."
>
> -Lloyd Greif, Founder, Greif & Co.

Step 2 - qualification

Practice makes perfect.

On the job training or learning as you do is common for most entrepreneurs. In the sales process, you will talk to one hundred potential customers to get five or ten prospects to get one or two sales, if you are lucky. Don't waste all those no's. Use the time to practice qualifying. Qualifying customers is essential to the process. Your call should steer the conversation in such a way as to identify the person in front of you as being able to make a purchase decision. Learn how the company makes a buy decision and strategize as to how you can reach that decision-maker. Your number one goal should be to know who makes the decision and why.

Who has the power?

Does the purchasing agent have decision power or are they acting on behalf of an engineer that needs a specification on your product who will then make the buy decision? Or is that engineer just gathering data for a purchase that may not happen for some time? If so, you must decide if you can afford to educate that engineer and perhaps gain a preferred position once that consumer is educated. But will that process be too time consuming for too little reward? You need to know why that potential customer chooses one vendor over another.

Step 3 - determine their need

Have you done your homework?

At this step, you must determine whether or not the prospective company is even interested in your offerings, which is reflected in the sales material that they previously received. You should already have a sense for their interest from probing in your cold call and pre-meeting conversation with questions like "are you currently buying products like this" or "have you considered buying products like this." The meeting is occurring because you already discovered what products they are buying and have qualified them. As such, your attention should now focus on their needs. Don't assume your product is the answer to a problem you have not yet even heard.

What's important to them?

What does this potential customer seek? Multiple suppliers exist in your industry as no product or service is free of competition. So, how does this prospect company decide which firm is best suited to meet its needs? Whether you are talking to the CEO, a vice president, or a purchasing agent, in your conversation, find out what is important to that company. What will prompt a "yes, I will buy?" What's the priority? Is it speed of delivery? How much inventory is typically on hand? Explore the biggest single problem that the company has experienced in the past with suppliers. The phrase, "what can we do to make your life better" should always be in the back of your mind.

Step 4 - sell your company

Brag.

This is the time to talk about your company, your associates, and what you stand for, but be careful not to spend time talking about you. Highlight the individuals that make a difference and their excitement for the job and about fulfilling the needs of your prospective client. Talk about your customers and how you satisfy their needs. It is not wrong to give names, but not as references. You are in a process of qualification and have not yet learned all that you need to know. Save some information for a later date. Be sure they recognize that you are a successful ongoing company and will be there to handle their needs for the long term.

> *"I make my cold calls from 10:00am to 2:30pm every day. Most of them are already people we've talked to, or are our customers and we're checking on an order. But we try to call at least five or six new stores a day and acquaint them with our line and be able to send them some information."*
> -Kim Camarella, Founder, Kiyonna Klothing

Step 5 - demonstrate your capabilities to fulfill their needs

Are you right for them?

If you have properly done your job thus far, then you should now have a well-positioned potential customer. You have successfully reached them, are having a meeting, and have begun the qualification process. You now seek to determine whether this company and these individuals are the right ones with which to be doing business. You have learned much about what they need and have told them about your company. It is now time to ensure that they feel absolutely comfortable that you are the company and you have the team that can deliver and with which they want to conduct business. At this point, success will only come if they are certain you are capable of meeting their needs. They then simply have to start the purchase process.

> *"Medical devices is a new market for us that we've been focusing on for 2-3 years. So, we look at doing trade seminars directed right at medical devices. They have very specific needs in that industry, so we focus right on those needs and the areas for which we have solutions. Our goal is to provide a very good answer for their needs."*
> -Pam Lopker, Founder, QAD

Step 6 - what do you need to get the order?

Ask for the order.

Salesmen refer to this as a test close. The only way to do it is to literally ask the question. "Mr. Prospect, we are interested in doing business with you, what would it take for us to be able to get an order"? If you have determined that this potential buyer is not the person capable of making a buy decision, then you may want to save this question for that meeting. Or, use this question to force the higher level meeting because if that individual cannot buy, then he or she is not the person with whom you should be speaking.

Uncover any obstacles.

If hidden objections exist, asking for the order will bring them to the surface. If they have a problem with company policies, if they have a commitment to another supplier in a contract, if they have a general problem with your services, or even a problem with the ballpark pricing you might have discussed, this is when they will arise. Listen to their obstacles, outline them, and be prepared to discover what you can do to resolve these issues.

Is it a complex sale?

For a simple sale, all of these details are handled by one individual. A sale could require multiple levels of approval, which makes it more difficult and is known as a complex sale. Multiple department heads may be in conflict and you need to recognize this. Be aware of the challenges and gain knowledge and practical experience in order to deal with them effectively.

Step 7 - get a commitment

Don't leave without a next step.

Every successful sales person ends a sales call with some form of commitment, a next step so that the process doesn't end. If the order itself or a sample trial order is not attainable, then you need to determine a commitment that will keep the process going. If there are many obstacles, it may not be the right time to address all of them. Instead, ask when you can schedule a meeting with the appropriate personnel who are able to make decisions and resolve any issues. If price is the obstacle, you should be prepared to identify your costs as opposed to list price to prove that you are not charging exorbitant prices. Whatever the obstacle, figure out how to address it.

Walking out of a presentation without a next action is totally unacceptable. Walking out without an order is disappointing, but it should then be just one step away.

Getting the commitment for action completes this process.

Chapter Summary

While the classic 5 step approach to sales and distribution channels is useful to understand how value is added along each channel in the process, it has slowly been eroding over time and new, innovative distribution methods have been created.

In considering your own entrepreneurial journey, determine the most appropriate sales channels for your product or service and bear in mind that, by definition, utilizing certain sales channels means that you must relinquish control.

After determining the appropriate distribution channel, you must make the sale. As you think about your own sales process, be sure to include the following in your approach:

- Initial approach,
- Qualification,
- Determine the need,
- Sell your company, demonstrate your capability to fulfill their needs,
- Ask for the order,
- Get a commitment.

Chapter Eight Exercises/Discussion Questions

1. Discuss the benefits and/or detriments to using the different sales channels.
2. Identify two companies who have changed their distribution models or added means of reaching their customers. Have they been successful? Why?
3. Identify two corporate alliances that have benefited both companies and why.
4. Think of examples of ways in which you can determine the customer's buying habits.
5. Think of an example of someone who made an effective sales pitch to you. What did he or she say that got you to listen?
6. Consider how the multi-step process will apply to your venture.

Journey Eight: Hard Candy

Dineh Mohajer was a 22-year-old premed student when she decided to take a summer off and work in an upscale boutique in Los Angeles. After buying a pair of baby blue shoes, she wanted some nail polish to match. When she couldn't find any, she decided to make her own. Mixing navy blue and white polish in her bathroom sink got her the nail polish she wanted and much to her surprise, it also led to Hard Candy, a company she didn't know she wanted. She effectively turned her problem into an opportunity and found a solution.

Dineh's first customers were her friends who really liked the colors she created. After baby blue, it was a natural progression to make lavender and other primary pastels. Her friends were not only willing to experiment and try the different shades she created, but they also truly liked her innovation in nail polish.

With such a large interest from those close to her, Dineh decided to take the polish to Fred Segal, the boutique where she was employed at the time. Being an employee, this was not a difficult sale, they liked her, were friendly, and allowed her shelf space. She was able to test and expose her concept. When she did, the response was quite positive, Dineh recalls that one young girl "came over and was freaking out and wanted to buy every single one. It was really a joke, that is now a big joke on me because it took over my life."

Hard Candy was an instant success. Soon buyers were flooding her dorm room (office) with phone calls wanting to purchase her funky colors that she gave equally as funky names, such as Trailer Trash, Luscious, Scam, and Fettish. The incredible demand led Dineh to take a semester off from school, which turned into two semesters and then three semesters and so on. She never imagined the polish would be so well received in the industry. As she recalls, "it was weird how many compliments I got because it wasn't a trend at all, it was just something I had hit on."

Dineh sold her polish to other high-end stores and celebrities became her primary customers because of the nature of this distribution channel. As a result, Hard Candy received a tremendous media blitz, which led to even more phone calls from buyers who recognized the benefit of Hard Candy's unique sense of style and fun.

But, her "project" got somewhat out of hand. She was approached and called by every store imaginable and went for months without billing because production and shipping were all consuming. She admits, "I had no idea what I was doing. There was no intention of it becoming what it did. I became this zombie. There were days that I would just be wearing the same thing for six days in a row, it just wasn't important."

Distribution became Hard Candy's biggest challenge. The incredible growth outran Dineh's ability to control it. She was overwhelmed and "accepted accounts because I had to get off the phone with people." Chaos reigned supreme and no checks and balances had been put in place to manage the process. As a result, Dineh was selling to stores in which she really didn't want her product. She had to determine which distribution channels made the most sense for her product, a challenge faced by many manufacturers. Rather than accepting all accounts, it may have made sense for her to sell to wholesalers or agents that could sell her product along with other products.

She determined that she had created an upscale product and wanted it to be sold in upscale locations. Her target store became "basically the stores that I shopped at because I was a consumer creating a product that I wanted within a group of other consumers that would want the same."

Limiting distribution to prestigious stores was not an easy task, but one that Dineh felt was very necessary in order to remain true to the brand that she was attempting to create. Hard Candy would have likely done a greater volume of sales if any and all accounts were accepted, but Dineh did not want to "jeopardize the integrity of the brand that I was trying to build and I just didn't believe in it. Building a brand is about staying true to the vision."

Going it alone was not a possibility and it was not until she brought in a national sales manager that Dineh was able to better control her distribution. Together, they developed a process, created a structure, and made people accountable for their actions, which enabled Hard Candy to build its brand in such a way that allowed Dineh to maintain her vision.

As an established business, Hard Candy is seeking to increase its distribution channels on the Internet and Dineh foresees this as a tremendous growth area.

What began as a summer project took over the entrepreneur's life. Hard Candy has been a phenomenal success and is now a $10 million-a-year business. Dineh declares "I love it, I hate my job. I love my job, but I hate it, I love my job."

Journey Eight Case Questions

1. How did Dineh's opportunity recognition occur?
2. What did she do to exploit her opportunity?
3. Who were Dineh's first customers? How did she leverage her early adapters into multiple customers?
4. What were some of the challenges faced by the entrepreneur as her company grew?
5. What distribution channels did she identify as appropriate for her nail polish sales? Why?

Chapter Nine
Developing Your Benefit

Chapter Nine Major Concepts

- Features versus benefits
- Stages of benefit development
- Tools for benefit development

Journey Nine: Strategic Partners

Developing Your Benefit

Customer is still driving force.

We now come to the final component of the concept—the benefit. Thus far, you have learned that the customer drives all aspects of the concept, which is why we first focused on clearly defining your customer. We then examined the many ways to sell and distribute your product or service in order to determine the most effective and efficient means of reaching customers and delivering their needs. We must now determine benefit needs. To do so, we must first ask what the benefit is and then determine how it will be developed and maintained.

What Is A Benefit?

Are you in love with your product?

Entrepreneurs often rave about the wonderful things that their products or services are capable of doing. Hearing about these different aspects of a product or service is always interesting and related discussions can be quite exciting. However, in contemplating such conversations that occur frequently in the entrepreneurial world, it usually becomes quite evident that the raving entrepreneur has built something that is faster, bigger, cheaper, wider, bluer, or greener, etc. Such a conversation typically ends without a sense for why this product or service is necessary. What is the problem that this entrepreneur is addressing? What is the pain that is being eliminated? Why is that specific product or service needed? These are the real questions and the answers to which comprise the essence of benefits.

What is a benefit?

In order to explore the development of benefits, we first need to clearly define a benefit.

A benefit is the value you receive from using a product or a service.

What is a feature?

Simply stated, a benefit is the reason someone would use your product or service. The opposite of a benefit—often confused with a benefit—is a feature.

A feature is what your product does.

What is the value received?

The benefit derived from using a telephone is that it enables immediate, clear contact with a third party. The ways in which a telephone works—speed, connection line, switching, access—are its features. To most people, these features are not important. Do you care that the speed of the telephone line is xx kilobytes per second? No, you care that as soon as you dial, you are connected to the third party you desire. It is the benefit, or the value, that you receive from using the phone that is important.

Features alone don't sell.

An entrepreneur's goal is to always deliver a benefit. Why do you drive a car? Do you drive the car because the transmission is a certain size, or the engine has a certain horsepower, or the car has certain automatic features, such as door locks. No. Your primary goal in buying a car is for the benefit of transportation, the ease of getting from one place to another. The specific model chosen may be a function of its features, but these features are not why you buy a car.

Think benefits—not features.

The Benefit Development Process

User is key.

The reason for using a certain product is the benefit it provides; therefore, benefit development is tied to the user. Benefits for which no users are interested are useless and make no sense. In the entrepreneur's vernacular, this would be developing a solution for which there is no apparent problem—the antithesis of the entrepreneur's goal. So, in proceeding to define your benefit, you must have a clear understanding of benefit development.

Benefit development is the process that first defines and then builds what the customers want.

What's the most important word?

So, we are back to the same premise that has guided us thus far—the most important word in the entrepreneurial world is customer. If benefit development were merely the creation of products and services with new features, then entrepreneurs would be no different from inventors or administrators armed with vast resources. In that scenario, there is no room for the little guy or the niche player who celebrates his or her smallness. However, that is not the case. Benefit development is really focusing on and constantly seeking to identify the current and evolving needs of your customers, and then fulfilling those needs. Therefore, benefit development has structure and purpose for the entrepreneur.

> *"There are so many women in the US that are bigger than a size 12 and a lot of designers only go up to a 12 or 14. So, my partner, Yvonne, and I thought that we could do a fashionable line for larger sizes."*
> -Kim Camarella, Founder, Kiyonna Klothing

> *"What we really try to do is best serve the customers' needs by looking at the market they're trying to address, the space they have, the budget they have, and then try to accommodate them that way."*
> -Michael Garvey, Founder, The Dumbell Man

> *"I keep in touch with our members' experience by being a member myself. I go home at night and I log on just like everyone else."*
> -Sky Dayton, Founder, EarthLink

> *"Sunday night at midnight and our biggest customer needs a load, we can do it. You won't get an answering machine here."*
> - Reggie Latham, Founder, ChemTrans

> *"The company I was associated with before I started QAD treated the customer really poorly. The customer would call with a problem and the employee would go, 'uuuhhhh, boy its always the stupid customer on the phone, do I really have to take that?'"*
>
> -Pam Lopker, Founder, QAD

> *"If I walk through the restaurant and I see someone not eating, I will still go there, get their plate, and convince them to have something else, so that they leave having a really good experience."*
>
> - Susan Feniger, Founder, Border Grill

> *"If the customer service reps are all busy, we actually have what we call the chime call where a chime dings on everyone's phone until it gets answered. And because we cross-train, everybody is able to answer at least 85% of the calls."*
>
> -Joe Kaplan, Founder, Superior Bankcard Services

Benefit development occurs in steps.

Every textbook and seminar seems to have a unique way of approaching benefit development. However, there is a common theme, which is that the various learning models are often stated in steps of progression. So, whether you use a three, five, seven, or nine step approach to benefit development is not important. What is important is to find what works for your business.

For illustration, we will examine a common overview of benefit development.

Step 1 - opportunity recognition

Find a problem that needs a solution.

There is no end to the search for opportunities. Before you begin to decide what you are going to develop as a benefit, you must know why you are developing it, which must be done in conjunction with the customer. As you learned, opportunity recognition is about looking for problems, confirming that they exist, and then proposing solutions. It is not about developing a solution and then looking for the problem. In other words, you must first identify the reason for developing this benefit. What is the opportunity?

Education may be involved.

An additional challenge is ensuring that the customers know what they need. You certainly can't give customers something that they don't know they need. Therefore, a critical part of the benefit development process is education. In listening to customers' problems, you need to educate them as to the different solutions

> *"Really in these newer markets, you're going to find a lot of exercise equipment in places that traditionally haven't thought about having them. And educating those consumers, whether they are a retail customer, a hotel owner or manager, or a university rec department personnel, is something that we can come in and do, because this is what we do on an everyday basis."*
> - Michael Garvey, Founder, The Dumbell Man

Guide customers to solutions.

available to them. They need to share their challenges and their pains. In turn, you must understand these issues and be aware of your ability and desire to solve them. You will then guide them to the solutions that you are capable of creating—even if you aren't sure of the details needed to do it.

Step 2 - concept investigation

As you talk to individuals and gather the information needed to transition from exploration to testing, you are moving from opportunity recognition to concept investigation.

Testing versus soliciting.

Investigating the concept requires that you test as opposed to solicit. Find out what is critical and of interest and perform the important primary research, which comes from direct contact with potential customers. Whereas opportunity recognition helps to determine what customers like, concept investigation asks what it would take for them to accept your solution and set of benefits that answers their problem. This is a different mindset into which you must transition.

A compliment versus a contract.

Be careful not to fall into the compliment, not contract trap as well. This is a difficult challenge many entrepreneurs face. A customer expressing an interest in your product or service and saying, "yeah, that sounds really great," is not necessarily a customer in a position to purchase. Even if they have both the desire and ability to buy, they may not feel that the value exchange point (price) is sufficient. Your price may be higher than the value they perceive, which will result in a compliment, not a contract.

Remember the earlier warning that the difference between a compliment and a contract is often bankruptcy.

Step 3 - design preparation

Seek to answer critical questions.

Combining that which has been recognized in step one and that which has been tested in step two results in design preparation. At this stage, you should organize a roundtable discussion among your associates who possess complimentary skills and explore the critical questions: What does the customer want, what will the customer purchase, and at what value exchange will they purchase it?

What is the value?

Do not turn this into an exercise in engineering. You should not be designing newer, better, more advanced features. Rather, this phase continues from the entrepreneur's point of view, which ask the questions: Where is value created and what is the problem being solved?

Pragmatism, not prophecy.

The nature of these sessions should be applied as opposed to futuristic. Maintain a focus on what can be accomplished relating to what has been recognized and tested and think in terms of immediate needs, not what future needs may be. Create a solution for the present that can evolve and expand in the future. Working in the future now may preclude you from experiencing the present at which time you should be launching your venture.

Determine general costing.

Likewise, design preparation should not be a cost accounting exercise. The goal at this stage is not to determine the precise costs of producing the benefit for that particular customer population. However, a general idea of cost should be maintained because it would be fool hearty to proceed forward without a sense for what it will take to build the perceived benefit and what the customer might be prepared to pay for it.

Discuss the many questions.

Once the team of associates is assembled, write down all of the challenges and opportunities learned to date. Throughout discussions, numerous questions will arise which you should also write down. In so doing, the following product development exercises will help maintain your focus.

Product development exercises

Building your brochure

Doesn't have to be expensive.

The first exercise is building a brochure. A brochure is an artistic and literal representation of your benefit. First and foremost, it articulates what is of value to customers—why will they use it. What benefit will be derived? The brochure must also highlight the features so that potential customers know how the benefit occurs (the features) in addition to knowing what is of value (the benefits). The final portion of the brochure should sell your team. Who will deliver the benefit? Why should they be trusted? Don't forget to add contact information to the brochure as well. Your customers have to know how to find you.

Let your creativity flow.

Going through this exercise is often a fun and exciting process. Allow your individual creativity to flow, but keep in mind that a formal, expensive, professional brochure is not expected. Rather, the brochure should be very detailed and should tell your story. What do you do for a customer? How do you do it? Why are you the company that can deliver? These issues must be clearly identified in the brochure.

Build the roadmap

It may be weeks or even months before a formal, professional version is completed. At this stage, you need a strong roadmap that will keep your team focused and portray your vision.

Brochure Example

Below and on the next page are pieces from the EDSG brochure, which is a startup company that implements Environmental Health Safety information solutions. Keep in mind that each brochure will be different and this one is tailored to EDSG's particular clientele. For purposes of reprinting, the presentation format has been changed here.

Welcome to EDSG!

Welcome to Environmental Data Solutions Group, LLC (EDSG), the industry leader in planning, evaluating and implementing environmental, health and/or safety management information systems (EMISs). Whether you know exactly how your EMIS should be implemented and are looking for expertise/resources, or would like input on implementation strategies, EDSG is your #1 solution provider!

Core Business. EDSG is the only company whose core business is dedicated to implementing EHS information management solutions. This means *YOUR* project is very important to us, and we are committed to your success.

Client Advocacy. EDSG is an independent information solution provider—not a software developer. We evaluate needs and solutions objectively and rigorously, and recommend what is best for *YOU*, the client.

Common Sense. Applying a common sense, business-based approach to each and every project results in good business sense based on your company's required return on investment (ROI). Nothing more and nothing less.

Creative. Our creative and innovative solutions have saved our customers labor hours and hundreds of thousands of dollars.

Competency. EDSG staff have significant experience in EHS and IT and provide more than just "number crunching."

Register with EDSG for a **complimentary analysis** and see how our approach can work for you. By registering with us, you will be provided access to EDSG's proprietary user Work Sheet Questionnaire. Based on the results, a complimentary analysis will be provided within 10 business days, identifying areas where an EMIS could improve your company's EHS performance and reduce EHS costs.

✔ Register today by calling EDSG at 888-888-8888 or email us at *xxx@xxxx.com*. Please be sure to include all pertinent information.

Environmental Data Solutions Group, LLC

ENVIRONMENTAL MANAGAMENT INFORMATION SYSTEMS
Needs Definition and Business Case Analysis

As integrated, business management information systems (MISs) continue to spread to all areas of services such as finance, sales, and inventory, companies must consider whether MISs should also include environ-mental, health and safety processes. To objectively answer this question, environmental, health and safety management information system (EMIS) needs must be defined and anticipated benefits quantified. An EMIS is justified if the benefits exceed the cost to purchase, implement, and maintain the system.

Direct and indirect benefits

System benefits considered must include both the direct and indirect benefits. Direct costs, which consist primarily of labor hours, permit fees, disposal costs, etc., are easily defined and quanti-fiable. Indirect costs, which typically include reduced risks and liabilities, improved company performance, EHS planning, etc., are more difficult to define and are less easily quantifiable. EDSG's successful program has shown that by statistically analyzing individual risk events over an expected project life, anticipated indirect benefits can be objectively and accurately quantified.

EDSG's methodology enables clients to:

- Reduce the EMIS analysis and selection period from years to months
- Select and implement an EMIS that by design, provides a positive return on investment (ROI)

Resulting in answers to specific questions including:

- Whether to buy an EMIS (the "go/no-go" decision)
- Software and licensing options
- How and when to implement

EDSG begins the process with a detailed needs assessment that is guided by the use of our proprietary survey questionnaires that address 20 environmental, health and safety and information technology topics. This is followed by a rigorous benefit analysis that addresses both direct benefits and indirect benefits. The software demonstration process provides the basis for system recommendations and a cost/benefit time line of cash flows.

The cost/benefit time line of cash flows is the basis to reduce costs, increase overall gains, and accelerate receipt of gains throughout the EMIS implementation.

Business case output is summarized in relevant technical and financial terms such as:

- Discounted Cash Flow (DCF) or Net Present Value (NPV)
- Payback Period
- Internal Rate of Return (IRR)
- ROI

The Business Case Output summarizes potential EMIS alternatives so optimal use of company resources can be determined. The right system can be selected and implemented. By design, desired benefits will be achieved.

✔ Register today by calling EDSG at 888-888-8888 or email us at ***xxx@xxxx.com***. Please be sure to include all pertinent information.

Define your value chain

What's the competition up to?

The second design development exercise is to ensure that your benefit is in harmony with your customer and your sales/distribution channel. This is where your competition grid comes into play. You should know as much about your competition as is possible so that you know what works and what doesn't in your market.

Which channels are best?

You already learned that your product or service will change as new, alternative distribution channels are employed. As a result, your policy on returns may be an important benefit if you are using the Internet as your primary sales channel. Home support may be the critical benefit for a technology product. In order to become sensitive to such needs and to refine your product offerings, you must study the actions of others—competitors and alternative products alike. These simple tasks will identify the cost of competitive products as well as the cost of each step of the sales and distribution channels being utilized.

Think about the value chain exercise that you had to perform. Where along the distribution channels is value added and how does that translate into a benefit for the consumer?

Build your timeline

What needs to be accomplished?

The third design preparation exercise is to outline necessary actions items in a timeline. Ponder all of the steps that will need to be taken from the present to some date in the future when your business can begin. Having already established the criteria for your benefits in a brochure, you are now able to identify specific actions that must be taken to build that benefit.

Not an engineering exercise.

By no means does this imply that you must become an engineer. Depending on your product or service, you will most likely need one in the future. However, for the present, you must identify the steps that need to be taken, how your energy will be spent, and how long the process is going to take. A timeline should be used as a road map that becomes increasingly detailed as you proceed and more clearly define both your own direction and that of your customers.

Therefore, building a timeline enables you to identify:

Critical issues.

- What you will do.
- How long it will take to accomplish each action item.
- The costs involved in starting, producing a first product (including design preparation), and ongoing supplies.

Entrepreneurial Exercise

This is your chance to perform the exercises discussed on the previous pages. So, get out your pen and paper and start making a list of all the benefits and features of your product or service. Identify them below.

Benefits: _____

_____

_____

Features: _____

_____

_____

Now, identify the distribution channels that you plan to use and what value is added at each step of the way.

_____

_____

_____

Finally, start to think about your timeline and identify what tasks need to be accomplished in order for you to start your business and how long each task will take.

_____

_____

_____

_____

_____

Compile the timeline in a format that will enable you to check each task off as accomplished.

⇒ **Tear out and move to your entrepreneurial road map binder.**

Step 4 - prototype building

Visual representation.

Building a prototype enables you to share your product or service with potential customers. At this stage, you need to create a visual representation that shows people how you will deliver the benefit.

Showcase your benefit.

Again, there is no need for an engineer at this stage either. While you may think so, it is not the case. A brochure clearly stating your benefits and features is, in effect, your initial prototype. By definition, a prototype is a means by which to showcase what you do and how you do it. This is your goal. Spending a great deal of money and effort on engineering a product is not.

More information, if necessary.

Further, you may want to have a secondary, more detailed brochure for any potential clients that warrant such attention. This brochure may contain images of a computer screen showing the input of data, the resulting reports, and how easily the process is adaptable to their world. Visualization of your idea is the essence of building a prototype, which enables you to involve the customer as you seek to recognize the opportunity and investigate the concept.

Prototypes can take many forms. Artistic renditions of your model product or your new fashion line are other examples. They provide the means by which to explore the worthiness of your concept.

Convert potentials into customers.

Delving deeper into this fourth stage puts you in a better position to elicit more information from your potential customers. Seek to convert interested parties into customers in hand and to be your early adapters.

What are the costs?

At this point you will also need to have a clear idea of an acceptable price for your benefit and of the cost to produce it. The cost of production must include both the marginal cost of each unit and the initial development costs allocated over some reasonable life, which should be identified in terms of units as opposed to time. For example, if your initial development costs are $10,000, you should determine how many unit sales you need to cover those costs as opposed to the number of days, months, or years that it will take to cover costs.

What will it take to get an order?

As you have learned, a concept contains three inter related components—customers, channels of reaching the customers, and benefits provided. This is even more apparent in this prototype building stage. The goal of demonstrating your prototype to early potential customers is to ask the question: "if our product were to deliver all of this at this particular value point (price), are you prepared to buy?"

Don't force a solution.

Only when you receive positive answers to this question is it time to convert your soft prototype into a hard prototype and produce your initial unit. Doing so earlier would indicate that you are trying to force your solution onto the market as opposed to developing a benefit.

Step 5 – alpha testing

Time to start building.

As you begin to build the initial production unit, everything that you have done to date will serve as a strong framework for the new actions you must undertake. Review your timeline and more clearly define your needs. Additionally, your price margin analysis needs to be more exacting.

Solicit feedback.

Ideally, you are fortunate enough to be producing your initial unit with a customer in hand, which means that you must factor in that customer's comments and quality concerns. Be sure to build this into your timeline to delivery because you are now under a time constraint and will instantly lose credibility if you promise to deliver and don't.

Don't lose your credibility.

There is another test of credibility at this stage which is the final functionality of the product produced. If you exceed your client's expectations in terms of function, but are extremely late in delivering, you've destroyed your credibility with this early adapter. Asking this initial customer to partake in the process meant that you made a promise to deliver and your tardiness indicates that you have not met your side of the bargain. The same is true for the opposite scenario. If you deliver on time, or even early, but the product does not do everything that you promised it would, then you have again lost your credibility, not to mention your client.

Start with in-house testing.

Upon completion of the initial unit, it should be tested in-house, which is the alpha test—the first test. At this point, you are primarily concerned with the functionality of the product. If it works once, that is great, but does not matter. You need to be sure that it works the same way twice. Additionally, the related issue is its usability. Its well and good if your engineers can use it, but can your clients. All too often initial products function extremely well but only in the hands of the experts. Likewise, if building a fashion item or any physical product, can it be manufactured the same way twice and will there be consistency of final product?

Why was Apple the leader?

Although there are many theories on why Apple Computer emerged as the industry leader in the early days of the personal computer, a majority of those who witnessed that era will point to Apple's consistency of production as the basis for their success. Many other firms had superior products when measured on a feature-by-feature comparison, but they lacked the ability to control development releases and produce consistent, quality machines.

Does it work?

After in-house testing is complete, the final challenge of the alpha testing stage is determining whether or not your customer can use it. First, you must determine the conditions under which you will expose it to them.

This is a delicate issue and you must be prepared. Your presentation must be done in such a way as to confirm that all of their benefit wishes, desires, and instructions have been met. In order to complete this first sale, you must reassure them that your mutual goals have been achieved and that their perception has been turned into reality through your first units produced.

Step 6 – beta testing

Say goodbye to the engineers and designers.

By definition, beta testing is secondary testing, which means that the first produced units have progressed to the point where functionality is exact and replicable. When this stage is reached, it is time to disengage the engineers, designers, or whoever was responsible for the process to this point. All those who's energy and love have given the project life are no longer needed. This is not an easy process for either party; it's like asking your children to leave home. But, the time has come for your benefit to stand on its own merit.

But, not too soon.

But just as there is an intermediary step as children leave home (going to college, getting a first job), so it is with your initial benefit. You have a responsibility to ensure a successful beta site testing. Remember a beta site is a controlled testing and while it must simulate a first shipment to a new customer, in actuality, it is not. As an entrepreneur you cannot afford a failure at this point, which is precisely the reason for this additional, beta, test.

Provide a safe beta environment.

Entrepreneurs often ensure a safe environment for beta testing by putting together pre-introduction education and providing technical or marketing (if a non-technical commercial item is being sold into a distribution channel) support services on-site during this beta testing. Your initial clients should understand that they are part of development and their benefit in being such is so that they could have an impact on the final product design and functionality. So, they have assumed a responsibility in being a beta site.

Glitches will exist.

As such, you must reaffirm your anticipation of a growth period and that you expect to not only find glitches, but also to discover areas that will need enhanced development. So, there should be a mutual understanding that once initial beta testing is complete and you have had the opportunity to rework your product, they will run second beta tests on the revised version of the product. It is only at that stage that they should test the product for volume and/or durability, depending on its nature.

Beta testing is where the rubber meets the road and you need to always be available during this period. You have worked too hard to leave anything to chance at this point.

Step 7 – ramping to production

Replicate in quantity.

It is now time to move full speed ahead. Enhancements and changes have been made based on both internal and external testing and you have built quality into both your culture and your products thereby incorporating your customer's revisions into the products. You are now prepared to build the final version of your offering.

Don't forget support issues.

In so doing, recall the session on guerrilla tactics. Relationship selling is a must in the new millennium and you need to be sure that your eye to the future is clearly focused. Build support into your product.

Can't afford to fail now.

Most failures at this stage are self-inflicted injuries. You should have anticipated every possible negative reaction and have plans in place to address these reactions. Murphy is right, failure always happens at the wrong time. So, be prepared to answer in the right amount of time—quickly.

Are no rules in entrepreneurship.

These seven steps are meant to provide an outline of the benefit development process. Your product or service may not go through all of these stages, or, they may go through many more. As you know, there are no rules in entrepreneurship and being able to figure it out as you travel the journey is critical to your success.

> *"The way our timeline works is that we're usually selling about three months before our products are actually going to be in the store, so we're about a season ahead of time. Usually in October and November we're selling for spring of the next year, which is going to be delivered in January, February, or March. So, we're selling way before we're delivering because we have to meet these minimums and because we have to place our order with the fabric companies so far in advance."*
> - Kim Camarella, Founder, Kiyonna Klothing

Rules of Development

1. Never build a product independent of a customer.
2. Never let your engineers develop your benefit.
3. Never build a product without knowing your competition.
4. Design benefit for your chosen distribution channel.
5. Build pricing into the benefit development process.
6. Build quality into your product and make quality the culture of your company.
7. Consider after market issues when designing your benefit including support, repair, and upgrades.

Chapter Summary

There is a fundamental difference between a feature and a benefit. Features are what your product does while benefits are where value is derived—why customers use your product or service. You will get into trouble if you fall in love with your product and its features and do not clearly define the benefits that you are offering.

As you know, there are no rules in entrepreneurship. Therefore, there is no correct number of steps to take in properly developing your benefit. But, the following steps provide a guideline that you can follow for benefit development.

- Opportunity recognition,
- Concept investigation,
- Design preparation,
- Prototype building,
- Alpha testing, and
- Beta testing.

Some tools that you can use throughout these stages of benefit development include building a brochure, designing your value chain, and developing a timeline to start.

Finally, you should always plan ahead for the future—anticipate how your benefit will evolve over time.

Chapter Nine Exercises/Discussion Questions

1. Articulate the difference between a benefit and a feature.
2. Identify the benefits that you feel your product or service offers customers.
3. Examine the benefit development process for the personal computer. How has it evolved over the years?
4. Determine ways in which you plan to add value to your product or service.
5. Have you identified the pricing structure of your product or service?

Journey Nine: Strategic Partners

Leveraged Buy Out

After successfully running the uniform division inside of a large apparel company, Mike Singer bought his business unit from the parent company. For several years prior to his leveraged buy out, Mike had successfully grown his division while the company itself experienced two bankruptcies.

Developing innovative ways to attract customers is always forefront in Mike's thinking and he wanted his uniforms to stand out from the competition.

Benefit Development

Licensing cartoon characters and putting them on uniforms was one idea that he pursued. As he recalls, "I really felt that licensed characters could bring a whole new dimension to our business and they could be a really fun, new product area that the customers would respond really well to." He was right.

The value of brand names is immeasurable and being able to leverage that familiarity was what struck Mike as a unique opportunity. No other pattern or design placed on a uniform would have the same recognition or history than such characters as Baby Looney Tunes, Garfield, Scooby Doo, and Peanuts. He knew this would be especially true for children and targeted the pediatric ward of hospitals. What better way to put a child at ease than to put familiar characters on the nurse's uniforms? When the sick children walk into the hospital and see the friendly faces, they will likely smile and hopefully forget where they are and why.

Product Differentiation

Mike viewed this as a great way to differentiate his products in the marketplace. But, he had to convince the licensors of the added value, a process that varies from industry to industry. He was able to negotiate agreements and convince the licensors that there was a clear fit for their characters on his uniforms.

Throughout the process and in growing his company, Mike recognizes the value in constant customer feedback. As he states, "You have to really stay close to your customers, you have to be open to feedback, you have to really be looking to get that feedback constantly from your customers. That's what really keeps you changing and keeps you on top of the marketplace. That's really where you have to be. There's not a lot you can do behind a desk."

Mike Singer's efforts demonstrate benefit development in action. He had a product that was rich with features, totally functional, and being used in the marketplace. But, he asked the question: How could I add value, how could I differentiate myself? How can I better satisfy my customers?

Adding characters created a new benefit that allowed his customers to not only feel better but also to better interact with their own customers.

"We really felt that licensed characters represent some of the most powerful brandnames in the world today. There's tremendous history and exposure that they have."
-Mike Singer, Founder, Strategic Partners

Journey Nine Case Questions

1. What entrepreneurial characteristics did Mike Singer portray?
2. How did his business evolve from being solely a uniform business to developing innovative benefits for the consumer?
3. How did he maintain his credibility while expanding?
4. How did he add value?

Chapter Ten
Money Tool Kit

_____

Chapter Ten Major Concepts

- The Blind Tour Approach
- Types of Financial Needs - The Classic Approach
- The Entrepreneurial Aproach
- Types of Money - An Example
- Entrepreneurial Tactics for Money Needs

Journey Ten: DeLeon Enterprises

Up Front & Personal: Harry Grimes

Financing A New Company - Money Tool Kit

Don't be afraid of money.

It is at this stage that many students of entrepreneurship freeze. Money scares and paralyzes them. They feel comfortable formulating concepts, finding and testing customers, understanding benefits, and determining sales channels, but figuring out how much money is needed to start a venture is a whole other ball game.

It's a tool kit.

Unfreeze yourself. It is not a different ball game. Learning how to calculate your financial needs is simply another entrepreneurial tool kit that can be learned and understood. To help you add money to your set of entrepreneurial skills, we are going to do three things. First, we are going to take a blind tour, which is a tool that will help you determine what funds will be needed to execute your concept. Second, we will analyze the classic approach, which is the way administrators view money. This will be contrasted with the entrepreneur's approach, which maximizes a limited number of resources and retains as much equity as possible.

Money is an enabler.

In understanding money, you must always keep in mind that money can only enable a concept. Remember the booster rocket analogy. Just as the rocket cannot orbit into space without the booster, a well-defined concept cannot be executed without money. But, the booster alone, or the money alone, will not function without the rocket, or the concept.

In the context of the entrepreneurial triangle, money is found at the bottom for just that reason. The customer, benefit, and product need to exist in order for money to be of any use. And, you, the entrepreneur is the one responsible for utilizing the money to enable the business as can be seen in the diagram below.

Don't lose sight of your concept.

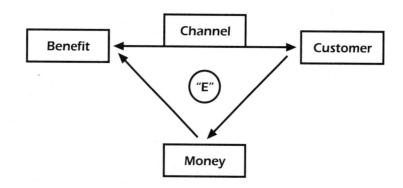

How are you going to use it?

If someone tells you they want to raise $1 million to start a business without having a well-defined concept, you should know what to tell them. It just won't work. Before money makes any sense, or is needed, you must know for what you need the money. What are you trying to propel forward with that money?

The Blind Tour Approach

Existing entity easy to understand.

An existing company is always easier to understand and finance by the very fact that it is existing. It has a record, either good or bad, it has a product line, personnel, a list of clients, a capital base and experience with some banks. But because it is existing, the company is apt to reflect more on the past. It will most likely be judged and understood based on its past track record.

New companies have no past. They only have the promise of a future. What then can they do to share this dream with knowledgeable money sources? How can a start up firm begin the difficult task of first understanding its own needs and then translating those needs to a third party in a credible manner?

Take a blind tour.

To help isolate the future needs of a start up company, bankers have often used a technique known as a "blind tour." The basic assumption is that a "would be" entrepreneur who is ready to launch his or her venture has so studied and considered it in their mind that he or she can see the venture as if it were a real entity. The planner or banker would then ask that person to lead him or her on a tour of this mythical facility. The early moments can be awkward and at times sophomoric, but the technique has been successful in starting the process of focusing the cash planning cycle.

Do a role play.

To assist in this tour, let us assume that you are the President of an about-to-be formed printing company. You have 10 years of experience as the general manager of a printing plant. You have saved diligently and now plan on approaching your bank for a loan. You want the bank to become the bridge between your dream and your future business.

Be prepared.

When you do approach the banker, you will need to supply him with many answers. First, how much money do you need to start this business? Second, how much can you contribute as capital? Third, how do you plan to repay him? These are not easy questions. But the answers are the basis for successfully raising funding, regardless of the money source chosen. In the banking industry your capital base is an important key but only if you can show your capacity to execute.

In order to learn how to perform a blind tour on your venture, beginning on the next page, we are going to walk through a conversation between a banker and an about to be entrepreneur, Harry Grimes, for illustration.

Up Front & Personal: Harry Grimes

Conversation between banker and about-to-be entrepreneur

Banker: *Good morning, I'm Bobby Banker. It's nice to meet you.*

Harry: *It's nice to meet you. I'm Harry Grimes and I'm interested in starting a printing business. I've got 10 years of experience and I think I can do a better job than the company I work for now.*

Banker: *That's good but what makes you think you can do better?*

Harry: *I do everything now. I run their place. From the time the order comes in until we bill it out, I do it all—artworks, print, cuts—everything.*

Banker: *That's very interesting. How can we help you?*

Harry: *Well I don't know much about banks and money and all that stuff but let me tell you what I do know. I know how to print. I've worked hard, saved what I could—it's hard with a family and two kids to support and everything. I looked for a long time and I've found some good used equipment. I could buy it and fix it up for $25,000—tops.*

Banker: *Is it available now?*

Harry: *Yeah, and like I said, I've saved as best I could. I've got $5,000 to put down and that's why I'm here. You guys want 20% down on a car or house so I figured that when I got to 20%, I'd come see you for the rest.*

Banker: *There really is no fixed rule on 20% but let's not talk about that just yet. Tell me more. You said you can do everything from the time the order comes in. Harry, how do you get the order in?*

Harry: *That's the good part. We've got a couple of big accounts at the shop that are just plain unhappy. They see me working and the company getting the big bucks. They'd like to see me go on my own. They feel, between the three or four of them, that I could sell $50,000 a month. No problem.*

Banker: *Hold on, you feel you've got $50,000 a month in sales, you've found the equipment for $25,000 and you want me to loan you $20,000 to start?*

Harry: *That's right.*

Banker: *Harry. I'm sorry but you're not ready to start. You've got more work to do.*

Harry: *Like what?*

Banker: *Like how much money you will need.*

Harry: *I know that. $25,000*

Banker: Harry, I wish it were that simple. Let me make a suggestion to you. Let's you and I go through a basic exercise that I put newly starting companies through. What I would like to do is to go on a blind tour of your plant with you.

Harry: You don't understand. It's not there yet.

Banker: I understand. It's just an exercise. Bear with me and let's see what happens. You should know in your mind exactly what you need and what it will take to start this company.

Harry: Sounds crazy but let's go.

Banker: Great let's start.

Harry: Welcome to my plant.

Banker: This is a great place. Where are we?

Harry: We're in a building?

Banker: I know but where? How much does it cost? Who pays the insurance? How long is the lease?

Harry: Oh, I see what you mean. I wasn't going to do all that until I had the money.

Banker: You're not going to have a chance to get near money until you do all of that and more.

Harry: I can't rent the place until I know what I can spend.

Banker: You don't know how to price until you know what you have to spend.

Harry: It seems like a chicken and egg story.

Banker: It's not. It's planning. And that's what you need to do. So go back to the question—How many square feet do you need, where's your building, and at what cost?

Harry: Well, I have had some preliminary conversations with a landlord about a 4,000 square foot building in an industrial area with good power. I think I can get him down to $3500 a month, which I think is a good deal.

FACT: RENT $3,500 PER MONTH

Banker: Harry, $3500, they'll probably want a deposit. We could be talking about $7,000 up front. Where's the initial $3,500 coming from?

Harry: I don't have it.

Banker: Harry, you just went bankrupt, it's over. You'll be out of business before you even start.

Harry:	O.k., I missed the deposit, so maybe we're talking about a little more money, but I still have the customers. I still have the experience, I still know where to get the equipment, I still have the down payment.
Banker:	I'm concerned that you still don't know how much money you really need.
Harry:	You made your point. I need to do some work. Should we stop now?
Banker:	No, lets keep going. We may see a few other obstacles to overcome. Keep the tour moving.
Harry:	Let's look at my equipment. I'm very proud of it.
Banker:	It looks to be brand new. Is it?
Harry:	Some is new and some I rebuilt myself. You're looking at $25,000 well spent.
Banker:	Harry these are large pieces of machinery. Did it cost much to move them here? And was it expensive to install and wire them?
Harry:	Not too expensive. All together maybe $2,000.

FACT - EQUIPMENT - $25,000 PLUS $2,000 INSTALLATION

Banker:	Harry only $2,000. Where did you get the money? It seems to me we've only looked at two things and you've gone broke twice. You just haven't done your homework.
Harry:	You're a very unkind man.
Banker:	No, I'm not unkind, you're hurting yourself, you're hurting you're family. You're asking for a $20,000 loan with $5,000 down and you need a rent deposit and you need to install your equipment, $5,500 that you don't have. That's more than you've even saved. How can you go forward?
Harry:	I've dreamt of this all my life, this has been my passion. I came in here for a few minutes and you've shattered it. I don't think that's very fair.
Banker:	No, what would be unfair is if I loaned you the money and let you start your business without enough resources and without the proper understanding of what it takes to start a business. So, do you want to keep going?
Harry:	Yes, let's keep going.
Banker:	What about the people.
Harry:	I think I'll need five.
Banker:	Who are they and what do they do?

Harry: *We have three full-time people. Charlie, my foreman, Jim, a senior pressman and Les, who does all our odds and ends and can repair most of our equipment. Oh yes, my wife Mary, does the books and she gets a small paycheck. So, counting myself, five people although one or two of them will be part-time. But payroll costs won't include me because I'm not going to pay myself.*

Banker: *You're not going to pay yourself. Aren't you going to be sad when you go home at night and you can't see the kids?*

Harry: *Why won't I be able to see the kids?*

Banker: *Because the house will be dark, there's no food, there's nobody there. They've left you. So, figure your monthly minimum, your car payments, monthly mortgage, etc. and add a couple hundred bucks on top of that and add that into your wages. So, when we add all that up, what is your full-time, normal weekly payroll?*

Harry: *$10,000*

Banker: *I agree. What about benefits, payroll takes, and other things?*

Harry: *What do you mean, payroll taxes and other things?*

Banker: *You've got taxes on the salaries, benefits you have to allow for, and most of the time, they add up to about 30-35% of your wages.*

Harry: *I didn't know that, I've never run a company. So, with taxes and fringe, just under $13,000 a month.*

Banker: *So, let's make sure we understand. The day you open, you're going to start to incur $13,000 a month in payroll and if your sales don't cover that, you're not only going to be bankrupt, you're probably going to have criminal penalties.*

FACT - PAYROLL - $13,000/Month

Banker: *So, let's just make sure we have that on the table. And, let's be clear about the other things we've determined. $5,000 deposit, $27,000 worth of equipment, $3,500 deposit and $3,500 a month. Have I got everything so far?*

Harry: *Yes, I think so.*

Banker: *Tell me about your supplies and inventory.*

Harry: *Well. I've got a great relationship with a company that supplies all the material, so that when I need it, I just order it.*

Banker: *How do you pay for it?*

Harry: *Well, when I get paid, they get paid. I've got a good reputation with them and they trust me, they know I'm going to be a good customer.*

Banker:	So, you buy just enough for the job?
Harry:	No, you always buy a little bit over because of spoilage and wastage.
Banker:	And, what about inks and other supplies?
Harry:	We always have to keep a supply of inks and things around.
Banker:	So, how much money do you need to buy these supplies to have on-hand?
Harry:	Let's see, $3,000, no, probably $5,000 would be a safer estimate.

FACT - INVENTORY - $5,000

Banker:	Strike three. Where are you going to get that $5,000? You just went bankrupt again.
Harry:	I see the point of your exercise. I guess we're done.
Banker:	No, Harry, what I promised you was that I'd help you understand what it took to start your business. It's not a question of being done or not done. Let's go through the rest of the exercise. We're not done. Let's finish the blind tour and then we'll take a look at how much money it really takes.
Harry:	Okay.
Banker:	When do you pay for the paper you order?
Harry:	Normal terms are due on delivery but these guys know me. I'll get 30 days in the beginning but someday I'll be back to quick pay.
Banker:	What types of clients do you service?
Harry:	All types. Some jobs are as small as $50 and some are $15,000. We're a general shop with all types of customers. The bigger clients I've told you about have given me letters of intention. That's my big ace. I've got $50,000 a month IN SALES. Would you like to see the letters?
Banker:	No not yet. Let's keep going. How do those customers pay?
Harry:	The small ones in cash, the larger ones in 30 days.
Banker:	Why are they going to pay you in 30 days, everybody pays in 60 days. Big corporations pay in 90 days. Why will they pay you in 30 days?
Harry:	Because I am a good supplier to them.
Banker:	But, Harry, 30 days. That means that whatever you're spending on payroll for that first month isn't going to happen. You're not going to get that cash in. How are you going to pay your bills if you are carrying those people for 30 days? You're financing them.

FACT - RECEIVABLES - ?

> *"The darkest moment of EarthLink was valentines day 1996 when our database and billing system melted down. We couldn't bill customers for two days. It was horrible, the backups had failed. It was brutal. I lived there, I was up for 48 hours straight down in operations. It was scary."*
> -Sky Dayton, Founder, EarthLink Network, Inc.

Develop your premises.

As the conversation continued, Harry and the banker developed a list of normal operating expenses, the gross margin Harry sought to maintain as he priced his jobs, and finally, Harry explained in great depth the future sales he felt he could get and, more importantly, why he would be able to get them. By using this blind tour approach, the banker developed the key premises that define the capital needs of a start up. He has not identified any loan capability or any potential income and subsequent profit that would be available for repayment, nor has the banker attempted to determine the probability of success. What has been developed and defined are the total capital requirements.

To finalize the exercise, these estimates must be put into proper perspective.

Types of Financial Needs – The Classic Approach

Different kinds of money.

Harry came to his banker with a list of capital equipment he wished to purchase. As far as he was concerned, they were his capital needs. In a way, Harry was correct, but not entirely. There are many aspects of starting the business and many facets of the funding that need to be understood.

Capital expenditures

Equipment and associated costs.

Capital needs represent the cost for all equipment needed plus appropriate taxes, freight, and installation. They are expenditures for physical items that have a life beyond one year or beyond the current operating period. Most potential entrepreneurs usually have an itemized list of equipment that is fairly accurate. Harry did. In our example his total was $25,000. In fact, he needed $2,000 of installation for a total of $27,000. He was 90% accurate but this was the first clue that he hadn't properly planned.

Soft costs ~ working capital

How much to keep afloat?

Working capital are the funds needed for doing business. Primarily, they represent the current asset portion of the balance sheet. The two primary items are accounts receivable and inventory.

To ascertain what is a reasonable receivable/inventory requirement, one must reverse the turnover ratios normally used by a financial analyst. That is to say, if one is reviewing an existing company that had $100,000 of receivables and annual sales of $600,000, the analyst would note that receivables turn over six times a year ($600,000/$100,000) or the turnover time is 60 days (360 days / 6 times). In our

*Average receiv-
able turnover?*

example of a new business, Harry assumed that he would generate average sales of $50,000 per month during the first year. In our interview he said that his major clients would pay in 30 days. If this is the case, then he would carry one month's sales as receivables or $50,000. If the average receivable turnover was 45 days, then he would carry average receivables of 1 ° months of sales. This would be a receivable balance of $75,000. A 15-day turnover would be $25,000 of receivables.

*Inventory
turnover.*

The inventory would follow the same basic rules. That is, the turnover rate of inventory must be determined and then the capital needs developed. In our ex-ample, Harry stated that he would carry only a few thousand dollars of inventory and would buy only for orders on an as-needed basis.

*What are the
terms?*

In starting your business you would have to determine the terms on which you would purchase material. For example, if you could buy an order and not pay for it for 45 days, then you would not have to pay for the material until you were paid by your client. If Harry were required to pay for the material in 10 days, then he would have to expend funds at least 20 days before funds were received (assuming 30 days receivable terms). The payable terms are critical since payables are in effect "borrow-ing from a supplier." As a result, they can reduce the amount of capital that must be raised from other sources. It is a fact that suppliers provide businesses with more credit than all of the banks combined. In addition to the primary soft cost of receivables and inventories (less payables), there are two other aspects of the current asset portion of the balance sheet to be considered. (It is really the working capital needs of the company that represent the soft cost.)

Some estimate of what prepaid items, such as insurance, must be funded needs to be made as well. It is reasonable to assume that Harry would have about $5,000 in prepaid items.

*Determine how
much cash on
hand is needed.*

The final soft cost deals with the cash on hand. Every company must have cash. Not in the sense of having a cushion for an emergency (which is necessary and is part of the capital needs), but rather the fact that cash must be physically in an account somewhere. How much cash is enough? It may be the one unanswerable question in all of finance. One rule which makes sense is to develop the premise of how many weeks of cash turnover the company should have. Considering the mail, etc, one can say that the working cash balance should total at least two weeks of average receipts. An equal argument could be made for one month's cash on the basis of turning over the cash 12 times a year. In our example, the monthly sales are to be $50,000. A two-week cash balance would be $25,000 of working cash. This is a bare minimum.

Summarizing all of these inputs we have gathered, we can show that Harry really has a need to be prepared for the following soft costs or working capital.

Cash	15 days	$25,000
Accounts receivables	30 days	50,000
Inventory	Arbitrary	5,000
Misc. Prepaid Items	Arbitrary	5,000
Total Soft Cost:		**$85,000**

Be wary of cash shortages.

The amazing fact is that Harry came to see the banker about financing a portion of the $25,000 of equipment he needed. Even without inventory, he needs better than 3 times that amount just in working capital. When these needs are not properly planned for in advance, then cash shortage will certainly follow. The banker may very well wish to help Harry. But, if Harry doesn't have control over his environment, there is little the banker can do. There is no greater sign of lack of control than such clear evidence of a failure to understand and anticipate cash needs.

You must be certain that adequate capital exists for both the fixed assets (equipment) as well as the soft costs needed. An old, but very true, adage is that most companies get into trouble because they have not adequately planned their cash needs.

Start Up Cost

Time frame until a sale varies.

When a new business is formed, there is a period during which fixed cost will continue to be expended in preparation for the actual beginning of production and eventual sale of product. This time frame varies. A used car lot is in business the day it opens. A steel mill may take three or four years from planning, environmental studies, construction of the facility, and debugging of the process. Certain individuals must be hired immediately and oversee the establishment of the process. Some will be added just before completion and be trained how to function and produce. In a small business, the potential owner may work part time as he establishes his own business. He may also run the business himself until orders are received and then he will only hire people on a part-time basis to complete them. In either case, once the decision to start is made, funds will begin to be expended.

Month 1: expenses, no income.

Start up losses are the losses incurred before the company reaches the break-even point. The first month you are going to have expenses, but no income. The second month you will have expenses and some income. It might be in the middle of the third month that your expenses will equal your income. But, until you reach that point, you will have losses, which are your start up costs.

Some of these costs may be capitalized by the accountants as part of the cost of machinery and equipment. Some may actually appear as start up costs on the company's balance sheet. The remainder may be directly expended as they are incurred. Regardless of the classification, these pre-start needs are cash expenditures that must be accounted for when the total needs of the company are determined. You must understand and accept this point.

Operating losses.

However, a second requirement for funds exists and is not as readily accepted. It is the operating losses per se, which are the actual costs of operations during the first several months that may or may not be covered by sales. By way of example, assume that the monthly fixed costs of our print shop are as follows:

Rent	3,500
Salary	13,000
Other	5,000
Total:	**$21,500**

Cover fixed costs for 3-6 months.

On the first day of operation, the company will spend $1,000 to open its doors ($21,500/20 working days). In all probability the business won't generate enough sales to cover the cost of goods plus this $1,000. Since these costs are not covered by sales, they must be accounted for and paid for by capital. Will the company cover its second day's cost? It's first week? First month? Obviously, there is no answer to these questions. The nature of the individuals, the amount of preordered sales, and the nature of the industry are all part of the answer. The classic approach to money says that when dealing with small entrepreneurial-type businesses, it is usually wise to plan on raising adequate capital to cover fixed cost for at least 3 to 6 months.

Don't underestimate.

It is important to recognize that Harry should have adequate capital to allow him the freedom to tackle the problem of starting the business. If he tries to start a business and at the same time is faced with the difficult task of feeding and housing his family, he is apt to lose both battles.

> *"At the time, we really needed the money to keep going. We needed money to operate, cash flow, the rent, the phone bills, everything. We needed a lot of that stuff. We were really scared that we wouldn't get the loan because it was taking so long. I think that was when we woke up and realized, wow, we might go out of business."*
> -Yvonne Buonaro, Founder, Kiyonna Klothing

The Plan

General guidelines determined.

We have in a very general sense and at a very simplistic level tried to walk through the establishment of a company. We have observed the obvious and the not so obvious. We have drawn a loose road map showing the progression from an idea to what hopefully will be a successful company. What we have developed is the criteria to assist in reviewing all of the financial ramifications of starting a business, as well as a general approach to use with existing companies as a means of exploring their cash needs.

The summary of our tour would result in the following schedule of financial needs:

Alot more than $5,000!

Fixed Assets		$27,000
Soft Cash		85,000
Start Up (3 mos.)	21,500 per mo	64,500
Total Capital Needs		**$176,500**

Classical rules.

Harry was shattered at this point. Many entrepreneurs have had a dream, had a passion, developed a concept, and walked into a money source and have been told that they are way off base in their financial planning. That's what happened to Harry. Harry walked into a classical source of money and was given a classical set of rules.

Summary

Don't let sales success destroy.

Both new and existing businesses are dependent on future revenues to continue. But success in sales efforts carries the responsibility of funding to adequate levels of working capital. Without such funding, sales success may very well destroy, as opposed to enhance, your chance of successfully raising funding.

The Entrepreneurial Approach

Are no rules in entrepreneurship.

But, entrepreneurs don't think in the classical sense. The rules that apply in the world of banking and according to the bean counters don't apply. Do you think the banker loaned Harry the money? What would your advice to Harry be?

Is it over for Harry?

Let's frame Harry in the context of the things that we have learned and in terms of feasibility. What is the ultimate test of feasibility? Who the customers are and how they will buy from you is what you determined in feasibility. What is the number one entry strategy? Starting with a customer in hand. So, Harry has all of the things from the feasibility study—industry knowledge, a defined customer, and a benefit for that customer. So, should Harry quit at this stage? No!

Get the contracts.

Think back to when we defined the difference between a compliment and a contract. Harry must turn his compliments into contracts and get the customers who have said they will do business with him to put their money where their mouth is. Harry must push aside the administrative mindset and embrace the entrepreneurial approach. Administrators think in terms of entire projects. Entrepreneurs operate in stages, take small steps, and manage the risk each step of the way. The banker shared the administrative approach with Harry, which is resource dependent and assumes full operation on day one.

Stage one needs.

Harry is in the first stage of operation and needs to operate as such. He doesn't need to build the business as though it were in full operation. He needs to build it for his first customer. Once that is accomplished, he can leverage that into the next three stages, one step at a time.

Outside the box thinking.

Instead of turning Harry away, the banker agreed to try to help Harry under two conditions. First, Harry had to agree to have an open mind and be open to new ideas. Second, he had to agree to schedule appointments with his potential customers and tell them that the bank was willing to back him with certain conditions. The banker told Harry that he had to ask his customers to sign a contract for an order and pay a 50% deposit on the order with the balance payable upon delivery.

Needed leverage.

Harry was not happy with this scenario. He felt this was a stab in the back of the people who were kind enough to agree to bring him business. But, the banker was experienced and knew that prepaid orders would give Harry leverage in the bank's mind and help to secure a loan. He also suspected that Harry had received compliments, not contracts. So, the banker convinced Harry and Harry proceeded to make his first sales calls.

Two signed the contract.

The majority of Harry's clients had complimented him and refused to put money down on an order at a new company not yet in existence. But, two believed in him and his ability to deliver. So, Harry collected 50% on two orders. This one guerrilla tactic enabled him to gain an extra $12,500.

Classical		Entrepreneurial
5,000	Harry's Savings	5,000
0	Customer Deposits	12,500
$5,000	**Total**	**$17,500**

Risk taker to risk manager.

The banker was leading Harry into an entrepreneurial approach and Harry was transitioning from a risk taker to a risk manager.

Recall the four stages of an entrepreneurial company:

Risk is now on Harry's shoulder's.

- Idea to first customer,
- First customer to multiple customers,
- Multiple customers to multiple customers and multiple products,
- Multiple customers and multiple products to harvest or reinvention.

With two customers in hand, the only question was whether or not Harry could fulfill those orders. As such, he was managing the risk, not taking risk.

Capital Expenditures

Size of operation factors in.

Another important differentiating factor between the classic and the entrepreneurial approach is the size of the operation. Harry wasn't going to be that big that fast and so the entire blind tour changes. He didn't need everything that he had originally thought, particularly in terms of equipment. When Harry assessed the needs of his first two customers, he realized that he didn't need such a big press, which meant that his equipment costs dropped by $10,000 to $17,000, which included installation and delivery.

Start Up Losses

Minimize start up needs.

The same reductions applied to his start up losses as well. When he thought about it, Harry realized that he didn't need as many people or as large of a building. As a result his start up costs dropped as well. Instead of the classic rule that 3 months of fixed costs were needed in the bank to get to break even, Harry was starting with an order. Since, it might take 30 days to get employees up to speed and things running properly, Harry decided he needed one month's worth.

Classical		Entrepreneurial
13,000	Wages	7,000
3,500	Rent	2,000
5,000	Other Costs	3,000
21,500	Monthly Losses	12,000
3 months		1 month
$64,500	**Total Losses**	**$12,000**

Working Capital

Rethink receivables and inventory.

Working Capital expenses were reduced in the same manner. Harry didn't have any accounts receivable because his orders were paid for in advance and on delivery. His inventory and prepaids were also lowered and his cash on hand requirements were eliminated.

Classical		Entrepreneurial
50,000	Accounts Receivable	0
5,000	Inventory	3,000
5,000	Prepaid Expenses	3,000
25,000	Cash On Hand	0
$85,000	**Total Losses**	**$6,000**

Vast differences.

Harry's total needs were therefore reduced substantially.

Classical		Entrepreneurial
27,000	Capital Expenditures	17,000
85,000	Inventory	6,000
64,500	Prepaid Expenses	12,000
$176,500	**Total Losses**	**$35,000**

One more effort

What a difference! And, all as a result of taking an entrepreneurial approach. But, the banker had one last piece of advice. He asked Harry to call the bank that had repossessed the equipment and ask if they would lease it to him instead of selling it to him. This eliminated his need for capital expenditures bringing his total cash needs to $18,000 and he had $17,500 in hand between his savings and the deposits received. He no longer needed $171,500 (176,500-5,000 savings).

The final solution

Harry only needed $500 to start his business.

> *"I actually had anticipated that it would cost me about $60,000 to open the first store. When it was all said and done, it was probably more like $85,000. So, even me having gone through an entrepreneur program and knowing that people typically underestimate capital needs, I still underestimated by 50% how much capital I would need."*
>
> -Bill Sanderson, Founder, Popcorn Palace

Entrepreneurial Exercise

This is your chance to perform your own blind tour. Take a moment to consider all of the costs that you will need to start your venture. Walk through a blind tour as the banker did with Harry and try to think of everything possible.

What capital expenditures will you need to start your business?

_____

_____

_____

_____

What working capital needs will your business have?

_____

_____

_____

_____

What start up costs are you going to incur?

_____

_____

_____

_____

⇒ **Tear out and move to your entrepreneurial road map binder.**

The Different Types of Money - An Example

How many types of money?

Now that you have seen how Harry could have done things differently, we will further outline the critical difference between the soft costs (working capital), capital expenditures, and start up costs.

Think in terms of candy.

To put the different types of money into perspective, think of a candy store. Candy retailers have learned that their business is extremely cyclical and about 48% of their business is done during Easter and another 27% takes place during Christmas. As a result, many candy stores are no longer stores, but kiosks in malls or elsewhere that are able to expand and contract with the seasons. In order to stock the kiosk, the candy store owner will need to use cash to purchase some inventory. This is considered his working capital because it will flow through the company and back to cash as he sells candy and then collects his receivables.

In other words, working capital is the money needed to run the day-to-day operations of the company. It is the money that you constantly have your eye on and that rotates through the business. These funds that cycle through the company make up the working capital as the diagram below indicates.

Working capital constantly cycles through the business.

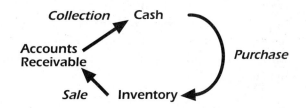

Cash exists in the business initially and by an action, it changes form. Making a purchase transforms it to inventory; selling turns it into accounts receivable; and finally, collection returns it to its original form of cash.

It's like the blood in your system.

A further analogy to help you understand this cycle is to compare it to the blood running through your system—your body. It's always there and is always needed and you're in trouble if you don't have enough of it.

Shelves are fixed assets.

On the other hand, if the candy store owner needs to purchase some shelves on which to store the candy, this is a capital expenditure. The shelves are purchased for a certain amount of money and become a fixed asset of the company. This money does not cycle through the company in any way. The shelves are not connected by an action back to cash, but instead are received as part of the cost of every sale. This is an important distinction to keep in mind when planning for the cash needs of your new venture and is exhibited in the diagram below.

Capital expenditures depreciate over time.

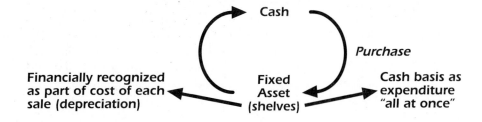

Cash used before sales are made.

Start up costs are the third type of money that have been discussed. These funds are used to meet operating expenses as opposed to purchase a hard or soft asset (shelves or candy inventory). They may initially be incurred either prior to the start of any actual sale or in excess of the income received from a sale. This portion of cash is used before reaching the breakeven point and is therefore the start up costs as the diagram below indicates.

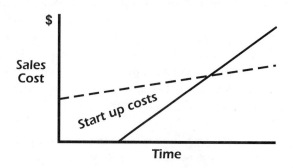

Start up costs incurred prior to breakeven.

Entrepreneurial Tactics for Money Needs

Think differently.

Previously, you learned about Harry, who was fortunate to have a banker willing to help him. It is now time to take the entrepreneurial approach to money a step further, while keeping the blind tour in mind. In so doing, the following concepts, which represent critical components of the entrepreneurial approach to money, should be kept in mind.

Map out stages

What needs to happen at each stage?

First, recall that entrepreneurs set goals which become the milestones or stages of their venture. In taking your blind tour, you need to write down everything that will take place and match those items against each stage of your planned journey. At each of the four stages of your company, there will be many tasks and developments that must occur. Write them all down. Be explicit. What needs to be accomplished to transition from idea to first customer? What are all of the elements that exist inside of the idea to first customer stage, the first customer to multiple customer stage, etc? How many employees will you have? How much are you going to spend on marketing and in what form? The blind tour built in stages gives you the framework from which to determine how much money it will take to start your business.

Triggers

What will cause things to happen?

Triggers are those things that cause an action to occur. You have mapped out each stage, you now need to know what will propel you from one stage to the next. As opposed to managers and administrators who think in terms of projects, entrepreneurs think of thing in terms of triggers. Instead of saying in month six, we will need to hire a new employee, entrepreneurs say, when we reach xx dollars in sales, we will need a new employee. Or, we will need new equipment to process the xxth sale. Your triggers cause you to bring in more resources and/or incur additional expenses, but only after the action has occurred. In effect, you pre-justify the action.

Expenses

Fixed vs. variable expenses.

There are two types of expenses: variable and fixed. Entrepreneurs prefer variable expenses because they are controllable. A variable expense is only incurred when something is sold. A fixed cost is an expense incurred regardless of whether or not there is a sale. For example, refering back to Harry's blind tour, a variable expense would be his use of supplies. With the exception of his modest supply of inventory on hand, Harry was only going to order materials when he received an order. Therefore, he would only incur the expense when he received his customer's order.

Variable leads to greater control.

A fixed expense on the other hand would be his rent. It doesn't matter if Harry has made a sale or not, he must pay rent every month or he will be thrown out of his building. As a result, entrepreneurs prefer to maximize their variable expenses and minimize their fixed costs, which gives them greater control as well as sufficient time to reach the next stage.

Break Even

Sales equal expenses is breakeven.

The point at which your sales equal your expenses is your break-even point. Entrepreneurs analyze the number of sales necessary to make their venture worthwhile. They do so by examining first their fixed and then their variable expenses, which enables them to calculate a break-even. By doing this at every stage, entrepreneurs are able to recognize the amount of sales they need to make and to determine their start up cost or "burn rate."

Sales Forecasting

Logic behind forecasting is critical.

Forecasting sales is a difficult, perhaps impossible, task. Yet it is also an extremely important aspect of the entrepreneur's financial projections because the logic behind your forecasting is critically examined by money sources before they will commit funds to your venture.

Which approach is right for your venture?

There are different ways in which this can be done. The "bottoms up" approach is to determine the minimum amount needed to be in business. In other words, it involves calculating the level of sales needed to cover both the fixed and vaiable expenses that are needed to get started, which gives you a sales target. A "most likely" approach is based on your personal knowledge. This can either come from customers in hand and how many orders they have placed at that particular stage or from knowledge gained from your distribution channels who already have their customers. Finally, a "capacity" forecast examines the upside and what will happen if measurable success occurs. Two aspects of this appraoch warrant some warning, however. Be careful not to be perceived as a dreamer, it is critical to be realistic at all times. This is your chance to show your vast knowledge of the industry and of your competitors. Use it to your advantage.

Don't be a dreamer.

There is no correct or incorrect forecast or method of forecasting. There is only valid, realistic, defendable logic or there is invalid "pie-in-the-sky" non-defendable assumptions. Logic beats assumptions.

Profit & Loss and Cash-Flow

Cash flow is lifeblood of company.

The profit and loss statement's primary function is to show how much profit (loss) an entrepreneur hopes to earn based on when a sale is made and costs legitimately incurred, as opposed to a cash flow which plots when cash is actually collected or expenses paid. While the P&L is extremely important to entrepreneurs and helps them to determine the long-term potential for the business, the cash-flow statement is even more critical because it dictates the actual funds available to the company at any given time. As has been stated before, many entrepreneurs have failed as a result of improperly forecasting their cash needs.

Thus, while the P&L is directly linked to the cash-flow statement, it does not track the actual inflow and outflow of cash. That is the function of the cash-flow statement, which determines how much cash is actually in the bank at all times.

P&L gives long-term profitability.

The primary difference between the two statements is timing. The P&L is the picture that tells how much money the business will ultimately make, whole the cash-flow statement tells when the business actually has or needs cash in the bank.

Cash Needs Assessment and Entrepreneurs Bet

How much total cash is needed to start?

The entrepreneur's bet is a term not found in most typical finance books because entrepreneurs assess money needs with an entrepreneurial approach, not a classical approach. As such, the entrepreneur's bet is the maximum amount of money needed to reach the cash break-even point and a cash needs assessment determines that amount—it aggregates all three types of money needed to start and begin to grow the business.

When does amount coming in equal amount going out?

Therefore, after doing a blind tour of your business, you must identify your findings in a cash needs assessment so that you will be able to intelligently seek the start up funding required for your business. The most critical component of the cash needs assessment is the sales forecasting because there is no basis for money coming in without a buyer. So, at that crucial juncture when the amount of money coming into the business equals the amount being spent by the business, the entrepreneur's bet has been reached.

Chapter Summary

Understanding money and how to properly forecast your financial needs in starting a new venture often frightens many people. It should not be a frightening experience. It is a tool set that can be understood and learned just as any other tool set.

Always keep in mind that money is an enabler and that it alone cannot start your business. Money should be framed around your entrepreneurial concept.

Recognize the different types of money and how much you need of each:

- Capital Expenditures
- Start Up Costs
- Soft Costs - Working Capital

Finally, be sure to take the entrepreneurial approach to money and think of creative ways in which you can finance the start up of your venture.

Chapter Ten Exercises/Discussion Questions

1. Explain the difference between the three different types of money requirements: capital expenditures, working capital, and startup losses.
2. Define the classical approach to determining financial requirements and how it differs from the entrepreneurial approach.
3. Identify unexpected financial problems in your business and how you might prepare for them.
4. Take a blind tour of your business.

Journey Ten: DeLeon Enterprises

DeLeon and the Company

Miguel DeLeon began his entrepreneurial endeavors as a teenager in Guatemala. But, he was not able to fully embrace this mindset when he first moved to the United States as he went to work on the production line of a defense manufacturing plant. While gaining vast industry knowledge, he was successfully climbing the ladder within the organization. However, much to his surprise, he learned, with just one week's notice, that the company was on the verge of bankruptcy.

Rather than sit idle, lose his job, watch his colleagues lose their jobs, and allow the company's customers to lose their supply source, Miguel seized the opportunity. He decided to buy the company and drastically alter its processes.

In addition to defense products, the company also produced custom electronics for certain clients, including components for equipment such as airport x-ray machines, guitar amplifiers, conveyer-belt systems for airport luggage, and airplane-trash compactors.

Miguel vividly recalls the day the Vice President of the bank informed him that there was only one week left before the doors would be closed. He recalls, "I'll never forget that in my life as long as I live because it was very painful to see my former employer, to see all my coworkers, to see their faces when we told them, there's no more company. I think that's the darkest moment in my life."

Finding the Money

Miguel knew that personally taking action was the only solution. After asking the banker what would be done with all of the equipment, he was informed that it would most likely be sold at an auction. Instead, DeLeon convinced the banker that he should be the buyer and was given two more weeks to find the money.

His original idea was to apply for a loan. He had determined that he needed about $150,000 to buy the equipment and maintain operations. But, classic money was not an option. The loan officer told DeLeon that his business could not be viewed as one that is up and running, but as a new company in which case it could not authorize a loan. So, DeLeon had to get creative in his approach.

His first thought was his customers. After many phone calls and personal visits, Miguel got his customers to change their payment terms to 15 days, which brought in some cash flow. Not all customers were willing to comply with the new terms, it took some good negotiating skills and time, but Miguel promised to deliver.

His second tactic was to talk to his landlord, who wanted a deposit and first month's rent up front. DeLeon made another personal visit. "I went down there and I talked to him personally and said, look, this is what happened. I had nothing to do with it, I just bought the assets of this company. I don't have the money to pay you rent or give you a deposit right now, but I'd like to stay in this place."

After considering his predicament, the landlord proposed a 3-year contract for $1000 less per month in rent. Miguel was ecstatic, but turned it around once more and agreed to commit for one year, not three, and his rent was reduced by $1000 a month.

Deadlines were fast approaching and Miguel was constantly thinking of ways to keep the company alive. "Between Thursday and that Monday, if I slept for two hours, three hours, it was too much. I was just too worried about making payroll, about getting money to buy pay the supplies and how I was going to raise the money to pay the bank."

He did it and DeLeon Enterprises was born, but not without sacrificing his children's college funds and every other penny he had saved over the years. He felt he had to do it, to commit 150% to make it work.

Eight months later Miguel secured a loan through a local nonprofit business development agency for more than $200,000. This enabled the company to cover its entire overhead expenses and take care of the payroll back up that had accrued. Miguel did not draw a salary for about 18 months from the opening day and even then it was not near the amount he had been getting paid from his former employer, it was primarily so that he could "quit living out of my credit cards."

The Customers

Once he had raised the money, Miguel needed to figure out how to maintain and increase his customer base. As Vice President, he had observed the entire sales process of the organization and felt that there were numerous areas that needed improvement. Specifically, he did not agree with the sales manager's approach. "The way he (the sales manager) was prospecting was not effective. He was not targeting the market that we were focused on," recalls DeLeon. "Its better to have 20 small ones (customers) than one big one that will give you one contract every two years." DeLeon saw many deficiencies that needed addressing.

After taking over the company, Miguel fired most of the executive staff and instituted entrepreneurial tactics. Personalized sales and project management were the critical factors in winning back clients. It was not an easy task though, as the former organization had not always delivered. As Miguel stated, "to establish a solid relationship with my customer, it took some time. It took a lot of personal meetings to show them that we were not working just for the profit, that we want to have a long term relationship with them."

One of the many benefits DeLeon Enterprises offers its clients is its open-door policy. Customers can drop in anytime they want without calling or setting up an appointment and check on the status of their orders. "We like to tell them (the customers) they can come anytime. That's how much confidence we have that this shop is operating properly," says DeLeon.

The company also tries to stay one step ahead of its customers and anticipate their future needs. As DeLeon's Operations Manager, Jay Prada, states, "sometimes, we like to do things before the customer asks for them. For example, we know a particular customer wants it a certain way. So, we try to have it ready before they ask for it. We can be ready to deliver it if they ask for it."

Success

Focusing on customer's needs, making the customer king, and employing entrepreneurial tactics has enabled DeLeon Enterprises to transition from a company on the verge of bankruptcy to a thriving enterprise. The new Sales Manager, Ray Payne, sums it up, "we always bend over backwards. If they need the job really fast, we'll rush it through, we'll get them out of a jam at times."

DeLeon reflects, "After the darkest moment of my life of closing the company and going into the unknown of opening up a brand new one, I am very happy and proud that I did it. Because that gave me the courage to work harder for this company because the odds of my company making it were like 1000 to one." DeLeon Enterprises is a thriving business that maintains a customer focus and personalized attention.

Journey Ten Case Questions

1. What guerrilla tactics did Miguel DeLeon utilize?
2. What characteristics did he display that enabled him to succeed?
3. How did DeLeon creatively solve some of his financial problems?
4. Did he stray from the classical approach to money? If so, how? What tactics did he employ?
5. Did he take a blind tour?

Chapter Eleven
How and Where Do I Find The Money?

Chapter Eleven Major Concepts

- The Rules of Money
- Knowing the Money Source Rules
- Friendly Money
- Assistance Money
- Professional Money
- Public Money

Journey Eleven: Zanart Entertainment Revisited

Up Front & Personal: Insight Into A Commercial Bank

The Challenge of Money

Is money truly frightful?

While the mere thought of money is scary to most entrepreneurs, the notion of *asking* for money is truly frightful. Yet without money, there is no business—no means by which to start the business and thus be rewarded upon completion.

Manageable and achievable.

However, in reality, raising money is perhaps the most manageable and achievable aspect of the entrepreneurial journey. Unlike customer searches and the constant challenge of finding and testing, the search for money is clearly defined. Suppliers of money are readily identifiable and most publish their rules of investment. The need to test for unknowns is eliminated.

Search for money is not abstract.

Similarly, the abstract methods used to develop and test products and services are not part of your search for money because this search is not abstract. The difficult issue here is not to define, but to meet the requirements of money sources. Once that is accomplished, money becomes available.

Thus, the great challenge of money is to follow the rules, and not to try to change or to get around them. Following the rules usually leads to success.

Rules Of Money – An Entrepreneur's Perspective

Rule 1 – Money doesn't create value

Remember the model business?

The early portion of this journey focused on the entrepreneurial mindset and the model business—what type of business is right for you. Reward systems and the underlying reasons behind the desire to start were also discussed.

Create value by doing.

The most common reason entrepreneurs want to start a business is to control their own destiny, to do what they want to do, and to have the lifestyle of their choice. While some define that as becoming billionaires, most entrepreneurs merely want a reasonable income that will afford a comfortable lifestyle. For them, the money portion of the journey is about doing what they want to do and having the ability to harvest the value that they and their associates have created. In other words, most entrepreneurs love the journey and their passion is for the journey—not the money. Learn from their message.

Value is derived from the "doing."

Money doesn't create success.

Also, commercially, money doesn't create value. Simply raising money does not mean instant success. The score only counts at the end of the game—not the beginning.

Money is the booster propelling the business forth.

Money has only one value for entrepreneurs—as the commodity necessary to execute a business plan. As such, money is critical. But the value of entrepreneurial efforts comes from the ability to design and then to execute the action plan in the face of "live competitors" in the business arena.

Upon successfully executing your vision, you have created value.

Rule 2 – Don't revert to thinking like an administrator

Grow your venture in stages.

Recall the earlier message that entrepreneurs are not administrators trained to think in terms of launching new projects with virtually unlimited resources. Rather, entrepreneurs are customer focused and recognize the need to grow a new venture in stages—not all at once. As Harry learned, creating a fully operational company in one step requires a great deal of capital that entrepreneurs do not have.

Are you seeking an instant title?

Thus, when searching for money, think in stages and determine where in the lifecycle your venture is. There is a big difference between raising money to start a venture and becoming president of a company that has been bought for you. People that want and seek a great deal of funding all at once are typically those that want to be an instant President.

Execute the vision.

Also, be careful not to search for money too early. Many good ideas fill the graveyards of dead ventures because too much time was spent searching for money and not enough time on executing the vision.

Rule 3 – What have you done to date?

Leverage accomplishments.

Ideas do not beget money. Rather, money finds individuals who have structured concepts, who know an industry, who have identified a customer, who have tested a benefit need, and who have built an execution plan. Once accomplishments have been made, money typically follows.

This is the value entrepreneurs bring to a money source. They are not popcorn heads with great ideas; they are disciplined, focused and zealous entrepreneurs. Their passion for the journey has brought them this far and unless they have accomplishments to leverage, they are without value.

Where is your passion?

So, if you are in the process of seeking money, but do not yet have anything to show for your business, perhaps it is time to rethink your passion for the journey.

Rule 4 – Learn the money sources rules before you play

Do your homework.

The process of raising money is time consuming and can be frustrating. Do not make it more difficult than it has to be by trying to raise money without knowing the rules of engagement. Recall the "wannabe" entrepreneurs who try to find or invent a perfect product without first testing the market. They have limited, if any, success and typically require a large amount of capital. Similarly, entrepreneurs who do not do their homework or take the time to learn the rules of engagement will also meet with limited, if any, success.

What are their needs?

Just as successful fundraisers or sales people must first learn the needs and desires of their potential investors or customers, so too must entrepreneurs learn the needs of their money source. In pitching your business plan, you are selling it to the investor. So, follow the same sales approach learned earlier in the book. Find out what thier needs are and then be convincing you can fulfill those needs.

What do the sources want?

And, what do money sources want? A former banker gives perhaps the best and truest, albeit generalized, answer to that question. He always said you need to know two things to receive money: 1) what will be done with the money and 2) how will the investor/bank get paid back? While the economy and society have changed a great deal since he first made that statement, the first question remains the same— what's the money for? In order to receive an investment, you must be prepared to clearly describe the ways in which you intend to use any money received.

Times have changed.

In today's jargon, the answer to the second question does change. Rather than asking how to get paid back, each source will most likely want to know: 1) what is the harvest, 2) what is the return, and 3) what is the collateral? Each source has a different requirement, which will be explored later in the chapter.

The three C's represent another set of guidelines taught in the banking industry. They help to define the basis for funding and are applicable to all money sources.

The three C's are basis for initial impression.

Character—what kind of a person are you? What is your track record? What are your ethical standards?

Capital—what do you have in the pot? How much hard work or sweat equity have you invested? What did you do without to get to this point?

Capacity—are you capable of doing what you say you are going to do? Do you have the ability and needed experience to get it done? Do you have a team of players with complementary skills? Is the market capable of accepting what you seek to do?

Knowing both the general rules of all sources and the specific rules of each money source is the key to attracting the funds needed to execute the plan you have built.

Rule 5 – Know the different types of money

Money is not money is not money.

While a rose is a rose is a rose, as Harry found out, money is not money is not money. In addition to different types of money, there are different sources of money and recognizing the different rules for the various types of money will enhance your ability to gain funds from the appropriate source.

Recall and be able to identify the difference between capital expenditures, working capital, and startup costs.

> *"The most important lesson I learned about raising money is that you want to make sure you raise it at the right time because if you raise it too soon, you're going to be giving up too much, its going to be too expensive. If you raise it too late, you're going to be negotiating from a position of weakness and not a position of strength. So, timing is so critical and so important."*
> -Bill Sanderson, Founder, Popcorn Palace

Entrepreneurial Exercise

With character, capital, and capacity being a basis for funding, it is important for you to be aware of your status within each of these categories. Take this time to consider your character, capital, and capacity so that when you are faced with a money source, you are properly prepared.

Character: What is your track record? What are your ethical standards? Identify an ethical situation in which you have found yourself and how you have dealt with it.

_____

_____

_____

_____

_____

Capital: What financial investment do you personally have in your start up? What about sweat equity? How many hours have you put into making your vision a reality?

_____

_____

_____

_____

Capacity: What is your background? Why are you capable of making this happen? Do you have a management team identified who will help to execute your vision?

_____

_____

_____

_____

_____

⇒   **Tear out and move to your entrepreneurial road map binder.**

Rule 6 - Timing the search for money

The oldest adage is that timing is everything. The antidote is that if timing isn't everything then it is at least 90% of everything.

Search for money before you need it.

When is the right time to get money? The experience of successful entrepreneurs dictates that the search for money must begin before you need it. The observation of one entrepreneur that bankers are individuals who give out umbrellas on sunny days and ask for them back at the first sign of rain has been proven correct. In other words, don't go searching for money on a rainy day. Walking into an investor or banker highlighting your accomplishments rather than waving your collection notices is far more likely to result in funding.

Always in the money hunt.

Entrepreneurs are always in the hunt for money. Just as they are constantly seeking new opportunities, new customer needs, or new distribution channels, entrepreneurs are always following their dream by passionately pursuing the components necessary to start their journey.

By always being in the hunt, you are searching for clues that will enhance the probability of success and that will enable you to further comprehend the identification and decision process of money sources.

Time your pitch.

While the search for money is continuous, knowing the buy-in process of the particular money source you are soliciting at that specific time means that you know when to approach that source and the rules by which that source makes investment decisions. Time your pitch.

> *"You need to understand what the deal is and what the benefit is to the person who has the money. When do they get their money back, how much do they get, do they get any control, do they get any management power, or do they just get their money back with a certain rate of return? Those are the things that you do need to know right up front."*
> -Debbie Esparza, Esparza & Associates

Rule 7 - Investors are more (not less) dependent on you after they invest

How much to give up?

There is a constant challenge, without solution, faced by all entrepreneurs—how much of the company should be given up for money? What percentage of the company is appropriate for investors to receive in return for the tools needed (not just money) for success?

Fear of loss of control.

The greatest fear is loss of control. Entrepreneurs constantly struggle with the notion that the company they have built from scratch will no longer be "theirs" and that the investors will own it.

When will you lose majority control?

However, nothing could be further from the truth. Inevitably, the entrepreneur's percentage of stock ownership will almost always fall below majority control. It is rare for this not to happen. So, the question is not if, but when that will occur and it

Increase the value through accomplishments.

is for this reason that entrepreneurs seek to grow in stages. Each stage is an accomplishment and each stage increases the overall value of the company. Raising an initial $100,000 may cost 20 or 25% of the company. But if the goal of that particular stage is met, then the next stage may support a value wherein the subsequent round of financing results in $600,000 for 20%—a $3,000,000 overall valuation.

Meet your milestones.

Control, as opposed to ownership, is only lost when entrepreneurs do not accomplish what has been promised. If an execution strategy is designed but not met, money sources will take action to protect their investment. Often, this means exercising their rights to control the board by electing additional board members. Alternatively, it may involve bringing in a new management team or a set of resident advisors, at which point, control is lost.

> *"Is this a strategy of a big fish in a small market or a small fish in a big market? A small fish in a big market is better because you've got a lot of potential from a growth standpoint. A big fish in a small market, you're potential is capped and that's not going to be as exciting to a venture investor."*
> -Lloyd Greif, Founder, Greif & Co.

While "nothing succeeds like success" is true, "nothing assures control like success" may be even truer.

Rule 8 – Consider the cost of money and the cost of opportunity

What's the alternative?

What is the cost of money? It is not what you pay in interest or what you give up in equity. The real cost of money is the opportunity you may be forgoing if you don't have the money.

What might you be forgoing without money?

All entrepreneurs have stories about tough "money" negotiations and how they held out—didn't cave in—because the cost of borrowing or ownership dilution was too high. Unfortunately the story almost always ends with an admission of how much money they would have made if they had caved in and taken the money despite its apparent "high cost." So the real question is how much did they loose in an attempt to save?

> *"When someone says, try to hold onto as much of the company as long as you can, I have to ask myself a question: what is the opportunity that you're looking at. I can hold onto that company for a longer period of time, but if the opportunity begins to evaporate, begins to go away during that period of time, have I maximized my values?"*
> -Gene Miller, Peregrine Ventures

Rule 9 – The first rule of engagement—never start without an introduction

Cold calls rarely work.

Since character and capacity are among the most basic money rules, it is only logical that they must be met first. Therefore, entrepreneurs making cold calls on investors are not likely to meet success because they are not able to sell their character. Without knowing the entrepreneur, a money source is unlikely to invest any time in even answering the call.

Referrals provide instant credibility.

On the other hand, if an associate refers you to a money source, then you come with instant credibility. This does not mean that an investor's background and other appropriate checks will be eliminated, it merely means that the money source is willing to speak to you and explore the opportunity. An introduction is just that, it is not a guaranteed investment. If your passion and vision are appealing to and meet the requirements of that particular source, the customary due diligence will then be performed.

A seasoned venture capitalist addressed a student networking session and shared that in 33 years of practice he had never funded a single venture in which the business plan came in the mail or over the wire.

Choose right advisers.

Choosing the right advisors, outside professionals (lawyers, bankers), and ultimately board members has as much to do with successfully raising funds as does any other component of your financial forecast.

Rule 10 – Don't fight their rules

Know what they expect.

Doing your homework, becoming credible in your industry, drawing a valid, logical, and defendable execution plan means that you are truly prepared and that you know what you need and why. But, to be ready to face money sources, you must also be knowledgeable about their rules and be cognizant of the fact that money is not money is not money.

Don't try to change someone's religion.

Upon learning their rules, be sure to play the game within them. Don't fight them. If one source does not do the type of deal you want, find another one. Your time is too valuable and the opportunity window is too tight to try to change someone's religion. There are other choices. For example, banks lend money—they don't invest. Trying to get startup equity money from a bank won't happen. Know that and don't try to change it. (While you might get a private investor to put up acceptable equity in order for you to receive a loan, don't confuse yourself, you convinced the private investor and the bank is merely a pawnbroker for the security.)

What's their niche?

Also be aware that money sources like and dislike certain types of investments and loans. Just as you have niches in your business, this is their right and responsibility. If they want to do apartments or high tech and not widgets, that's their choice. If you are selling widgets, don't waste time with the ones who fund high tech. Find another source that understands and likes your niche.

Qualify the source.

But beware of a source's capacity. How much of one type of investment or involvement in one industry does that source want? Always remember that a good sales person starts by asking questions—qualifying the buyer/investor.

Finally, do not ask about or tell money sources what you are willing to pay. Instead, ask what types of deals they have done—find out the price later.

Sell your journey.

In almost every negotiation the price point is directly dependent on how much money sources know about you and your journey. Spend your time selling that. When they are interested they'll tell you what kind of prices they are accustomed to receiving for deals like yours.

> *"It's an estimate on the part of the Venture Capitalist as to what the situation needs. Do we need brilliant technology, do we need superb marketing, or do we need someone who can build an organization and build it rapidly to take advantage because this opportunity may not be around for a long period of time? So, it begins with a judgement, what does the situation need?"*
>
> -Gene Miller, Peregrine Ventures

Knowing the Money Sources Rules

What are their rules?

With the rules of money in place, it is now time to explore the individual sources of money and learn their specific rules and criteria.

While there are no absolutes, one key aspect to finding the appropriate source of money is to align the various money sources with the stages of your business. In a general sense, money sources change as your company grows over its lifecycle.

As a result, general categories of funding can be matched against the company's stage as shown in the diagram below.

Company Lifecycle

Align sources with stages.

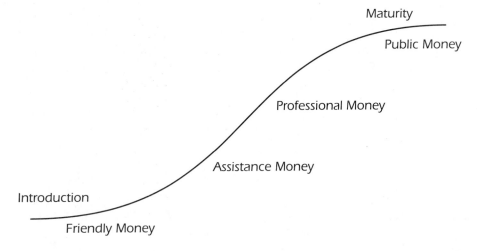

In addition to the timing of your lifecycle, there are five other points of differentiation between the various money sources. Having knowledge of these will increase your probability of success.

Know their points of differentiation.

1. Reason for investing—Why do money sources invest? What are their primary and secondary considerations? Each source will have different reasons for investing.
2. Effect of investing—Do sources want their money to be a true investment, which reduces the entrepreneur's equity or do they want to make a loan, which does not affect ownership? Or, do they want both?
3. Form of repayment—How will the source be repaid? Some sources look to the entrepreneur's ability to earn profits to get their funds back (usually a loan source) while other sources will often require a harvest—a sale or an IPO—to get their return.
4. Rate of return on investment—What is the rate of return to be expected? What are the differences in the rates of return among various money sources? Do all charge the same? Why or why not?
5. Level of control—Which money sources will have a greater need for control over the venture? Which ones don't want control? Why?

Know what they expect.

Keeping both the timing of the lifecycle and the five key points of differentiation in mind, let's review the specific sources of money.

Sources For Money

Friendly money

Friends and family invest in you.

In the very early stages of a start up, entrepreneurs tend to attract money from a close circle of individuals they know. This is primarily because these friends know the entrepreneur's character and capacity and are willing to invest in the person, not the business. At this stage and from this source, the investor usually does not seek a great deal of additional information and puts money down because he or she believes in you, the entrepreneur, whatever your idea may be.

Level of investment usually modest.

Many individuals start companies with the financial and emotional support offered by family. Most people have an aunt or uncle with whom they are closely aligned and who may wish to be part of the excitement of a new start up. The amount of investment is usually modest, but adequate for the entrepreneur to gain his first targeted accomplishment.

> *"My uncle really wanted to support me. So, he wrote me a check for $10,000 right on the spot, and I didn't even know what to do with it. The fact of the matter is that I had the first 10 grand, and the first money is the hardest to get. At that point people started jumping in behind him and saying, well, gee this thing is going to work."*
> -David LaMontagne, Founder, Vessel Assist Association

If you are fortunate enough to be offered this type of friendly money, you need to be sure that you understand the rules of acceptance. These differ depending on the category of friendly money as defined below.

Three types of friendly money.

Friendly Money – sources that invest in you, the person, as their primary motivation. There are 3 categories of participants. They are:

- Family
- Cocktail Circuit
- Customers & Suppliers

Friendly money comes early.

Maturity

Public Money

Professional Money

Assistance Money

Introduction

Friendly Money

Family

Family investments can be emotional.

Family is obvious. They know and love you and that's why they will get involved. But be careful of family because once money is accepted, you pay it back. Family members are driven by your success, which is the format of their return. And, when successful, they will expect to be paid back with some upside. Certainly some interest on the money or some ownership (modest) as a thank you.

Agree to terms in advance.

You would be wise to get the repayment understanding in advance. In the entrepreneurs world that is known as "making all bet's on the first tee." Prior to starting the match, outline the money rules and once the game starts, the rules can't be changed.

What happens if you fail?

On the other hand, should you not succeed, recognize that you may have an emotional responsibility to repay your family, even if it requires you to mortgage or second mortgage your house (if not already done). Or it may mean a second or even third part time job. Family commitments are stronger than the money itself. For this reason, family money is the most expensive because it always has to be repaid. Issues of stock appreciation or rates of return are secondary.

Cocktail Circuit

Angels are divine guardians for you and your firm.

This phrase has been used to describe the range of investors who are motivated to invest in you but are one step removed from family. Historically, "angels" comprise the primary subgroup of this category of investors and as the name implies, they are viewed as divine guardians for you and your firm throughout its life. They are

Be wary of angels.

motivated to invest in you and may even seek to guide you as a guardian angel would. But, the name also depicts a kindness or gentleness, which is not true. Angels are professionals with vast amounts of experience and who are not shy about expressing their opinions.

What strangers have you met?

This category also includes professional and/or trade-related contacts and even individuals you meet through social networks at cocktail parties—thus the name. All of these people represent important strangers you meet along your journey. And, when the time is right for this source of money, it is available to assist you with early round funding.

Like the mystique and excitement.

As opposed to the desire to see you succeed that motivates family, this group gets involved because they love the mystique and excitement of being part of a start up. They also love the thought of potentially being part of the next Microsoft, AOL, or Intel. This combination of excitement and greed does require a more formal set of engagement rules. There is no altruistic motivation—their primary reward is to make money.

They do expect a large return.

Their rules almost always include an issuance of stock and they typically expect a big harvest either from an IPO or a sale of the company. While their initial joy is being part of a success, their ultimate goal is to be the next start up millionaire. A return of less than 10 times their early round investment money would be a disappointment.

Nature of angels has changed.

The ongoing evolution of angels is a new phenomenon. In the past, angels have typically been wealthy individuals who brought money and talent in the very early rounds of funding. They also brought their experience of managing growth. Today, angels are of the same cloth but are forming into BANDS. There are several such BANDS throughout the country that range from loose associations to formalized groups. In many of these formal groups there are rules governing each member's annual investment minimum as well as the amount of time each is required to invest to perform due diligence on clients sponsored by other members of the BAND.

Highly selective process.

To gain access to a BAND, the selection process varies, but is also somewhat formal. First, those seeking funds need to be sponsored by a member of the BAND who then arranges for a presentation to a small screening group. If successful at that level, then a presentation is made to a larger screening group and then eventually to the full angel consortium.

Wide spectrum of angel investors.

Therefore, angels now cover a wide array of investment types. At one end of the spectrum, they are the independent, experienced, and wealthy individuals acting as mentors and investing in the character of the person and excitement of the start up. At the opposite end, angles are functioning as venture capitalists, but with their own funds.

In all cases, the key ingredient is that they are still investing in you, but with strong expectations on a stock position and a large upside return.

> *"They (angels) might even lend a hand in terms of helping you—making a recommendation in terms of bringing in a management team or a member of management to strengthen the company where it might be weak. Or as we said, an angel can act as a mentor in terms of, not only the management team, but also in terms of their own experiences and the pitfalls that early stage companies might have."*
>
> -Lloyd Greif, Founder, Greif & Co.

Customers and suppliers

Why are they friendly money?

The largest source of new venture funding comes from the individuals and companies from whom you buy or to whom you sell—your customers and suppliers. Yet these sources are often overlooked as a source of money and curiously classified as Friendly Money.

Selling yourself.

However, they should not be overlooked and the reason they are considered friendly money is because just like family and cocktail circuit friends, they know you and are often willing to take a chance on you. Being well known in your industry means that your contacts not only know you, but they also know your character and capacity.

Can offer special terms.

Suppliers can easily offer you normal trade payment terms or extended terms because this represents a controllable risk for them. Despite the fact that you are a new company with a financial statement that may not warrant credit, they trust that you will turn the inventory. The supplier's upside is a loyal, long-term customer. If perhaps you do fail, then inventory can be seized by them much more efficiently than by any other entity. (This may require that they perfect certain liens and Uniform Commercial Code filings).

Ask for payment in advance!

Customers, particularly those that are familiar with you, are not only able to make buy decisions, but they are also able to negotiate special payment terms that are favorable to you. Such terms could require them to pay you sooner than industry norms. It is not uncommon for initial customers to agree to pay on delivery or even put down a deposit in advance. In return for such terms, you may have to grant certain concessions to your client, such as earlier delivery time or price breaks. However, the cost of agreeing to these needs is quite small if the up-front or advance payment enables you to minimize your working capital requirements in the start up phase. Establishing such a mutually beneficial relationship with a customer provides you with money assistance as well as the credibility to further negotiate with other money sources because you have a customer in hand and can leverage this accomplishment.

> *"We launched the company by attracting three initial customers who gave 50% deposits with their orders. Having these in hand we were able to go to the cocktail circuit and raise the remaining funds with minimal dilution of equity."*
>
> -Mark MacWhirter, co-Founder, ShopTrac

Entrepreneurial Exercise

Since friendly money is the most common source for money in the early stages of a venture, take this time to identify potential sources of friendly money that might be willing to invest in you and/or your company.

What family members do you know that might be willing and able to take a chance on you? What would their expectations be in return?

_____

_____

_____

_____

Who have you met on the cocktail circuit that loves the excitement of a start up and would want to be part of yours? How many strangers can you list to whom you could pitch your idea?

_____

_____

_____

_____

Do you have any customers or suppliers that would be willing to work under special terms? Have you built good relationships with these potential money sources?

_____

_____

_____

_____

⇒   **Tear out and move to your entrepreneurial road map binder.**

Assistance Money

Moving through the lifecycle.

Introduction

Friendly Money

Assistance Money

Professional Money

Public Money

Maturity

Legislative initiatives.

Assistance money is an umbrella term for the various legislative initiatives that help start up firms. Various government entities have passed legislative acts that require these money sources to give loans, make investments, and provide grants and other such monies.

The SBA is primary source.

The primary example is the Small Business Administration. (SBA). Whether it is a direct SBA loan (rare) or an SBA guarantee to a bank or other financial institution (more common), the federal government has bankrolled many an entrepreneur.

> *"Assistance money is the kind of money that you can get access to through the government, like SBA guarantees or there are a number of community and economic development incentives and initiatives throughout the area for example."*
> -Debbie Esparza, Esparza & Associates

Are you a minority?

The government also offers a variety of minority programs that serve as money sources. Generally referred to as Section 8A loans, they are available to certain gender or race minorities.

Local or regional Economic Development Councils also provide counseling, education, and funding either through assistance loans or through direct funding of the programs.

> *"We went through a program called the women's prequalification program where they first review your business plan and then send it onto the SBA and say we've already looked at it, it looks great, will you fund it. So, we went that way, and then Bank of America came into the picture and we got one of the fastest approvals that the lady who did our package had ever seen."*
> -Kim Camarella, Founder, Kiyonna Klothing

It's not easy.

However, getting these funds is difficult. The motivation for assistance money is clearly stated—government's desire to assist start ups. But, in order to obtain that assistance, you must work within the constraints of a government office that is required to adhere to a fixed and lengthy bureaucratic process. The red tape can be exhausting. Don't overlook this as a source of funding because it is viable, but know the rules under which money will be granted and heed the following words of caution.

What's the security required?

<u>Don't expect a gift</u>. Almost all agencies are required by law to take all that you have as security—even if the security is illiquid or doesn't fully secure the loan. You will pledge the equity in your house. You will pledge any stocks or bonds. You will give a blanket guarantee that pledges everything.

Time consuming.

<u>Don't expect an easy change down the road</u>. All start ups desire to grow under control, however it does not always happen that way. You must recognize that receiving assistance money takes time. If you are dealing at arms length with other money sources, e.g. a bank, and your business is growing at an accelerated rate or you need a new piece of equipment, then requesting a loan for additional working capital or new machinery is relatively straight forward. So is the answer—either yes or no—in a short period of time. However, the same is not true of all agency backed lending. The red tape will be present and a response may be too late to assist your growing pain.

> *"It took me about a year and a half before I got some money—a little working capital—from the valley development economic center which is an institution funded by the department of commerce."*
> -Miguel DeLeon, Owner, DeLeon Enterprises

Professional Money

Continuing on the road to success.

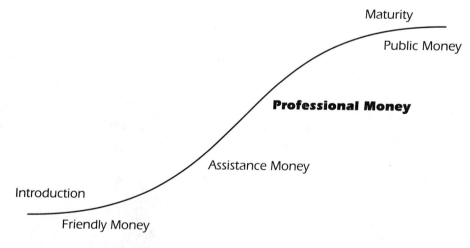

Beyond the start up.

Professional money is termed "professional" for two primary reasons. First, at this stage, entrepreneurs have made many accomplishments and reached a level of growth such that their business is now a going concern and no longer a start up.

The business is rapidly accelerating rather than simply surviving and the entrepreneur is now a professional in every sense.

Dealing with pros.

Second, the money sources themselves are experienced professionals who have seen much in their careers. Their rules are stringent and you must be fully prepared because the game is more exacting—it is professional to professional.

Venture Capitalists

VCs are the most visible.

Venture capitalists are the most well known professional money source. They are the folklore heroes that gave birth to the technology age by funding many of today's high tech leaders. Apple Computer and Intel are among the top tech firms that secured early venture capital money. Upwards of 1,000 venture firms existed during the technology surge of the mid 80's.

But the least likely to help at the true start up stage.

Yet for all the lore and glamour, this segment accounts for less than 2% of early stage money deals done. Venture money is rarely made available to a start up and may actually be the smallest source of money.

Strict requirements.

However, there is a great deal of hype surrounding venture capitalism. The reason for this is that if you are able to judge your start up and needs against the very demanding rules of a VC, then your preparedness is likely to serve you well when dealing with any money source. It forces you to set internal standards for your fundraising. Being ready and having done the necessary homework to meet a VC's requirements (even though you may not be the type of firm they finance), means that you are prepared to face the rules and regulations of the SBA, an angel, or any other money source.

Expect huge return in a hurry.

You must understand two critical points when dealing with venture capitalists. First, they seek investments with very large upsides and want to propel your company into mach speed. They are also in a big hurry and want this growth to occur in a relatively short period of time. They expect you and your firm to blossom on a time schedule that meets their needs and their goals. In other words, merely doubling or tripling your market share may not be considered sufficient.

They want to cash out.

Second, venture capitalists aim for liquidity at the right time. Therefore, they must see a harvest in the form of either an initial public offering (IPO) or a merger. Their investors require them to show returns and expect more than just paper profits. Thus, involvement with a VC typically means that your business structure will change at the end of the relationship and your company will either be public or sold.

Exceptions to every rule.

Every rule has exceptions and VC money is no different. Despite the fact that venture funds are usually associated with the emerging stage of a business, there are hundreds of VC deals done much earlier. This happens when the founders of the company have strong industry experience and proven management capability. These two attributes can lead to almost any type of money at any stage. Prime examples are the founding of DreamWorks SKG by Spielberg, Katzenberg, and

DreamWorks, Intel - strong history.

Geffen, and of Intel by Moore, Noyce, and Grove, three strong established players in their industry. Neither group had any problem raising funds. But, we are all not Spielberg or Grove.

> *"Nothing is a better predictor of future success than past performance. And so you're always going to look and see about their past. If someone has the traits to be a winner, it doesn't matter if they are 25, 30, or 50 years old, it'll show up somewhere in their past. You will see that."*
>
> -Lloyd Greif, Founder, Greif & Co.

VCs play hard and fast.

In sum, venture capitalists are professional sources of money that play hard and fast. They want equity, but will allow management to run the organization as long as goals are met in a timely manner. However, they will interfere and take charge rapidly if goals are not met. In the end, they expect a harvest and at least a fivefold return in a maximum of five years.

Can be worth the effort.

But, suffering through their high rejection rate and demanding standards can be worth your effort. If your firm does fit their criterion, the VC firm will not only help you manage your company, but it will also drive you to that successful conclusion.

> *"When you talk about venture capital and high rates of return on an investment, you're talking about a mathematical calculation that has at least 3 components—the dollars up, the dollars back, and the time it takes to get them back. So a dollar put up today and 2 dollars coming back a year from now, or 2 dollars coming back 4 years from now, are going to give different rates of return. The pressure that's going to be on you is to get the 2 dollars back in a year, rather than in some distant point in time."*
>
> -Gene Miller, Peregrine Ventures

Hard Asset Lenders

Collateral enters the picture.

The other professional money sources are equally as professional and play by equally as demanding rules. They are hard asset or secured lenders and the nature of their deals is based on both the company and its collateral, that is, you and your accomplishments to date (although the proportion of reliance on the company and on the individual is different for each deal.)

Track record and asset being financed are key.

Accounts receivable financing is when collateral is most important. Secured lending companies will view the actual receivables as their primary source of repayment and the borrowing company's financial condition will be the second priority. However, the borrowing company will need to show past performance and some stability because the secured lender will assess the borrowing company's ability to collect receivables. This is easier to show for a going concern as opposed to a start up. But first and foremost the hard asset lender will examine the asset itself rather than the track record of the company, therefore, start ups can use this as a money source.

Lenders monitor and can take over.

Once a loan has been made, lenders will often become involved with a company and audit books, confirm balances with customers, and even direct customer payments to their mailbox address so that they can use the checks received to pay the borrower's loans. In effect, lenders monitor the company's pledged assets on a daily basis and because of this amount of additional work they perform, their fees and interest are very high. Rates in the neighborhood of prime plus seven percent plus fees are not abnormal for a fully policed accounts receivable loan. For loans with less risk (better company financial statements) the rate might be prime plus a few points with lower fees if the lender does not have to exert as much control.

Track record determines terms.

Similar lending arrangements are made for inventory, but with less strict regulations. While it is difficult to borrow on inventory, hard asset lenders will do such transactions. In many cases they will actually impound the inventory—by putting a fence around it—while it sits in the borrowing company's warehouse. Lenders do this if the borrower's financial condition does not warrant better terms and there is a need to protect the asset.

Factors are expensive.

Factoring is another form of receivable financing whereby the factoring company actually takes ownership of the receivable as opposed to allowing the borrowing company to maintain ownership while the lending company lends against the receivable. Factors will often have the right to approve customers in advance. When the borrowing company sells the receivable to them, it doesn't receive the funds immediately, rather it gets money when the customer pays. However, if necessary, the factorer will lend money to the borrower until the collection occurs. Factoring is a very expensive alternative with fees ranging from seven to ten percent of the receivable for purchasing it plus prime plus ten percent for borrowing. Thus, you should only explore this option if absolutely necessary.

> *"A factoring company is the kind of situation where once you're in it, you can never pay them back because you are constantly borrowing and they hold a certain percentage of your receivables. So, every week you borrow money, you get $10K for payroll money, you give them receivables of 10, they'll give you 8 maybe or 7500, but you are constantly borrowing because as soon as the checks come in, the checks go to them. So, its like being in quicksand."*
> -Carolyn Colby, Founder, Colby Care Home Health

General equipment is easy to lease.

A final form of hard asset lending is leasing. A leasing company bases its decision on the equipment being leased. If the equipment is widely used and not some custom piece designed for a specific purpose, then it is easier for a leasing company to repossess and resell the equipment if the borrowing company is unable to meet its financial commitments. Today, leasing is readily available for many small purchases, such as office equipment and computers. Manufacturers or resellers of the equipment give the best rates because they are most knowledgeable about the true value of the equipment and have an established distribution channel in which they can resell the equipment should there be default on payment.

Larger leases more difficult.

Larger leases, especially leasing of equipment with finite lives (larger computers) will be decided not on the equipment itself, but on the firm's ability to make payments. To receive such a lease, a company will need to show financial capability to raise funds.

Professional Money Summary

What's the cost to you?

Entrepreneurs must be aware of the differences between the various types of professional money and understand that some money may be a commodity that comes at an unaffordable cost.

What business are you in?

If you are considering a hard asset lender and financing through receivables, you must consider the high rates involved and ask yourself what the vital area of your business is. Are you creating value by delivering goods and services or by financing customers? Did you start this company to bake specialty breads to sell to wholesale chains or to police receivables from customers?

What makes sense for your business?

Be sure to understand what business you are in. Return to the model business and assess the business that is right for you. What do you want your business to be about—managing a factoring company or running your business. While these options may make sense for certain businesses, be sure that if you choose to pursue this type of money, yours is a business for which it makes sense.

Public Money

Latest stage money is public.

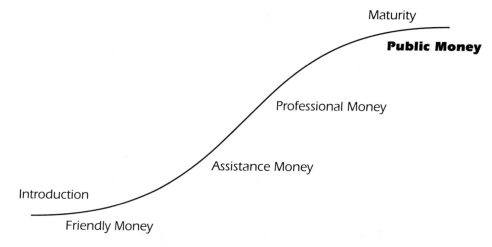

Mature businesses go public.

Historically, this source for money services established or mature companies. In effect, it is money available to any business that qualifies and thus the name "public." Businesses seeking public money typically have solid management teams and proven track records. They have a dependable business base and their growth can be forecasted with reasonable accuracy. Being well-entrenched means that the risk factor is lower and therefore the options for funding are greater.

Commercial banks

Classic bank as money source.

Banks comprise the most prevalent form of public money. Banks today have subdivisions and affiliates that enable them to perform many, if not all, of the functions of other money sources. For purposes of this discussion, focus is given to the classic bank as a money source, that is, the bank as a commercial lender—one that lends money to a business.

Banks don't take a lot of risk.

Again, entrepreneurs must be aware of banks' rules. Because their margins are so small, they are not in a position to take on a great deal of risk. They can not and will not act as venture capitalists and therefore, they do not take an equity stake in a business. Similarly, they do not act as hard asset lenders because of the manpower and overhead necessary to administer such loans. Their primary goal is to reinvest their depositor's money at a margin that will earn interest for the depositors while also allowing a profit for the banks' shareholders.

Banks require collateral.

If a bank is the source of money that you seek, you must recognize that banks will require stocks or bonds of some secondary source to assure repayment. You may want money for inventory or accounts receivable, but if you don't sell or collect to a level that you have projected, a bank will have no sympathy and will demand repayment from your secondary source. In some states, it is even legal for the bank to ask for a second mortgage on your house.

Will you second mortgage?

Are you willing to sign over your house? Are you willing to guarantee and give secondary collateral? If you want to control the outcome of your business and your desire is to receive the most flexible terms and best rates, then the answer is yes. If you need and want the bank, then you should be prepared to do what it takes to receive a bank loan.

Be ready for the unexpected.

In business the unexpected always happens. If you have a chance to bid on a large order that requires additional inventory, then you need to make a quick decision and bank funding may be the only option. Therefore, you must be willing to make those sacrifices and confident enough in your ability that you would put a second on your house. If the unexpected does happen, consider the other sources. Friendly money is not always liquid and receiving funds from angels may take weeks or months, not to mention the loss of equity. Similarly, assistance money is slow and you may not have the explosive growth to attract venture capital. So, in certain situations, banking is your best option—it's fast and affordable.

Your banker should be your friend.

Therefore, you need to be very close to your bankers and keep them informed so that they are not surprised by an unexpected request or a change in your business. Every business needs a bank, albeit not for loans, but for daily operations. Therefore, establishing a good relationship with your banker from the outset may prove helpful when the unexpected occurs.

Up Front & Personal: Insight Into A Commercial Bank

The leader at a recent seminar asked participants to turn to the person next to them and introduce themselves. After a few moments passed, the leader regained the group's attention and asked the audience how many people would loan the person next to them $100,000. The attendees were puzzled. One stated that he certainly didn't know that was the reason for the introductions. The leader recognized this, but asked if they were able to get a general feeling for the person they had just met. All agreed that they had. The leader then explained the "character" rule of banking describing that people are judged within the first several moments of making contact with a banker.

The leader then allowed them to have another few moments to continue their conversation now knowing the purpose. They did.

When he regained their attention, he asked the audience how many would be interested in being part of the opportunity the person next to them offered. A majority of hands were raised. He then tried to pinpoint them and asked how many were prepared to loan the person next to them $100,000 for 90 days. A few asked at what interest rate, but most were quiet with lowered hands.

The leader then placed a deal on the table. He suggested that if they agreed to make the $100,000 loan for 90 days, then, if the person receiving the loan successfully accomplished everything promised in the introductory conversation, they would receive the $100,000 back with a $500 bonus. The leader continued and said that if the person receiving the loan did not do everything promised, then the lenders would not get any money back. The audience was silent except for several who made comments that anyone who would do that would be crazy.

The leader then explained that the profit to a bank, after paying depositor's interest and meeting personnel and overhead costs, would be $500 on a 90 day $100,000 loan.

The message is clear. The return dictates the amount of risk that can be taken. While this is a money deal that no one would do, it is a deal done everyday by bankers all over the world.

The point of differentiation (and a good part of why they can make these loans) between banks and most other sources of money is that banks require two forms of repayment. First, they demand interest on a regular basis. Second, before lending any money, they must know what will happen if your plan doesn't work out. What will they receive if they don't receive their money back? They require a secondary, independent piece of collateral that they will have the rights to if you default on your payments.

As a result, banks are a large source for commercial funds that can be bought at reasonable prices and without having to give up equity.

Investment Bankers

I-Bankers enter late in the game.

Investment bankers are available at various stages of growth. If you have the background and track record, they could support you in earlier stages just as the venture capitalist might. However, historically, investment bankers become involved with more mature and established companies.

They only get paid when they produce.

Investment Bankers are in the fee business and are commission players. They will find money or provide service for a fee. When they produce, they get paid. If they don't achieve results, they don't receive their payment (except perhaps for certain expense reimbursements).

They represent you.

Unlike their cousin, venture capitalists, who first raise a fund and then invest in various opportunities, investment bankers act on your behalf to find investors. Deal requirements are usually a minimum of 8 figures on the low end and the money you receive is not theirs.

Must make sense and cents.

Their services are often linked to the liquidation of your firm—finding a buyer at a price that makes sense and cents. Sense being a strategic fit and cents meaning at an acceptable price.

Continuation of VC role.

In many ways, the investment banker continues the work of the venture capitalist either by finding additional funding at non VC rates or by selling the company to liquidate the shareholders.

As you learned in Chapter Four when lifecycles were addressed, many entrepreneurs have difficulty facing the question of whether or not to sell their business—their baby.

Should you sell?

While this is a difficult question, when examined logically, the answer becomes clear. In determining the correct course of action, entrepreneurs must ask themselves if they like to manage and/or if they are effective managers. For some the answer is yes. They feel comfortable managing and want to take their business to a new level. Others feel that the day-to-day operations are not exciting and that becoming a manager would be the antithesis of their goals and dreams. Therefore, freeing the value that they and their shareholders have created and gaining liquidity from it to enhance a lifestyle or to start over again is a good option. What is right for you?

Are you a manager?

The investment banker can assist both of these needs—expansion funding or liquidation.

Going Public - The IPO

What's your goal?

For many entrepreneurs becoming a public company is the pinnacle of their journey. To go from having a simple idea to being President of a NASDAQ or NYSE firm is the crown jewel. Others feel it is the best way to maximize their return, gain liquidity, and leave. A third feeling is that it is the alternative to selling to a third party.

Extremely costly and time consuming.

Going public is a very risky and expensive process. Meeting all legal and accounting requirements, paying the underwriter's fees, and preparing the documents for the pre-marketing of the deal can cost millions of dollars. Additionally, the amount of time that an entrepreneur and his management team must devote to the entire process is vast. And it takes away from the time spent running the business.

Control out of your hands.

All of the preparation doesn't even guarantee a public market. The underwriters control most IPO's and if they believe that market conditions (downturn in economy, higher interest rates, too many offerings at one time, etc.) are not favorable for a successful sale, then they can and will pull your offering. If this happens, your efforts will be seen solely in the cancelled checks for expenses paid. Therefore, an IPO is a risky proposition that requires careful consideration.

Raises lots of money though.

If an offering is successful, then the amount of capital raised will be significant. If this occurs and is your goal, then congratulations. If you have determined that your business needs funds to compete (acquire other companies, large marketing campaigns, new technology implementation, etc.), then going public and offering additional stock in secondary and tertiary rounds means the IPO is right for you.

Severe emotional drain as well.

However, you must recognize that, in addition to monetary expenses, being a public company also has emotional costs that are not insignificant.

Annual auditory and legal filings, including internal staff time for preparing data for the outside firms comprise the monetary costs. Costs of $300,000 to $700,000 for a small cap stock IPO are the norm.

Pressure from Wall Street is intense.

The emotional cost is higher. If you started with a vision for the future, you now have a 90-day vision for the street. You will live under a microscope and the first time you fail to meet a quarterly expectation, the market will severely punish you. Your stock price will drop and your shareholders will be irate.

Short-term profits or long-term results?

To compensate and to prepare for a down turn you may become obsessed with short term profits and cut needed future technology to meet short term earnings. But, you will be challenged regarding both the 90-day window and the five year direction of your firm.

SEC has strict guidelines.

If your goal in an IPO is immediate liquidity, be sure you examine the rules under which you take your firm public. The Securities and Exchange Commission rules governing insider sale of stock are significant. It is not easy to sell stock when you run the company. Not only does the SEC impose rules, but your shareholders will question your every move. They will wonder why you are selling. Since you are the president, do you know what the future holds? What are you not sharing?

Weigh all options.

In the end, a successful IPO raises vast amounts of equity, but at great cost. If your business needs multiple rounds of funding, then the public market may be right for you. But, be sure to consider all options carefully.

A summary diagram of money sources is found on the next page.

Money Sources

Basis Of Funds	Friendly (Invest In Person)				Assistance (Secondary Motive)			Professional (Money Changers)				Public (Spread Management)	
Major Types	Family	Cocktail Circuit	Customers	Suppliers	Gov't Loans	Tax & Asst	R&D Grants	Fin Co	Hard Asset / Leasing	Venture Capital	Comm. Banks.	Investment Bankers	IPOs
Why Involved	Love, Mystique	Greed	Profit	Expand	Regulations	Savings, Expansion	Regulation, Expansion	Return	Return	Return	Return	Return	Return
Ownership: Rent or Buy	Buy	Rent	Both	Both	Rent	Both	Both	Rent	Rent	Buy	Rent	Buy	Buy
Repay Source: Operations / Liquidation	Liquid.	Both	Oper.	Oper.	Oper.	Oper.	Both	Oper.	Oper.	Liquid.	Oper.	Liquid.	Liquid.
Anticipated Return	10X 5 yrs	???	Sales, Purchases		Jobs	10 to 15%	5 to 10%, Royalties	6 to 8	3 to 5, Basis Points	5X in 5 yrs	Prime to 2 over, Basis Points	5% fee, Warrants	Fees
Control	Pressure	Next Order			Limits	Minor	Indirect	High	None	Total	High	Contract	Regularity
How to Find	Known, Introduction	Industry Contacts			Long List	Long List	Long List	Long List	Long List	Intro	Long List	Intro	Intro
Project Life Cycle	Start Up				Early Lift			Emerging Company				Maturing Company	

Chapter Summary

It is impossible to deal in absolutes when discussing money. The rules and moods of money sources are constantly changing. As an entrepreneur you need to understand and stay abreast of the changes either directly or through your associates and network of contacts.

As a general overview remember the following:

- Money is a commodity that enables the execution of your vision. It does not have value unto itself and by itself can not create value.
- In every money equation—regardless of the source—you, the entrepreneur, are the most important component. People will judge you (character) and your ability to deliver (capacity) before they even consider the business proposition.
- Money sources are usually tied to progress points on the entrepreneur's journey. Look to the sources that match where your business is. Know the needs and rules of each source and anticipate your needs well in advance.

Further, match your money source against the stage of your company as the diagram on the previous page indicates.

Chapter Eleven Exercises/Discussion Questions

1. Identify the importance of the three Cs.
2. At what time is it appropriate to start seeking investments?
3. What are the differences between the things with which a professional investor is concerned and those with which people offering friendly money are concerned?
4. Contact a venture capitalist or an investment banker and ask what he or she looks for in a start-up company.
5. How will you determine what portion of your company you will give up for an investment?
6. Discuss the advantages and disadvantages of taking a company public.
7. Under what circumstances is it appropriate to seek an investment from a customer or supplier?
8. What would be a good reason to consider applying for an assistance loan?

Journey Eleven: Zanart Entertainment Revisited*

Investor to Public Market for Secondary Offering

The investor gave Zanart a $500,000 bridge loan in February 1994 at 10 percent per year. The principal would be paid at the closure of a public offering or on any other permanent financing arrangement. In addition to the interest payments, the loan granted 250,000 shares of stock in the expected to be public company and a warrant to purchase another 250,000 shares at $4.00 per share.

The investor's funds were to be used mainly for working capital (specifically to finance additional inventory and accounts receivable), to acquire new licenses and to add key management personnel, including a CFO and a national sales manager.

When the offering was delayed and certain capital requirements needed to be met pursuant to the letter of intent from the investment bankers, the investor agreed to convert $100,000 of this loan to equity at $4.00 per share. This left the note at $400,000 and gave the investor 33,333 additional shares of stock. By the fall of 1995, the investor owned 283,333 shares of ZE, approximately 10 percent of the total number of shares then outstanding (2,902,983).

Public Offering Timetable

During March 1994, Arthur Andersen LLP was engaged to do the required audits and accounting work preparatory to the secondary offering. These were the first full audits that ZE had undergone, and they entailed a great drain on management time and money over 12 months.

The company talked with several underwriters. The investor was able to introduce ZE to a senior executive at First Equity Corporation, investment bankers of Miami. They were excited about doing a deal with ZE and the investor.

In October 1994, Todd Slayton was hired as chief financial officer. Todd is a CPA, received his MBA in Corporate Finance and Financial Accounting from USC in May 1991, and was a senior consultant/accountant with the middle market practice of Deloitte & Touche in Los Angeles.

The grueling and frustrating process of writing a prospectus and preparing the SEC registration ran from November '94 through March '95. This process involved the coordination of no less than six parties: the company, the company's counsel, the underwriters, the underwriter's counsel, the auditors, and the SEC.

There were constant hurdles to overcome in order to make the deal happen. There were several SEC filings with continuous changes based on its comments, upgrading the financials (certain financials grew "stale" over time), amendments, and endless tinkering with the language and presentation. Todd commented in hindsight:

This road was wrought with surprises at every turn and several potential events that could have been "deal killers" were skillfully avoided.

The offering called for ZE to sell 800,000 units at $6.00 (the original plan called for 1 million units). Each unit consisted of one share of common stock and one warrant allowing the redeemer to purchase a share of stock at $6.00 within five years. First Equity had the option to sell an overallotment of shares of 120,000 units (the "Green Shoe").

The "red herrings" (prospectus) were printed in early April and Tom, Bob, and Todd hit the road. The roadshow involved a multimedia presentation to brokerages and private offering meetings with potential investors. The three reflect:

The process was incredibly stressful.

The slide presentation which posed the question "Why Invest in Zanart?" had five main points:

- Product innovation and market niche
- Emerging channels of distribution
- Stable of blue chip properties
- Strong relationships with licensers
- Dedicated management surrounded by successful businesspersons

The roadshow was a success and the three returned home exhilarated and ready to jump through the final hoops to close the deal.

After a final night of endless pone calls, cold sweats and nervous stomachs, the deal was declared effective by the SEC on May 11, 1995 (commencement of trading), and the final prospectus was printed. The deal closed one week later on May 18, and the company received a check for $4,188,000 on that day [$4.8 million gross proceeds less 12.75 percent ($612 thousand) in commission and fees to First Equity]. The investor was repaid immediately. On June 28, First Equity exercised the overallotment of 120,000 shares and ZE received an additional check for $628,000.

Summary of Offering

The offering is summarized as follows:

- 920,000 units sold at $6.00 for gross proceeds of $5.5 million
- Yielded approx. $4M after commissions, expenses, fees, repayment of debt
- Funds in US Treasury Fund at brokerage earning 5.5-6.0 percent

Operations

The Company's products are manufactured by a coordination of vendors mainly in Southern California. The Company uses three printing vendors and various independent artists to produce the prints. Warner Brothers Stores (approximately 50 percent of revenue) buy mostly framed products that are finished by a firm with a framing facility adjacent to Zanart's offices in Van Nuys. Most licensed merchandise (both matted and matted/framed) is assembled by a vendor located in Gardena. The Company uses other vendors as "over-flow" producers as needed.

Zanart grew out of its small warehouse space in Van Nuys, and in August 1995, leased approximately 10,000 square feet of space adjacent to the Gardena vendor's 75,000-square-foot warehouse and set up the main distribution facility. Gardena is where most raw materials and finished goods are maintained and where most shipping of licensed merchandise takes place. The facility has an Operations Manager and two to three warehouse staff.

The Company has 16 full-time employees including officers. Other than the three officers discussed previously (Tom, Bob, and Todd), there is another four-year veteran of the company, Vice-President Mark Politi, who coordinates the Warner Bros. "show" and is key to overall company operations.

Sales are headed up by a National Sales Manager who attends trade shows, makes visits to national key accounts, and manages the more than 25 outside "rep" companies, which show Zanart's lines. He is supported by a sales coordinator, a customer service manager, and order entry staff.

The Company recently established an internal art department with an Art Director to create ads and displays, sell materials, catalogs, new product prototypes, and so on, using the latest computer equipment.

ZE also recently hired a Director of Special Projects to coordinate the development of a Zanart web site on the Internet, oversee catalogs and ad placements, develop programs for home shopping channels, and assist in other new business development.

The company has a Novell network with ten Windows-based workstations with Windows-based accounting software designed for small to mid-sized companies. Accounting Staff consists of a staff accountant (who also handles accounts payable) and a customer service manager (who also handles accounts receivable, credit, and collections).

Journey Eleven Case Questions

1. Was the initial public offering a success?
2. What other money sources could they have utilized to expand? Was an IPO the best choice for them at that time?
3. How should they use the funding? What should their next steps be?

Chapter Twelve
Feasibility - Part Two

Chapter Twelve Major Concepts

- Feasibility Recap
- Timeline & Financial Premises
- Sales Forecast & Cash Needs
- Sensitivity Analysis
- Feasibility Made Simple

Journey Twelve: Avanteer Revisited

Feasibility Recap

Chapter six introduced the concept of feasibility by defining it as the way entrepreneurs think and a means by which they become successful. Prior to that point in the journey, the focal point was you—the traveler—and on exploring who you are and whether or not you are suited for a journey in entrepreneurship.

Do you remember feasibility part one?

In Feasibility Part One, the focus began to shift from an examination of who you are to a study of the tasks you need to accomplish—what you do. As opposed to searching for the great idea, entrepreneurs develop skill sets, the first of which is opportunity recognition. In a constant search for new opportunities, entrepreneurs study each idea in light of current and changing trends. As the opportunities are recognized and begin to take shape, they are then defined in terms of a concept. Successful concept definition is dependent on the proper identification and testing of all three components of a concept—a customer, a sales and distribution channel, and a benefit. Initially, the customer is of greatest importance and entrepreneurs seek to involve the early adapters in the definition of the channel and the benefit.

Ideas are filtered through the feasibility funnel.

This entrepreneurial thought process is best described as a feasibility funnel. Ideas abound at the top of the funnel and then pass through a series of filters. In order to filter down through the first funnel, an idea must be considered contextually—in terms of what is happening in that particular industry, what patterns of change are occurring, what is the state of the art of current product offerings, and where in the lifecycle is this industry? Upon being defined as a concept, the idea is able to progress through the filter. If a proper concept is unable to be identified—no customer, sales channel, and/or benefit—then a variation of the idea or an altogether new idea must be placed at the top of the filter. Only when the idea can be stated as a concept will it continue deeper into the funnel.

As was explained in chapter six, one idea can have hundreds of permutations and they are best assessed as part of a concept grid. Since entrepreneurs have the perseverance to continue and a strong passion for the journey, they must therefore be careful to maintain a sense of realism in assessing the components of an idea. The desire to launch a business can become so great that entrepreneurs have a tendency to rationalize the customer test or justify impractical pricing models. Enthusiasm may lead to over-simplification in costing, underestimation in terms of manufacturing costs, or unrecognizable complexity of a sales or distribution channel. Any of these events will lead to certain disaster.

Tool kits aid in the feasibility process.

Chapters Seven to Eleven discussed entrepreneurial tool kits, which are the means by which to successfully execute all portions of a concept. Entrepreneurs use their tool kits to appropriately define and test a customer, recognize changing patterns within an industry, and design, build and communicate their benefit. The final tool kits examined were money related and dealt with identifying the amount of money needed and how to raise that money. Critical to raising money successfully is knowing how much money you need, the source for that money, and the rules of that source.

Financial Feasibility Funnel

With these lessons in mind, it is time to complete feasibility. Returning to the funnel, the assumption is that a concept has been defined and the components of the concept have been tested.

The funnel.

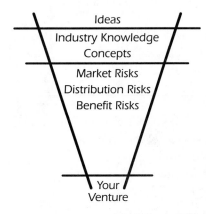

The next filter in the feasibility funnel is financial feasibility, which combines the accomplishments of the three previous filters.

Enter: financial feasibility.

Time Line

Need to identify action items.

Financial feasibility begins by merging the blind tour with a clear definition of the stages of execution that you have designed for your new venture. While the blind tour identifies what is needed to build your company, the stages define your timeline of action. As you have learned, entrepreneurs are not project-driven; rather, they build their ventures in stages so as to maintain the greatest degree of flexibility throughout the journey.

For example, a simple timeline could consist of the following information.

Stage One – Secure beta customer in hand. Actions needed:

- Complete customer test
- Build prototype
- Finalize brochure

These represent your action items. Then, you must identify the person(s) responsible for executing each action item, which could be you, an associate, or you may elect (need) to have outside professional assistance. Thus, the action plan would expand:

Stage One – Secure beta customer in hand.

Who is responsible for what?

Actions needed	Person to execute
Complete customer test	Self
Build prototype	Special Systems Group
Finalize brochure	Creative Design Inc.

The next question is evident—what does it cost to complete each task? You may perform some of the action items while working for sweat equity, any expenses involved should be recorded. Professional fees must also be listed, even if received for a discount.

Financial Premises

What is your logic?

In creating this timeline, the goal is to build a model that defines both the cost and the premise underlying the cost. Remember that readers of your feasibility or business plan will view your model to understand your strategy, priorities and approach and they will be heavily influenced by the logic underlying your model.

Incorporating the costs and premises, the model is completed as follows:

Stage One – Secure beta customer in hand.

What costs are involved?

Actions	Person	Cost to execute
Complete customer test	Self	Travel to trade show - $ 2,500
Build prototype	Special Systems Team	Per quote - $11,000.
Finalize brochure	Creative Design Inc.	Estimated by company - $6,000.

These are not detailed financial models.

The purpose of this introductory text is not to give detailed examples of financial models; however, it is necessary to recognize that you will need to develop the skills to build such models or find an associate/outside professional to assist in this process. While financial models are a critical part of the entrepreneurial journey, they are second to the overall vision of the project being developed.

Sales Forecast

Forecasting is not an exact science.

Financial feasibility continues into subsequent stages and becomes complicated by the addition of multiple new variables, the most important of which is the sales forecast. As discussed earlier, entrepreneurs recognize that a forecast is, at best, a sophisticated or processed guess. Experienced readers will not hold you responsible for a 100% accurate portrayal of the future; however, they will demand a clear description of how both the forecast and the timeline were determined. Again, the logic behind the number is more important than the actual number.

On the other hand, expenditure levels are controllable and able to be accurately identified. Therefore, failure to control expenses will lead to instant demise.

Cash Needs Assessment

Remember working capital and start up costs?

Another variable in the money model is defining the need for non-action money—working capital and start up losses. How much working capital will it take to support your endeavor? Identifying the amount and reason for that amount are the first tests of the validity of your financial model. For example, if a beta customer is your goal in stage one and you are offering price concessions to attract that customer, perhaps you should expect cash assistance in terms of a deposit or up-front payment. If that customer is not willing to offer such assistance, then how will you rationalize to investors the fact that your new venture is putting up all of the money and carrying all of the paper?

Further, it is necessary to identify the length of time it will take to reach break even and how you will support the losses. Inaccurate estimates in these areas will likely lead to both insufficient (or no) funds and irate investors or bankers.

Upon completion of the financial feasibility model spreadsheets, entrepreneurs can view and test their sense of reality. Are the goals and tasks identified able to be accomplished in the necessary time frame and for the right cost?

Sensitivity Analysis

Must develop "what if" scenarios.

In order to test this last question, entrepreneurs must examine their model and develop a series of "what if" scenarios. In essence, entrepreneurs must ask themselves what can go wrong. In so doing, all variables—both positive and negative—need to be identified. Often people will "what if" themselves to death regarding negative possibilities; however, positive occurrences could be just as deadly. For example, if sales materialize faster than expected and production capabilities are not able to keep up, then quality and time to delivery may suffer. Additionally, actual field use could result in a need for modifications to the offering, which are not able to be made because production is back-logged. Many early fatalities in a new venture result when leaders accept more sales orders than they should and then fail to deliver consistent quality.

Different variables can alter whole course of action.

The most likely variable that must be reassessed is time. The creative process is typically not done on a schedule and many unknowns can occur. Thus, you must create "what if" scenarios that allay investors' fears regarding potential increased sales, longer time to market, and/or a need for additional contracted associates.

Timing is critical.

A second highly scrutinized variable is time to break even, typically caused by slower than anticipated sales growth. Despite the fact that you have forecasted a series of events that everyone knows are not controllable, you are still expected to control them. So, what is your backup plan? It is critical to be careful in crafting such a plan because if it calls for raising more money, then your logic shows a level of uncertainty that will make investors wary and your success in raising funds will be limited. Similarly, if you do not have answers for "what if" scenarios, it shows a lack of preparation and again, you will experience the same perilous results in raising money.

Pricing can be tricky.

Another very common and related challenge is pricing. Many entrepreneurs have successfully met sales forecast levels but inadequately planned for the effect of price competition and pressure to lower prices. Equally difficult can be manufacturing cost overruns.

A final difficulty arises when expenditures are higher than anticipated. This often results when early associates join the firm at lower than market rates and over-produce. Having moved beyond the initial stages of growth, it becomes necessary to offer more competitive salaries in order to attract talented employees. Additionally, you may need more than one employee to accomplish the same number of tasks that one of your original over-producers could.

Have you considered these and other possible "what if" scenarios and do you have answers?

Financial feasibility conclusion

Three critical questions.

In the final analysis, financial feasibility seeks to answer three questions. The first is quantitative, the second is qualitative and the third is competitive. They are:

1. How much and what type of money is needed?
2. Is it a worthy opponent for you (is it worthwhile - profit plus salary plus life style plus upside)?
3. Is it worth while to stakeholders and therefore can it be funded?

Are you a quitter?

What happens if the answer to any or all of these questions is no? Do you abandon the project? Do you give up? If your thoughts were leaning toward yes, then you are not a true entrepreneur. The answer is no. You don't abandon the project, you persevere. If the answer is no, then you must return to the top of the feasibility funnel and begin again by changing the benefit or the channels—whatever is necessary—until your concept can be proven and you can answer yes to all three questions.

Entrepreneurial Exercise

This is your chance to help a friend. Review the Feasibility Made Simple description on the next pages and then come up with a list of the ten first questions you would ask a friend coming to you for help in starting a new business.

1. _____

2. _____

3. _____

4. _____

5. _____

6. _____

7. _____

8. _____

9. _____

10. _____

⇒   **Tear out and move to your entrepreneurial road map binder.**

Feasibility Made Simple

There are a number of steps involved in preparing to test the feasibility of a new venture. This somewhat simplified overview was generated so that you may properly guide your best friend, their child, or someone at a cocktail party when they want assistance evaluating their great idea. It is a structure that simplifies and explicitly identifies twelve steps that should be taken to determine the viability of an idea.

1. Take the idea to a concept by discussing the difference between the two.

There is a critical difference between an idea and a concept and people always want to revert to their idea or product instead of focusing on the customer and the benefit—the more important pieces. Be sure to focus on your benefit and why what you provide will make your customer's life easier.

2. If you want to catch a mouse, make a sound like a cheese.

By definition, doing this means acting like a buyer. Examine the competitors, how they reach the customers, and what benefits they are delivering. This will help to answer many of the questions in the feasibility made simple process if you are able to gain access to useful information. Guerrilla tactics come in handy during this step. If you dress in a suit, put a pack of pencils in your shirt pocket, and carry a clipboard, people will often assume that you are important and should be given answers.

3. Have them draw a competitive profile of their competitors.

This builds on number two. Examine the competitive process in order to determine how to enter the market. You are seeking to learn not only who is in the industry, but also how they execute their plans. Distribution, pricing, and sales tactics are paramount.

4. Patterns of change.

Most opportunities for entrepreneurs happen at the time of change in basic structures. By way of example, think about the confusion surrounding the Internet. Companies such as Amazon, Yahoo, and eBay acted on this pattern of change in society and have built successful Internet companies as a result. What are the patterns of change in the automotive industry?

5. Market size.

Is this a worthy opponent? Live by the 11th commandment—Thou shalt not lie (BS) to thyself! Be careful not to confuse the size of the niche in which you are operating to the size of the entire market. This is a crucial distinction.

6. Customer buy basis.

Despite many efforts at analyzing the competition, the perceived customer is constantly changing and evolving. Recognizing this enables you to remain one step ahead of their changing needs. You must always be able to inform your customers of what you can do to serve their needs and provide their benefits.

7. Time line and event definition.

All plans are time sensitive and time is always the enemy for a start up. Laying out your plans in a timeline enables you to stay ahead of the competition. You need to have a series of events to execute as well as identifiable triggers for next actions.

8. Initial penetration of the market.

If there is truth to the entrepreneurial approach, it is here. Often there is only one opportunity to secure your initial customer. How will you do that? Identifying that process will eliminate the allure of the market and enable you to focus on the specific reality of your product.

9. Plan for success.

What to do when that first order is received? Plan your actions before that first order is taken. In other words, have an operational plan in place. *The devil is in the details is a wise proverb.*

10. Product evolution.

A basic idea may start the race, but the finish line will be different from the start. While the culture and values of any business should not change, the product should. The best initial penetration plan is to develop the final product with a customer. Be sure that there is a vision to take it to the final stage.

11. Financial plan.

Achieving profitability must factor into the equation. Is this concept financially feasible? Not just does it work, is it a worthy opponent—worthy of your efforts—but is there a large enough return and level of excitement to attract money? Likewise, does it have an exit strategy to harvest the crops?

12. Support.

Having a personal and professional environment conducive to starting a business is critical. Life and entrepreneurship are about people. Is there a formal and informal team in place? Are outside advisors willing to monitor your path? Is there a supportive and involved spouse, lifemate, and/or other family?

Feasibility Conclusion

Is no finality to feasibility.

In reality, there is no definitive conclusion to a feasibility study. A grade of pass or fail cannot be rendered. There is not even a final **written** feasibility report. The only finality to feasibility is that there is no finality. Reports can be written to show where you are along the journey and what you have discovered up to that point; however, it is never final because it is constantly changing.

One change can effect everything.

Feasibility is a series of tools used by entrepreneurs to methodically assess an idea and to meticulously gather the necessary facts that will enable them to determine under what conditions they will go forward. It is an individual approach to a complex challenge. Further, it is dynamic and entrepreneurs must recognize that a change in any one component could have far reaching and complex effects on each and every other aspect of the study.

Go or no go?

The "go or no go" decision in venture formation is typically based on two or three key points in the plan. What points are most critical for your venture? Herein lies the excitement of entrepreneurship because in each plan and for each individual there are unique decision criteria. What constitutes a worthy opponent? Is the equity share significant enough for you? Typically, it will be less for a first time entrepreneur than for a serial entrepreneur who is starting a fourth or fifth company. You will have to decide on your own.

Within feasibility, there are typically three focal points most often explored, examined, and debated.

Three primary points.

1. Proof of a customer inside a viable niche at acceptable prices.
2. Functional and flexible financial models that also provide rewards that meet the needs of all players.
3. Definition of the vital area, the most often missed variable in a feasibility and/or business plan. It is inevitable that others will replicate your offering in the future, nothing is that unique in today's world. However, every business should have a vital area—a way in which it is superior to the competition—that enables it to stand out from the crowd. And, the vital area does not necessarily have to be a point of differentiation because, in the long run, superior performance is more important than just being different.

The final feasibility challenge

Can you identify the "conditions under which you will go forward?"

This is the only real and complete challenge or question that must be answered.

Chapter Summary

Feasibility is the essence of entrepreneurship. It seeks to define the conditions under which you will move forward with your new venture. Chapter Six introduced you to this very important concept and this chapter completes the structure of testing ideas and concepts, i.e., feasibility. In order to perform a complete evaluation of an idea that has been transformed into a concept, you must examine the financial ramifications of your business. A crucial part of financial feasibility is the sensitivity analysis and being sure that you are prepared to answer many "what if" questions.

Perhaps the most important aspect of feasibility is determining how to proceed if you discover that the idea/concept you have been exploring is not financially (or otherwise) feasible. This does not mean that you should quit. Quite the contrary. Rather, it means that you either develop a new permutation of the idea or you recognize a new opportunity and filter it through the funnel.

With this approach, the feasibility funnel will constantly be revisited and should always be kept in mind.

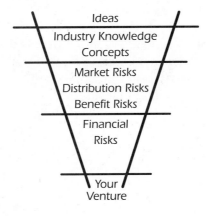

Chapter Twelve Exercises/Discussion Questions

1. Define six different "what if" scenarios and identify potential ways of handling them if they were to occur in your business.
2. What are four different actions needed in a timeline for success in a new venture?
3. Explain why a feasibility study is never truly complete.

Journey Twelve: Avanteer Revisited

Stefan Bean and Tony Rochon formed their company, Avanteer, to develop collaborative Java-based technologies. In the early stages of development, they made a conscious decision not to seek venture capital because they wanted to build value before bringing in investors. As Tony comments, "The longer you go and the more you build up your assets and your reputation as a company, which is what we tried to do, the more people start coming to you and the more leverage you have as a company. You have more options."

Preparation

After two years of developing their product, honing their business plan, and scraping to cover fixed costs, Tony and Stefan felt ready to step into the complex world of professional investment. As do many entrepreneurs, they got their original funding from family and friends. Pitching to Lloyd Greif, a prominent investment banker who gets hundreds of requests for capital investment every month, is a completely different scenario.

Stefan and Tony had done their due diligence and were armed and prepared with a projected use of funds. The money would enable them to pay off debt, hire personnel, complete product development on Funtopia, and begin to pay salaries to management. They were seeking a $1.5 million investment for which they were willing to part with 30% of Avanteer. However, the terms had to be favorable or else they would not accept a deal.

Having practiced and reviewed their presentation numerous times, they were confident. As they introduced themselves and began their pitch, Greif sat and listened.

Their business plan described the Funtopia game site, the Funtopia engine, and the training and consulting that they were engaged in primarily to bring in revenue. Bean informed Greif that the Funtopia engine was necessary to run the Funtopia game, therefore, they were not really two separate products.

Fatal Flaws

Greif commented, "It's not two products, it's two businesses, isn't it? Who do you sell this (game) to? You sell this to the end consumer, right? Who do you sell this (engine) to? You sell this to another business, right?" Greif pointed out that as a start up company, they were focusing in multiple directions with multiple products, not the typical model of a successful start up.

Another issue he identified was that they did not have a "gaming" expert on their management team. Rochon countered by informing Greif of a newly formed alliance with a third party company, Big Grub. But Greif was still concerned—"They didn't pull their team together as a complete package and frankly, I'm not even sure they saw that they had a missing link until we discussed it. Because if they had seen that missing link, then they would have mentioned that third party joint venture company in the business plan. They would have mentioned it in their presentation. They never did, its like they didn't even think about it. That's scary, that's a very scary prospect." If they wanted to succeed in the gaming industry, he suggested they seek an experienced individual to join their team.

Greif also pointed out that their mission statement referred to global communications, which was not in alignment with their business plan focus on gaming, consulting, and training, or their oral pitch.

Even the name of the company raised concern in Greif's mind. Bean and Rochon chose Avanteer, a combination of avant-garde and pioneer. Greif indicated that typically someone who is avant-garde is appealing to a small audience. More importantly though, in the venture capital community, pioneer has the connotation of someone who "has arrows in his back and is dead. He's the one who paves the way for somebody else to come through and make the money."

Unlike friends and family, professional investors get involved for a financial reward and often expect a 50%-60% return on their investment. Therefore, they scrutinize each and every deal with a very careful eye. According to Greif, it only takes one fatal flaw to break a deal and the Avanteer business plan had at least three. Lack of a gaming expert on their management team and a focus on multiple business models were the first two.

The third fatal flaw was their overly optimistic financial projections. Greif noted the critical importance of being realistic, cutting costs to the bone where appropriate, and spending significant dollars on advertising. Of the $1.5 million that Avanteer was seeking, 20% was for management salaries and only about 17% was for advertising. As he stated, "The four top guys were going to pay themselves roughly $72,000 a year. A venture capitalist is going to want to see the management team getting their benefit from equity, not from cash. So, you want them to have living expenses, but if you're an entrepreneur who's getting started and the company hasn't generated any money, you can survive on something less than $72,000 a year. And you should."

In concluding their meeting, Greif advised that they focus their business model, find a gaming expert, and reevaluate their financials. He felt the real test would be to see how they handled his advice. What would they do next?

Mentor

After collecting themselves, Bean and Rochon decided to meet with their mentor to discuss what had taken place. Bill Sanderson, Founder of Popcorn Palace, had been advising them throughout their business development.

They gave Sanderson the one-line summary: "He grilled us pretty good."

Having just received and read their updated business plan, Sanderson commented that the plan articulated a "work in progress" or what they had been doing in order to keep the business alive as opposed to their vision for the future. Rather than write about what has been happening, in order to attract investors, a business plan must identify the opportunity in the specific market that you wish to enter. He stated, "investors don't want you out there doing 100 different things or even 10 different things because they know you will not be able to concentrate and stay focused."

Sanderson asked Bean and Rochon if their vision for Funtopia was still the same—to focus on the game site. They admitted that they had been receiving more requests for the engine than for the game and were contemplating the merits of a shift in their business model. Sanderson was encouraged by their ability to recognize this need. A business plan serves that exact purpose—to guide an entrepreneur through the process of discovering the focus that is most desired in the market.

Tony and Stefan were discouraged by this advice because it meant that they had to continue scraping by until they had better defined their market. But, they were also inspired because it gave them greater focus and new goals to achieve. Sanderson was impressed: "They've been doing this for quite some time now. I think it's a sign of their sticktuitiveness and determination. All entrepreneurs have the same story to tell. It's not a straight line; there are bumps in the road. There are good days and bad days."

In addition to his advice and encouragement, Sanderson also offered to introduce them to a friend in the gaming industry who might be willing to join the team and provide the expertise needed to complement their management team.

Bean and Rochon have demonstrated passion, perseverance, enthusiasm, and integrity on their journey. They're willingness to learn from every experience will prove vital to their ultimate success.

Journey Twelve Case Questions

1. What were the fatal flaws that Greif made Stefan and Tony aware of?
2. What are the differences between the things with which a professional investor is concerned and those with which people offering friendly money are concerned?
3. What did Tony and Stefan need to change about their model in order to please an investor such as Greif?
4. Is public money the type of money they should be going after? Or, is another source more appropriate for them at this stage?
5. How was their meeting with Sanderson? Were they excited or did the meeting with Greif diffuse their enthusiasm?
6. What entrepreneurial characteristics did they portray?

Chapter Thirteen
The Business Plan

Chapter Thirteen Major Concepts

- When to Write the Business Plan
- For Whom to Write the Business Plan
- What a Business Plan Is Not
- What a Business Plan Needs To Accomplish
- Writing the Business Plan

Journey Thirteen: EarthLink Network, Inc.

The Business Plan

Business plan - ultimate document.

Almost all studies of new ventures seem to be focused on the business plan. This document (or structure) has been given a level of supreme importance by both the popular press and many educators.

Or is it?

However, when talking to successful entrepreneurs, the business plan is often portrayed as an after thought—something done subsequent to starting the business. One prime example is Wayne Huizenga (Blockbuster, AutoNation, Republic Industries). He was presenting his entrepreneurial journey to several hundred students when one commented that with his record of success, he must put together a great business plan. Huizenga was a bit flustered by this and replied "No, not really. We did a lot of homework before starting and had several test operations running smoothly before we actually wrote a formal business plan. We always had a vision but the plan came later."

With that in mind, let's explore this critical part of the journey—the business plan—by putting it into context.

B-plan is strategy for birth.

What is a business plan? In essence, it is the written articulation of your business and the strategy for its birth. It states that which you want to do and how you intend to do it. In other words, a business plan is a road map for the execution of your journey.

When do you write a business plan?

Constantly changes.

A business plan is constantly changing and the minute it is finished, it's obsolete. With every new step taken, your knowledge base increases and therefore the overall direction changes. As a result, so does the plan.

Feasibility is essence.

This is why the true essence of entrepreneurship is feasibility and the testing of your concept rather than the actual writing of a business plan. Entrepreneurs think in terms of feasibility and execute with a business plan.

Always writing.

So, the answer is that you are always writing your business plan because it is continuously evolving.

For whom do you write a business plan?

A business plan has many purposes and is written for different groups of individuals. However, there are three primary categories.

For you

Are you prepared?

First and foremost, the plan is your confirmation that you are fully prepared. With your execution plan designed, you must be confident in your ability to communicate that plan in a professional manner. Thus, for you, the business plan serves as a written articulation of your needs and goals for execution.

How will you become victorious?

When exploring money sources, you learned of the entrepreneurial phrase "all bets on the first tee." As well as being the basis for all bets, the business plan is also the first tee on which those bets are made. It is your battle plan that includes a comprehensive listing of key targets to be achieved in order to reach final victory.

Outlines all details.

Thus, the business plan should be used as your strategic tool that gives direction to your organization. The benefit development strategy detailed in your plan will explain the products and services that you offer. Your operational plan will identify how you plan to run the business on a daily basis. Details of your sales effort will develop from the sales strategy you explain in the business plan. Not only does the business plan explain the intricacies of your venture to outside contacts, but it also helps you to know where your company is going internally.

> *"The best business plan I've seen is one from a baker who was planning his second store. The first store was up and running and he was doing okay. For the second store, he thought he needed to borrow $50K. Rather, he developed a plan to leverage the resources of his first store to start the second store. Baking at night, sharing the employees, and leveraging some of the leases and equipment, he was able to open that second store without borrowing the $50K."*
>
> -Debbie Esparza, Esparza & Associates

To attract associates to join your team

As you learned in the beginning of the book, entrepreneurs are not lone wolves and can not exist by themselves. It takes a team to make a touchdown.

Takes a team to make a touchdown.

Therefore, your plan should clearly state the vision for your company and tell potential associates and investors what the company is about.

Good talent is tough to find.

Good team members are not easy to recruit and you must first recognize that you are competing for talent. The business plan shares your vision and enables potential associates to study your goals thereby providing them with the information needed to decide whether or not your vision and leadership warrants their time. Is it a worthy opponent for them? What does success bring? How and to what extent do they share in your potential success?

Considering the vast competition for talented individuals, recruiting good team members is difficult at best. The business plan is necessary for this challenging task.

To attract funding

To launch a business does not necessarily take a lot of money. We have explored many examples of low cost start-ups throughout our journey.

Money becomes necessary and cheaper.

But as you progress through the initial start up phase and start to reach critical mass, money becomes both an affordable and a necessary commodity.

Individuals, not plans get funded.

So, the business plan is your "invitation" to a money source. Its purpose is to begin a discussion that hopefully becomes a negotiation and then a funded deal. It is merely an "*invitation*" because a plan can only start the process. A business plan by itself has never been funded; the individuals who write and who execute the plan receive the funding.

> "*The investor wants to know: what is the idea, how is it unique in the market place, who's doing it, who comprises the management team, and how much money do you need in order to execute? Also, if they give you that money, what's it for and what's it going to look like for them.* "
> -Bill Sanderson, Founder, Popcorn Palace

Articulation of your concept.

So why do you write a business plan? Because putting your thoughts on paper is the most effective way to articulate your concept and the way in which you plan to execute that concept. It can then be used to attract resources to both join and fund your company.

> "*When you're starting a company, it's very important to set out on paper exactly what you're objectives are, the strategic focus for your business, and how you think your going to get there. Nobody's going to give you any money unless you have a business plan that's well thought out.*"
> -Sky Dayton, Founder, EarthLink Network, Inc.

What a Business Plan Is Not

Don't operate backwards.

Many entrepreneurs make the mistake of trying to start the entrepreneurial process backwards. Instead of exploring themselves (model business), choosing an industry, learning and working in that industry, and then looking for opportunities and testing them, they begin by writing the last document first—the business plan. Their hope is to raise extraordinary amounts of money and then play CEO for a startup.

Is no guarantee.

In so doing, they typically seek a formula for the perfect business plan and want to know what to say and how to say it. They search for a "fill in the blanks" or "connect the dots" solution that will guarantee a successful business plan. And, there are many texts, software packages, and web sites that make that promise—all but guaranteeing how to write the perfect business plan.

Read as many samples as possible.

Some of these formula-based software packages suggest tactics to excite readers, such as to "sell them on the upside." Others list buzz words or phrases that promise results. While it is reasonable for you to review such packages or texts, remember that your plan is your journey and therefore, can not be a copycat. In fact, ideally, you should read as many feasibility and business plans as possible. This will give you a good background to develop your own plan.

12-steps to success!

Other publications offer even greater promises. Beyond the business plan, they offer such things as the 12 steps to start a business—a how to, step by step, book to open the business of your choice. Promises of start up formulas for a variety of different businesses do exist in the marketplace.

Is no formula.

But there is no one formula for a successful business plan. Just as your journey is unique, so too is your business plan. There is no series of questions you can answer to reach success. It's not about writing the plan or even about the planning. It is only about your vision and your execution of that vision.

What A Business Plan Needs To Accomplish

Three critical questions.

In its most basic format, the plan needs to answer three critical questions. On the surface, they seem like very simple questions, but in reality, each is extremely complex. They are explored below.

Why you?

Why are you the person that can execute this plan? What is your background? What do you know about this industry? What do you know about managing a business?

Who's on your team?

But "why you" is not only about you. It's about the collective you—the associates joining you. What kind of team have you assembled or plan to assemble? Are the skills complementary? Do your backgrounds and experience form a mosaic that covers both the industry and the skill sets needed to execute? Are sales, distribution, product and finance represented?

What accomplishments can you leverage?

The critical third component of "why you" that must be articulated in your plan is the accomplishments to date made by you and/or your team. Your business plan should cover many topics that you have explored and tested. If learning the industry, defining and testing customers, examining competitors, and other tasks have not been done and you have written a "business plan," then what you have is a novel—a work of fiction. It is not a business plan. Are you all about ideas without a basis in reality? If so, it's time to start over.

Need hard facts.

Your plan must present what you have learned through feasibility and include not only your vision, but also the data and facts that support that vision. It must share <u>what you know</u> and <u>why you know it</u> rather than merely state what you believe and for what you hope.

The critical question of "why you" represents the first act and if done well, it sets the stage and earns the right to continue.

> *"I think when you look at business planning, when you're starting a company, its very important to set out on paper exactly what your objectives are. What the strategic focus of your business is and how you expect to get there. For one thing, nobody's going to give you any money unless you have a business plan that is well thought out."*
> -Garry Betty, CEO, EarthLink Network, Inc.

Why now?

Get beyond the cynicism.

With great merit, many believe that timing is everything. If readers of your plan are comfortable with your passion and your capability, then you have passed the first act and they begin to believe in you. Recognizing that you are the person that can execute this vision enables them to move beyond a feeling of cynicism.

At this point, the question becomes does the world need your product or service? If the answer is yes, then the question is why isn't someone else already doing it?

> *"Investors want to know where is the pain? Where is the problem you are solving?"*
> -Gene Miller, Peregrine Ventures

What's the competition?

The heart of this challenge is the current position of known and unknown competition and recognizing when is the best time to start your venture.

Timing deals with a series of factors explored in the model business. Is your idea in the early stages of a promising market? Or is there going to be education involved—do people know they need your product or service?

How much education is involved?

In terms of the model business, do you prefer a recognized market wherein a segment of the population is already willing and able to buy your prospective product or service? You also explored your desire for a perceived need. Is yours a product that is seeking a home? Do people know they need it or must you allocate greater resources to marketing because there will be a learning curve involved? The cost involved if you are the first to market can represent a tremendous challenge. And if you are successful, then why will you dominate in the next stage? You may be educating a market for another company with a distribution channel and/or established product line that will then take over the market. Be careful not to be the scout for a competitor who can dominate the next stage with vast resources.

Is it a solution seeking a problem?

If there is no perceived need for your product or service, then perhaps there is no identifiable pain and therefore no real need for your offering. If such is the case, then unfortunately you are merely a solution looking for a problem that may not exist.

Lifestyle or harvest?

Another differentiating factor in the model business is whether or not you want to pursue a lifestyle venture or one with an exit strategy. Timing may be more critical if there is an exit strategy involved. Additionally, you must examine the regulatory nature of your market. Have any new laws been passed that would help or hinder your success? So, take a moment to review the model business and determine the way in which timing will effect your business and strategy.

Don't be late either.

The other aspect of "why now" deals with being late to market. The cost of being late can be disastrous. If the opportunity has already been exploited and the market is saturated with others who have developed the benefit or established a distribution channel, then you must have another point of differentiation or don't bother entering the game. What do you offer to compete? If the competition has established solid relationships with customers, then how do you plan to catch up and surpass them?

How will you win?

Building on the work of the feasibility study, a business plan must recognize the competition and identify its strengths, weaknesses, and the means by which you will win market share.

Not about a calendar.

"Why now" is not about a calendar. It's about market positioning and competition. What is your vision of these critical areas? What does the future hold in terms of both market acceptance and the level of competition?

If not timing, then certainly timely market position is everything.

Why me?

Not up to reader to answer.

While it may appear that readers of your plan should answer this question, they should not. Potential investors will answer only the question of whether or not they will invest the time and energy necessary to go from a business plan to a deal and do all the homework necessary to explore if this makes sense and cents.

Tell them why.

To assist the process and enhance the probability of receiving funding, you must answer all three questions for them. Why you is outlined by the team you have assembled. Why now is answered through the positioning of your product or service in the marketplace. Likewise, why me must be answered with a compelling argument that the money source you are seeking is right for your particular stage of the journey.

What do you plan to do?

Such a convincing argument requires a clear identification (articulation) of the stage of your business as well as a strong focus on the goals you plan to accomplish to reach the next stage of your journey. Recall the money source diagram and determine where you fit on the grid. Anticipate questions that will come from investors so you are prepared to handle them.

Can you answer the questions?

Depending on the stage and purpose of your plan, be sure that it answers the following questions.

1. Is this plan written to recruit associates to join your team? If yes, what is their benefit? What's in it for them?
2. Are you trying to complete development of your benefit for a series of early adapters? Will family and friends or individual angels have their needs met?
3. Are you seeking a first customer who will be strategic to the company? Will they have favorable pricing or equity to bind them to the company forever?
4. Are you looking for an informal or a BAND of angels to go from first customer to multiple customers? How are you meeting their needs and attracting them to your vision?

What stage are you at?

Entrepreneurial Exercise

The three whys are a critical aspect of writing your business plan. Take this time to consider them.

Why are you the right person to launch this new venture?

_____

_____

_____

_____

Why is now the most appropriate time for you to launch this venture?

_____

_____

_____

_____

Why is the person you are asking to read the plan the right person to be reading it? Are they reading it as a possible investor, mentor, partner, or associate?

_____

_____

_____

_____

⇒　**Tear out and move to your entrepreneurial road map binder.**

Some Words to the Wise

Some basic concepts are important to keep in mind when writing the business plan. Be sure to follow the below listed recommendations in writing your plan.

Write precisely.

Be concise. If you are too verbose and take a hundred pages to describe your vision, investors will tune out and decide that you are not focused enough.

Don't make generalizations.

Be specific. Talking in generalities detracts from your credibility. If you learned something from a reliable source, quote them directly or state clearly where the knoweldge came from.

Do a reality check.

Be realistic. Perform a reality check on your plan. If you look like a dreamer, potential investors will lose faith. Also, if there are any issues in the past or present that are negative about you or your business, be sure to state them up front. It is likely that investors will learn of them anyway during thier due diligence; therefore, it is better for them to be told at the outset. It is likely they will look favorably on you for being honest and for your ability to learn from the situation. If they don't, it's time to search for new investors and/or associates.

Express simply.

Make the description of benefits readable. Be clear and direct in explaining your product or service. Investors are not likely to be impressed with arcane knowledge of your industry or technology. Use lay language and focus on the big points, expressed simply.

Be focused in all areas.

Be proportionate. Do not spend the majority of your plan on one topic. If you focus heavily on your product or service and have a short discussion about your sales strategy, the reader may conclude that you are a guy in love with your product and don't know enough about selling to reach your customer.

Writing The Business Plan

Several common components.

As you should know by now, there is no formula for the perfect business plan. Therefore, there is no fixed set of components that should be included in the plan. It is up to you to decide what is important to your business. However, several common elements to a good plan should be given strong consideration for inclusion into your plan. They are described below.

Executive Summary

Some only read the executive summary.

This is perhaps the most critical component of your business plan. Many investors will read only the executuve summary. Therefore, it should act as a directory to the sections that follow as well as highlight the most significant points about your plan. An overview of you and your team, your customer, your market, the benefit you intend to deliver, and your financial projections should be given. Since it is a culmination of your complete plan, it should be written last when you are confident about your strategy within each section.

Concept Statement

Four concise, yet descriptive paragraphs.

The concept statement is a single page with four short, succinct paragraphs that act as a blueprint for the reader. Remember the concept statement that took so long to develop? That should be the first paragraph—a 25-35-word statement of your business concept. The second paragraph should contain a clear and concise, yet simple definition of your customer. The third, a paragraph describing your sales and distribution channels. The final paragraph should be a definition of your benefit and why it is valuable. The basic idea behind your concept statement is to provide a single page with a core of your business concept to which the reader can quickly refer if there is any confusion elsewhere in the plan.

Body of the plan

Management Team

Who will execute?

This is where a description of you and the team you have assembled to execute your vision is found. Any key sales, technical, marketing, and production people should be included. This is the group that promises to turn your vision into reality and therefore, must be reliable and capable.

> *"If you have someone experienced in an industry for a long time, you'd want to put that right up front, because that's a big selling point."*
> -Bill Sanderson, Founder, Popcorn Palace

Customer and Market Niche

What's your niche?

The most effective customer and market niche sections include a detailed description of your customer including the types of companies or people that are your customers as well as their buying decisions. Clear identification of your customer niche and how you intend to exploit that niche are essential. Refer back to the testing of your customer and what you learned in so doing. Did you get any contracts or just compliments? If you got a contract, a first customer, you should explicitly state that in this section.

Sales Channels and Their Costs

What's your channel?

In this section, you should clearly describe the way in which you plan to reach your customer and why. Why have you chosen the sales channel that you have? Do you plan to hire a sales force or use direct sales? Investors will seek a detailed analysis of what sales channel will work for you and how much that channel will cost.

Benefits Package

Focus on why, not what.

In this section, you must be careful not to spend too much time detailing the product or service that you intend to offer. Rambling on for pages about the benefit may cause the reader to believe that you are in love with your product or service and are seeking funding to enjoy your favorite pastime—building the product. The focus should be on why a customer will buy your product or service, not what the product or service does.

> *"My succinct, 15-page business plan talked about this company that would make connecting to the Internet easy for millions of people who were going to join the Internet in the coming years."*
> -Sky Dayton, Founder, EarthLink Network, Inc.

Organizational Plan

How will you operate?

This section should indicate how your comapny will grow past the genesis team—the founders and key early members. It is reasonable to have positions that are not yet filled because they will be, with added investment. Additionally, a brief job description for each significant position and why that job is important should be included.

Financial Section

Use words, not numbers.

Often the most misunderstood part of a business plan, this should not be pages of figures nor should it contain tremendous detail. Your use of funds should be described in words, not numbers. Ideally, this will be for developing your benefit and sales channels, not fat salaries and unnecessary additional employees.

Growth Plan

How will you grow?

This is directly linked to the patterns of change occuring in your industry. How is your niche growing and what forces are pushing for expansion? You should describe how you and your team plan to handle growth. Investors tend to look favorably on large markets with a great deal of potential for growth. If your market niche is relatively small and you intend to dominate, it may mean there is limited room for growth.

Appendices

Extras?

The appendices are made up of important items that don't have a clear place in the main body of the plan. You may feel it necessary to include some as part of the actual plan and, again, that is up to your discretion. Just be wary of increasing the length of your plan such that it becomes overwhelming to the reader. In either case, none of the appendices should be longer than two pages.

Time line - This should be a simple, one-page graph of the actions you plan to take, projected into the future.

Competition Grid - You should have already created a competition grid from earlier, which can be adapted for this section. Be sure that you clearly convey the essence of your competition and how you intend to compete.

What will add value and enhance your plan?

Pricing Model - This is an identification of the price at which you will be selling your benefits and why. It also includes a description of the value you intend to deliver.

Market Action to Date - What have you already done in the marketplace? Identify what you have learned about your market from primary research.

Resumes - While you have given a description of the key points about your management team in the body of the plan, you may want to include complete resumes in the appendix if they provide a depth of experience worth showcasing.

Executive Summaries

It should be written last!

Upon completion of the main body of the plan as well as its appendices, it is time to write the executive summary. It should not exceed three pages in length and should include a synopsis of each section that you've included in the plan, written to highlight the key points of your business concept.

Some Final Thoughts

With your business plan written, your journey begins to accelerate. You are now doing. Seeking associates and investors as you battle your competitors for customers is your goal.

A few thoughts as your journey continues.

The essence of entrepreneurship.

- Entrepreneurship is about the creation of value and creativity; it's not about money or resources.
- Entrepreneurship is a journey of passion, doing a thing you love to do.
- Entrepreneurship is focusing on your customer, not being overwhelmed by the market.
- Entrepreneurship focuses on benefits, not features. That's the entrepreneur's secret. It's about the value that you create.
- Entrepreneurship is not about about planning, it's about doing—it's tactics, execution, accepting failure, living with experimentation.
- Entrepreneurship is about teams, your ability to attract the right people with complementary skills, to round out the package—then lead them with your vision.
- Entrepreneurship involves managing risk, not taking higher risks or being foolhardy.
- Entrepreneurship involves accepting chaos, confusion, and ambiguity-and where you step outside the box to find the solution.

Entrepreneurial Exercise

Since every business plan is different, you must consider what components will be included in your business plan. Consider the most important aspects of your concept and the reasons that certain sections should and should not be included.

What does the outline of your business plan look like? Identify the sections of your plan and a brief description of the primary contents of each section, including the appendices.

_____

_____

_____

_____

_____

_____

_____

_____

_____

_____

_____

_____

_____

_____

_____

_____

_____

⇒ **Tear out and move to your entrepreneurial road map binder.**

Chapter Summary

The business plan brings together everything you have learned about your industry, your market, your customers, your suppliers, your distribution channels, and your financial needs. While it can serve many purposes, it's primary goal is to execute your vision.

In writing your business plan, be sure that you understand and can clearly articulate the three why's. Knowing why you, why now, and why me should prepare you to face money sources and other readers of your plan.

Remember that all business plans are different and just as with entrepreneurship itself, there is no formula for success. Try to consider what are the most important and critical elements of your business, which are the items that should be discussed in your plan.

Don't underestimate the importance of the executive summary—many will only read that.

Chapter Thirteen Exercises/Discussion Questions

1. Create an outline for your own business plan. What will be the critical components for you?
2. Volunteer in class to verbally pitch your concept as if it were to an investor, customer, or associate.
3. Think of one potential customer, one investor, and one associate to whom you will give your business plan and why.
4. Look through your entrepreneurial road map binder and pull together the various exercises you have completed. They should help you create your business plan.
5. What is your execution strategy? How did you intend to make your vision a reality?
6. Can you answer the three whys?
7. Clearly articulate your concept statement.

Journey Thirteen: EarthLink Network

In November of 1993, Sky Dayton tried to log on to the Internet. When it took him 80 hours to accomplish this modest goal, he was frustrated and inspired: He would start an Internet Service Provider (ISP) that focused on customer needs and service.

To turn this vision into reality, Sky founded EarthLink Network, Inc. in 1994. The company has grown to become one of the nation's largest ISPs—boasting upwards of 1.3 million subscribers. At 26, Sky was the third-youngest person listed on the 1998 Forbes "High Tech's 100 Wealthiest."

Early Background

Sky's interest in computer technology stemmed from his early introduction to the field by his grandfather, an IBM Fellow. He had to convince his parents to purchase a television set so that he could use it as a monitor.

Throughout his childhood, creativity and experimentation were advocated. Never being told what he "should" do, Sky was always encouraged to figure things out for himself. His first entrepreneurial venture was a candy store that he and a friend wanted to start, but his parents decided not to fund them and therefore, this attempt at a start-up failed. He also recognized and exploited an opportunity in window washing as a result of his chores at home, but quickly recognized that the business would not scale.

His desire to control his own future and capitalize on opportunities led him to forgo a college education in pursuit of his own business ventures. Immediately after graduating from Delphian School, a private boarding high school, Sky apprenticed for three months at an animation company. Shortly thereafter, he co-founded a successful coffee shop, Café Mocha, in West Hollywood, California, with an initial investment from his grandmother. His interest in coffeehouses stemmed from his love of meeting and interacting with strangers, the primary happening at such a location.

While running the coffee shop, his interest in computer graphics led him to seek a job in the industry, so he worked in the darkroom of an advertising studio. The company was expanding and one day, he noticed a room full of new computers. After asking the office manager to lunch, he convinced her to hire him to run the new computer graphics department. Not knowing the first thing about these new computers, he locked himself in the room and learned all he could as quickly as possible. After mastering the computers and successfully running the division, he moved on to a larger firm for a short period of time.

In 1992, while still managing Café Mocha, he co-founded Dayton Walker Design, his own computer graphics boutique that served entertainment industry clients such as Disney and Universal Studios. Then, in 1993, as he describes it, "I became enthralled with the Internet, and everything else in my life went to hell."

Starting EarthLink

After his troubling initial experience trying to get on the Internet—a medium he felt was going to "turn the world's communications infrastructure upside down"—Sky conceived of EarthLink. He recognized the pattern of change in society—that the Internet was going to be the next mass medium—and knew he had to be a part of the revolution. He sold his stake in Dayton Walker, wrote a business plan, and sought investors.

The EarthLink business plan was about a 15-page document that described the Internet, the process of connecting to the Internet, and how the company would facilitate the connection of millions of people to this new and upcoming mass medium. At that time, people were not familiar with the Internet; therefore, the three critical paragraphs described the ultimate vision of the company and the tactical process that outlined how the company was going to get to market quickly.

Business plan in hand, Sky then had to find the $100,000 he needed; so, he started calling everyone he knew. A friend at boarding school's father agreed to meet with him. Sky handed him the business plan and the potential investor responded: "I'll call you."

The next day, Sky received a call and was told not to talk to anyone else about the plan. He and another gentleman made the initial investment and received 40% of the company in return.

In reflecting on the value of money, Sky recognizes that EarthLink would not have been possible without that initial funding. Even though he gave up a large percentage of ownership in return for the investment, he received a great deal more than just cash and knew that beginning to build the company was more important than finding another source of money that might not have required as much ownership. Industry contacts, resources, and expert advise were worth the loss of ownership and 60% of EarthLink was better than 100% of nothing.

So, in the Spring of 1994, Sky launched EarthLink Network, Inc. He made efficient use of his limited resources and bought all used furniture, phones, and other equipment. He also bought only what was needed at that start-up stage, particularly a limited number of computers that would enable first customers to receive the benefit of Internet access.

He founded his company with an eye toward the customer. Instead of devoting significant resources to developing proprietary networks, a new interface, or content, as other ISPs have done, Sky focused on providing painless initial sign-on, superior customer service, and unequalled technical support. In addition to offering a low rate [$19.95 a month for unlimited access], EarthLink was one of the first to offer phone help, custom icons, and a print newsletter. Using these tactics, EarthLink's member retention rate is much greater than its competitors.

Perseverance

Sky has a strong focus on not giving up and pursuing every angle possible to determine the best means of accomplishing his goals. His initial thought for EarthLink was to create a software package that would be enabled by an Internet Service Provider. His benefit was user-friendly connectivity as opposed to connectivity itself. After spending several months pursuing this idea and building prototype designs, he realized that what was missing in the marketplace was the connectivity itself. He found a need in the market that was not being filled and recognized that he could and should solve that problem for the masses.

Sky also lived by a call ratio that exemplifies his sticktuitiveness. He recalls "I had so many people tell me I couldn't do what I've done, so many people not return my phone calls, I used to have a ratio that if I got one call back for every ten calls I made, I was doing well."

Growing EarthLink

Transitioning from a start-up to a professionally managed company is often difficult for entrepreneurs, as they are not willing to delegate or allow others to assist in the growth of "their baby." However, in early 1996, Sky broke with tradition when he recognized that EarthLink had grown beyond his ability to manage it. As he recalls, "it is difficult when you're in the driver's seat to jump out while the car is moving and a turn is coming. But there is no other choice—that is the only way to grow a business."

With this foresight that a startup needs a seasoned executive to complement the entrepreneur, Sky hired Garry Betty as President and CEO to take over the day-to-day management of the company. Garry is credited with being the youngest CEO on the New York Stock Exchange when he served as President and CEO of Digital Communications, Inc. He also served as senior vice president for sales, marketing and international operations at Hayes Microcomputer Products. Garry brought his experience in taking entrepreneurial companies to the next level to EarthLink.

What is ideal about the two is the fact that they have complementary strengths and tal-ents. They recognize the value that the other brings: "It's been a good balance, I'm a little bit more conservative than Sky because I've been there before and Sky helps push the organization to achieve greater results than it would have if he wasn't pushing," says Garry.

In addition to Garry, Sky, with the assistance of his investors and Board, recruited other seasoned executives to help him run the company. He believes strongly in delegation and making people responsible for their actions. Along the journey, Sky continuously relinquished control, while at the same time never lost sight of his responsibility to take action should it be necessary. He knew that he had to give up control in order to maintain control. Through this process, he began to work himself out of a job.

Sky's theory of hiring is to hire from the top down so that people could grow into their jobs and scale with the company as demand increased. He also believes strongly in incentivizing employees with stock options and brought in executives who shared his vision and were therefore willing to reduce their salary in return for equity ownership in the company. He always paid himself less than he paid his employees.

In growing the company, there were definitely times of turmoil. One notable "meltdown" is fondly referred to as the Valentine's Day Massacre 1996 when the entire database and billing systems failed and the back up refused to load properly. Sky recalls the horrible time with the system down for two days, having to work down in operations for 48 hours straight, and flying a database expert in from San Diego to recover as much of the data as possible. But, he persevered, returned operations to working levels, and coaxed the company through the time of trouble. In coping with such difficulties, Sky stresses the importance of being able to "cope and organize, cope and organize, so you're never fixing the same problem twice." He never wanted to have to put out the same fire twice and recognizes the value of learning from mistakes.

With Sky as its vision and Garry as its execution, EarthLink has grown dramatically, from 1995 revenues of $3 million to almost $175 million in 1998, a 5700% increase. After its initial public offering in January 1997, Sky retained 14.3% of the company, which currently has a market capitalization of approximately $1.8 billion.

In September 1999, EarthLink announced a merger with MindSpring, a company that started at almost the exact same time as EarthLink as a result of its founder, Charles Brewer, experiencing the same connectivity frustration and difficulty that Sky had. It is a synergistic merger that creates the dominant number two (to America Online) ISP. With this merger, Sky truly worked himself out of a job and is turning over the Chairman title to Charles Brewer. He will retain a seat on the Board.

The New Model—eCompanies

As a result, EarthLink was just the beginning of Sky's Internet career. His latest efforts have led to the formation of eCompanies in June 1999, an Internet incubator that recently closed its first venture-capital fund by raising $130 million in 60 days. Sky co-founded eCompanies with Jake Winebaum, former chairman of Disney's Buena Vista Internet Group, which created the highly successful Disney.com, ABC.com, and ESPN.com web properties.

Throughout his career at EarthLink, Sky identifies both his best and worst decision as choosing to discard the many business plans that came across his desk. It was his best decision because it enabled him to maintain focus on EarthLink. It was his worst decision because there were so many great opportunities that he wasn't able to pursue.

However, in slowly working himself out of a job, Sky was able to review some of the business plans that he saw, which led to the notion of eCompanies. Over enchiladas at a taco stand in Burbank one evening, Sky and Jake conceived of eCompanies because of their belief that the Internet is currently only about 20% developed. Sky stated that they decided to "build a company that can build companies, not any single product or service, but a focus on companies themselves."

So, the focus of eCompanies is not only to invest in Internet companies, but also to assist in their development as Sky feels that "it takes three things to make a successful Internet company: a great idea, capital, and gutsy execution. There's a glut of ideas and capital in the market today, but execution is scarce. Execution alone has become the difference between success and failure for an Internet startup." The incubator, otherwise known as the accelerator, provides the critical services start-ups need in seven key disciplines: strategy, finance, recruiting, creative, technology, business development and marketing.

With Sky and Jake as its driving force, eCompanies will attempt to change the way internet start ups get to market by attracting entrepreneurs into their incubators with immediate funding and a commitment to be up and running in 90 to 180 days.

Sky and Jake's strategy is simple yet radical—replicate the success of EarthLink by bringing experienced investors and proven execution experience into an Internet start-up.

Journey Thirteen Case Questions

1. What was the opportunity that Sky saw that led to his desire to create EarthLink? What about eCompanies?

2. What entrepreneurial characteristics does Sky portray?

3. How did Sky manage the growth of EarthLink? Does his strategy differ from typical entrepreneurs? If so, how?

4. What were the keys to the success of Sky and Garry's relationship?

5. Should Sky have given up 40% of his company for $100,000? Why or why not? What other alternatives did he have?

6. What patterns of change did Sky view as critical for both EarthLink and eCompanies?